# IN SEARCH OF NEPTUNE

## THE NATIONAL TRUST

Charlie Pye-Smith

# IN SEARCH OF NEPTUNE
## *A Celebration of the National Trust's Coastline*

PHOTOGRAPHS BY JOE CORNISH

*For Sandie*

First published 1990
Copyright © 1990 by Charlie Pye-Smith

The National Trust, 36 Queen Anne's Gate, London SW1H 9AS
Registered charity number 205846

British Library Cataloguing in Publication Data

Pye-Smith, Charlie, *1951*–
    In search of Neptune: a celebration of the National
    Trust's coastline.
    1. Great Britain. Coastal regions. Description & travel
    I. Title
    914.1'04858

ISBN 0-7078-0106-0

**Acknowledgements**
The author and publisher are grateful to the following for
permission to reproduce copyright material in the text: Faber
and Faber Ltd, for the lines taken from 'Going, Going', published
in *High Windows* by Philip Larkin; William Heinemann Ltd, for
extracts from *English Journey* by J. B. Priestley, copyright ©
1934 by J. B. Priestley; David Higham Associates Ltd, for the
extract from 'Who Do You Wish Was With Us' by Dylan Thomas,
published by Dent in *The Stories of Dylan Thomas*; Oxford
University Press, for extracts from *The Matter of Wales* by
Jan Morris, published in 1984.

All photographs in this book are by Joe Cornish

**Maps**
The maps which appear in the text are drawn by Neil Hyslop.
Properties owned by the National Trust are identified in
rectangular boxes.

Designed by Gail Engert
Phototypeset in Monotype Lasercomp Sabon 669
by Southern Positives and Negatives (SPAN), Lingfield, Surrey (7190)
Printed and bound in Italy by Amilcare Pizzi s.p.a.

HALF-TITLE: *The sea front, Swanage*

TITLE PAGE: *Fishermen at dawn on Dunwich Beach, Suffolk*

The coastline of the British Isles is the one feature which differentiates this country from the rest of Europe. Throughout our history it has been subject to invasion both by man and the elements, but it has protected us in times of war and given us enormous pleasure in times of peace. No one can walk the clifftops and shorelines of Britain and remain unmoved by the fickle sea and the natural sights and sounds which convey so many moods and impressions that cannot be detected further inland. In terms of formal ownership the coast has a complex history, but exploitation and spoilation over the last two centuries, as well as the legitimate development of areas for commerce and industry, have in some places made it a cause for shame instead of a pleasure.

When the National Trust first alerted us all to what was happening, and set out to save 900 miles of the remaining coastline, it soon secured support from Esso. We are delighted to join in celebrating what has already been achieved and to push for yet more effort to carry on the task and make Enterprise Neptune complete. As a company we have to use part of the coast for our own facilities, in particular our refinery on Southampton Water, and we are very aware that industry and natural beauty can sit uneasily side by side one another. We try hard to minimise any potential adverse effects of what we do, and we like to accentuate the positive effects of our activities. We feel an obligation to strive to help preserve as many of the remaining unspoilt coastal areas as possible. Therefore we have supported this book in which the visual images photographed by Joe Cornish appear alongside Charlie Pye-Smith's text, capturing something of what it means to us all that Enterprise Neptune has succeeded so far.

Sir Archibald Forster
*Chairman and Chief Executive, Esso UK plc*

*Embleton Sands, Northumberland*

# Contents

# Introduction

A STEEP ALLEY climbs away from Barmouth's main street towards the hill behind. You pass cramped cottages with tiny gardens, then after a while the tarmac runs out and a short walk leads you up to Dinas Oleu, four acres of heathy hillside with little to recommend it apart from the view. When the weather is fine you can see across the wide mouth of the Mawddach Estuary to the gentle hills beyond. This being Wales, the views are just as likely to be curtailed by rain, in which case the far side of the estuary will be no more than a misty blur, the sea and the sky the same sombre colour as the slate-roofed, grey-stone town below.

The modest nature of Dinas Oleu belies its historical significance. When Mrs Fanny Talbot told her friend the Reverend Hardwicke Rawnsley that she was going to give Dinas Oleu to the newly formed National Trust, of which he was a founder member, she could have had little idea that this was the beginning of a vast movement to save Britain's coastline from despoilation. Her thoughts then, in 1895, were entirely parochial. 'I wish to put it into the custody of some society that will never vulgarise it,' she said, 'or prevent wild Nature from having its own way . . . I wish to avoid the abomination of asphalt paths and the cast-iron seats of serpent design . . . '

During the next century the National Trust was to take over more than 500 miles of coastline in England, Wales and Northern Ireland. Initially, there was no grand plan: from time to time the Trust was given properties by generous landowners; sometimes it bought them. In 1925 a local appeal in Northumberland raised the money needed to buy the Farne Islands, famous for their seabird colonies. Two years later the son of Alfred Lord Tennyson bequeathed to the Trust land in the Isle of Wight where his father used to walk. Just before the Second World War the Trust acquired White Park Bay, a magnificent sandy beach on the Antrim coast. Over twenty years later it was given the nearby Giant's Causeway. And so it went on: in dribs and drabs

OPPOSITE: *Surf rushing between the mainland and the island of Carrick-a-Rede, Co. Antrim*

*Carn Galver tin mine, West Penwith*

came beaches, islands, villages, cliffs and headlands, and by 1965 the Trust had taken possession of 187 miles of unspoilt coast.

During the same period, of course, many stretches of coast had been ruined. Industrial development accounted for some; the growth of towns and suburbs for others. Pressures on the coast increased after the Second World War as more and more people headed to the seaside for their holidays, fuelling the demands for carparks, golf courses, marinas and caravan sites. Post-war planning legislation, though in many ways exemplary, was powerless to prevent much of the coastal development.

Fears for the future prompted the Trust to mount a survey of the coastline in 1963. Of the total 3,000 miles of coast, one-third was found to be developed beyond any possibility of conservation, and a further third was thought to be of little interest. The remaining third – something over 900 miles – was considered outstanding and worthy of permanent preservation. An audacious campaign to save this coastline was launched by the Trust in 1965 under the title of 'Enterprise Neptune'. Within four years Neptune funds had enabled the Trust to buy a further 100 miles of coastline; by 1980, 220 miles had been acquired by Neptune, thus bringing the Trust's coastal holdings to over 400 miles. In 1988, the 500th mile came to the Trust in the form of one of County Durham's coal-blackened beaches.

*In Search of Neptune* tells the story of these last twenty-five years, but it is as much about the people of the coast as about the National Trust itself; and it is as much about fishing villages and farms as about beaches and cliffs and wildlife. I have been selective: rather than traipse round the whole coast, I confined myself to ten areas, six in England, two in Northern Ireland and two in Wales. I began one autumn and ended the next; my memories now are not just of people and places, but of incidents and seasons too. Scores of people have helped to shape this book. My thanks go not only to those I have written about, but to the many others, unmentioned here, who entertained and enlightened me on my journey round the coast.

Charlie Pye-Smith
*November 1989*

# 1

# *Crumbling Cliffs*

SOME PEOPLE love mountains but loathe flatness; others feel ill at ease in high country, preferring instead the broad skies and brooding emptiness of fens and plains. Few landscapes are universally admired: most have both champions and detractors. However, I have never heard anyone express dislike for the seaside. This is curious, for the British coastline boasts a remarkably rich variety of landscapes, and a diversity of types might be expected to elicit a diversity of reactions. Inevitably, each of us will have our preferences – perhaps for the remote and unremitting cliffs of Pembrokeshire or Cornwall; perhaps for the gentler landscape of Dorset, where sandy beaches and undulating cliffs are found in easy coexistence; or perhaps for the vast, muddy expanses of the east coast estuaries – but all of us, it seems, love the seaside.

So why is the coast universally loved? Is it because the sea has a redemptive quality? Does its presence render the mundane interesting, the unsightly agreeable? Yes, I think it does, but there is more to it than that. Most of inland Britain is clothed in soil and vegetation: we see the outer layers of flesh, but we can only guess at the nature and texture of the skeleton and innards. But wherever land meets sea, the former is stripped naked by the latter; nature has pared away the flesh to reveal the guts of the beast. Coastal landscapes are honest landscapes: by baring their geological souls they tell us about the past, and through them we catch a glimpse of what goes on beneath the hinterland. One is struck, too, by the physical vulnerability of much of the coastline, especially along the eastern seaboard. So soft are the cliffs around Robin Hood's Bay, on the Yorkshire coast, and at Dunwich, in East Anglia, that one measures their recession in feet and years, not inches and eons. Their fragility emphasises the frailty of human endeavour, for the crumbling of the cliffs has been accompanied by the loss of towns and villages, churches and cottages.

The coastal landscape round Robin Hood's Bay is possessed of a fluidity

OPPOSITE: *The crumbling cliffs below Dunwich Heath*

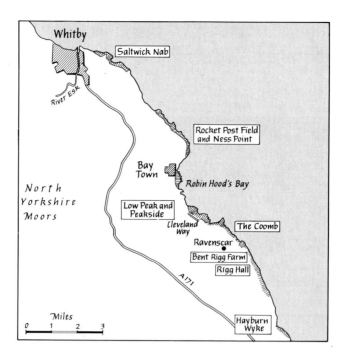

well understood by those who live there but indiscernible to the casual visitor. The cliffs are the texture of marzipan and they are gradually crumbling away. Were it not for the sea wall, which was built in 1975, Bay Town would be even smaller than it is: over a period of two centuries some 200 houses – or about half the old town – have fallen away into the sea. Nature has been only partially restrained by the wall and every year great chunks of soil and shale slip seaward as Robin Hood's Bay, which stretches some four miles to the south of Bay Town, eats further into the hinterland.

In his *Guide to Robin Hood's Bay*, William Dalton, Bay Town's Congregational minister from 1880–1912, claimed that 'for a delicate constitution no better climatic conditions can be found in these Isles . . . the greatest difficulty has been encountered by every medical man who wished to live upon his practice'. I spent a weekend in and around Bay Town in mid-August and it rained and blew almost without cease. Down by the quayside chilled parents in anoraks clutched beers and whiskies while their blue-fingered children skimmed shrimp nets through the rock pools. This should have been harvest time, but the fields of oats beside the old railway line lay uncut and beaten down by the rain. The leaves on the oak and willow in the scattered woods had yet to take on their autumnal colours, but they had lost the green sheen of sap-rising summer. Everything apart from the red-berried rowans had a weary look about it. Flowers were few and solitary: thrift on the cliffs, harebell and knapweed in the meadows, red campion and herb robert in the woods.

Most of the eight miles of Yorkshire coast belonging to the National Trust

*Looking north over Robin Hood's Bay*

is to be found round here. (Robin Hood's Bay lies within the North Yorkshire and Cleveland Heritage Coast; it also falls within the North York Moors National Park.) The Trust owns a chunk of cliff and pasture to the north of Bay Town, and much longer stretches of coast to the south, beginning at Boggle Hole, sweeping out past Ravenscar and taking in a further four miles of cliff down to the nature reserve of Hayburn Wyke. This coast is full of drama, the scenery being exceptional and the towns quixotic. Wherever you go you will come across reminders of the past – of the fishermen, Methodist preachers, quarry workers and lifeboatmen who once lived here.

Bay Town is a hybrid. The old port's cobbled streets and pantiled cottages, many of which date back to the seventeenth century, cascade down the hillside to meet the North Sea. Then higher up, and on flatter ground, is the red-brick suburb built in Victorian times. The former oozes charm; the latter is grander, more pretentious and distinctly lacking in prettiness. The tiny gardens spattered among the winding alleys of the old port are full of ragged rose bushes, fuchsia and montbretia; the more capacious plots in the new town are trim and ornamental: this is a world of crazy-paving and hydrangeas, lace curtains and landladies. You can almost smell the petty snobberies.

During the last century Bay Town was one of the most important fishing ports on the Yorkshire coast. In 1820 there were 130 fishermen working thirty-five cobles – the flat-bottomed, high-bowed boats of Viking ancestry – and five larger ships. You can still see cobles on the slipway in front of the Bay Hotel, but only two people make any sort of a living out of fishing now. Most cater for the tourists and weekend visitors, and indeed tourists have been coming here for a long time: in his guide of 1914 the Reverend Dalton listed sixty-three places to stay. It says much about the town that it now has two museums, one in the old Wesleyan chapel, the other in the old reading room and library. The latter has a delightful notice on the door which reads: 'Members have the use of TWO COMFORTABLE ROOMS which may be heated by putting a penny in the slot of the gas fires . . . The library contains 2,281 books.' Needless to say, this is no longer a world of Nonconformist, cod-catching autodidacts whose dialect is intelligible to the Danes and double-Dutch to the English.

I particularly liked the general store beside the Bay Hotel. Tacked on to its outer wall are some old-fashioned enamel advertisements of the sort more commonly seen in Islington antique shops than out in the open. One is for Rowntree's Elect Cocoa, one for Brooke Bond tea, and the other for Spratt's

*The general store, Bay Town*          *Mel Cunningham*

meat-fibrine dog foods. Next to the store is possibly the smallest launderette in England with just two machines. Indeed everything apart from the Nonconformist churches is cast in miniature. Even the lobster I ate at Ye Dolphin Hotel was of the Bonzai variety. I recommend, both for eating and sleeping, the robust Victoria Hotel, which overlooks the old town from the edge of the new. During my stay it was virtually taken over by a beery and liberally tattooed party of airport police who had come to do some wreck-fishing for cod off Whitby, a sport which the landlord described as murder.

Looking south from the Victoria Hotel, or from the slipway outside the Bay Inn, the views are spectacular. Topping the sea-cliffs are fields of corn and grass, behind which are more cliffs, a dirty purple beneath the richer purple of the heather moors above. Beyond the bay the lower cliffs rise dramatically to jut into the sea, and here, some 600 feet up, is the town of Ravenscar, which is where I met Mel Cunningham, the Trust's warden. A wiry, bearded man, Cunningham looked like a shepherd. Having taken a degree in biology at London University, he worked for a while as a local-authority ranger in the Wirral before moving here four years ago. We sat in his kitchen and chatted before setting out along the cliffs. It was Sunday and he was wearing a boiler suit and Wellingtons. I asked him if he always worked at weekends. 'Yes,' he said, 'there's always something to do, or people like you turn up.' It was said in the nicest possible way. Cunningham enjoyed the work and he liked living at Ravenscar. His kitchen has one of the finest views in England: the sort that makes estate agents reach for a hyperbole.

Ravenscar looks as unprepossessing as it sounds. If you follow the Cleveland Way south from Bay Town you will pass Cunningham's house and enter the 'town' near the main gates of the Raven Hall Hotel, a sprawling building set in lovely gardens whose trees have been bent backwards by the fierce easterly winds. It is said that the hall was built for King George III, who fled here during his bouts of lunacy to be treated by Dr Willis, the owner. According to the hotel's brochure, 'In the gardens, iron trees were created with tin leaves which jingled in the breeze. The inside of the Willises' house had many mementoes of the King, including a framed order of the Privy Council giving Dr Willis permission to flog the King when necessary to aid treatment of his illness.'

The Willis family eventually lost the hall when one of their number challenged a man from London to a woodlouse race and backed the more lethargic of the two creatures. Mr Hammond, the new owner, was a driving force behind a company which was set up to turn this windswept and inhospitable headland into another Scarborough. Lunacy, it seems, was

*Robin Hood's Bay from the cliffs at Ravenscar*

endemic. A railway was built, the land was divided into plots, and roads and drains were laid. Only a handful of the 1,500 plots found buyers, the company went bankrupt, and with it died the dreams of an esplanade and all the other paraphernalia which goes with seaside resorts. 'And that,' explained Cunningham, 'is why Ravenscar is called "the town that never was".'

We made our way past the hotel and drove down a grassed-over cinder track beside some fields owned by the Trust. Ravenscar's attractions are those bequeathed by nature rather than the developers. The few houses built at the turn of the century to the south of the hotel are monumental and unattractive. Outside one stood a yellow Rolls-Royce, the property, said Cunningham, of someone who was a 'star turn' during the summer season at Scarborough.

After a while we ran out of track, abandoned the Land Rover and joined the Cleveland Way, a long-distance footpath which begins inland at Helmsley, crosses the North York Moors, then runs down the coast from Staithes to Scarborough. We followed the path south until we came to a disused coastguard look-out. The views from the cliffs were imposing: from 600 feet up the fulmars wheeling over the waves looked like specks of dust. The inner cliffs on which we now stood were scruffy-looking affairs, their colours those

*The cliffs below Ravenscar*

of offal: dirty grey, liver brown and muddy purple. In places they were streaked green where weeds and creepers grew. Sandwiched between these and the sea-cliffs, on the gently sloping undercliff, was an isolated world of scrub and heath. Among the trees to be found here were elm, ash, sycamore, alder, willow and hazel. 'It's glorious in the spring,' said Cunningham. 'There's nothing particularly rare, but the primroses are lovely, and there are roe deer and badgers living on the undercliff.'

There are two ways to get from Ravenscar to Bay Town. By car it is a distance of some thirteen miles; there is no road across the bay and drivers must head back on to the moors and make a long loop round. By foot it is a little under three miles. Cunningham is more privileged than most and he can drive between the two towns on the old railway line. The Whitby to Scarborough coast line was opened in 1885 and closed down eighty years later. It had one of the steepest inclines in the country, the line dropping some 430 feet over five miles of track north of Ravenscar. We joined the track near Cunningham's home and stopped at the site of some old brickworks. These had been set up in the lee of an alum quarry at the end of the last century to supply bricks for the town that never was.

In many ways this is the most interesting part of the Trust's estate on the Yorkshire coast. The land was acquired for its beauty rather than anything else, but it is of profound geological and archaeological interest as well. I have vague memories of childhood visits to the bay: like most children of that time, and I dare say this, I spent many hours chipping away at the cliffs in search of fossils rather than paddling in the waves. The coast here is famous for its ammonites and belemnites, primitive members of the family of marine molluscs whose living representatives include octopus and squid. Belemnites, which were a prototype for today's cuttlefish, look like little black torpedoes; they used to be known as thunderbolts, as that is what people once thought they were. Ammonites have the appearance of curled-up horns, getting their name from Ammon, the ancient Egyptians' ram-headed god. Local legend claims that St Hilda of Whitby, finding this part of Yorkshire infested by snakes, prayed for their removal, cut their heads off, and drove them over the cliffs. Their contorted bodies turned to stone; hence the ammonites. The only other place apart from Dorset where I have seen ammonites is 12,000 feet up in the Nepalese Himalaya. There they are highly prized by Hindu pilgrims, who see them as symbols of the deity Vishnu. In both places shopkeepers know they are on to a good thing and they sell them to passing tourists.

Most of the rocks exposed here are about 160 million years old and they

*Eroded rocks, Ravenscar*

belong to the Jurassic period. The lower cliffs in the bay consist of alternating beds of shale and limestone: ammonites can be found in the shale and shellfish fossils in the limestone. However, hammering is dangerous as it can set off avalanches; it also breaches the Geological Association's code of practice. Behind the cliffs a shelf of sandstones and ironstones is covered by clays deposited during the last Ice Age; this is poorish-quality land but the farmers manage to grow corn in their fields as well as grass. Then, ranging up the massive cliffs to the west, come the rocks of the Upper Lias Series, alum shales topped by beds of sandstone.

The alum industry was the first of England's chemical industries, and shale quarrying began at Peak – as Ravenscar was once known – at the end of the sixteenth century. The process of extracting alum – whose main use was fixing dyes to wool – was bizarre and messy. According to a historian of the early nineteenth century, the alum works along the Yorkshire coast provided 'a spectacle at once pleasing awful and magnificent'. The shale was dug out of the cliffs by hand and laid in piles up to 200 feet wide and 100 feet high. These were roasted slowly on a brushwood fire over a period of several months, occasionally for a year or more. The resulting residue, which was brick-red, was washed with water then treated with an alkaline solution. Stale human urine was ideal for this purpose and the local population obliged.

One of the earliest descriptions of the alum works comes from Daniel Colwell, a London merchant who visited the area in the 1670s. 'Alum is made of a stone digged out of a mine, of a seaweed and urine,' he wrote. 'The mine of stone is found on most of the hills between Scarborough and the River of Tees in the county of York. It is of a blewish colour . . . The best urine comes from poor labouring people who drink little strong drink.' It took anything up to 100 tons of shale to get one ton of alum. Much of the coastline round here shows the massive scars of quarrying, and the alum works themselves were evidently a tourist attraction: the manager of the Guiseborough works further north produced a guidebook in the 1850s, presumably to save himself the bother of showing visitors round.

I returned the following day to meet Jonathan Sharpe, an archaeologist temporarily employed by the Trust. His office was in an isolated cottage where the manager of the alum works used to live. Sharpe was both pleasant and prickly; had he been in a novel by Trollope he would have found himself with the same name. He had arrived at Ravenscar in April and he expected to leave in December, by which time the archaeological survey of the old alum works would be complete. He had one full-time assistant and up to seven part-timers, all paid for by the Manpower Services Commission (MSC).

The Trust has some 40,000 sites of archaeological interest on its properties. These range from the rare and magnificent to the commonplace and modest: from Avebury Rings and Hadrian's Wall to medieval rabbit warrens and roadside churn-stands. It is currently carrying out an examination of these sites, and the survey of the alum works was part of this lengthy programme. 'This is perhaps the best-surviving example of a seventeenth-century chemical plant in Britain,' said Sharpe. He felt that the Peak works should be scheduled as an ancient monument, although he agreed that as the site wasn't under threat of destruction there was no immediate need to bestow upon it the protection that goes with ancient-monument status.

Apart from the house, there is only one roofed building at the alum works: a barn, now used by the Trust as a store, which boasts walls from various centuries. Below this, on the sloping ground above the sea-cliffs, are the ruins of the old works and here and there can be seen bits of rusty machinery. When the tide is out the remains of the old docks at the foot of the cliffs are visible; across the shore run some tracks, gouged out of the rock, along which wagons were once pushed. Here the alum was loaded on to schooners, in which it was taken to other ports in England and as far afield as Turkey, Russia and America.

At present the alum works are dangerous and therefore out of bounds to the public. Whether or not the Trust will shore up the ruins and make them safe remains to be seen. If it does, I hope it will resist the temptation to set up an interpretation centre; a simple noticeboard would be quite sufficient. One of the main attractions of this roadless stretch of coast between Ravenscar and Bay Town is its emptiness and the lack of tourist facilities. Admittedly, the Trust has a shop in Ravenscar, but it is small and inobtrusive. 'Even in summer,' said Cunningham, 'it's quiet along here, although Ravenscar seems to get more visitors now than it did when we came four years ago.'

One tires of the way tourist boards promote the countryside with their glossy brochures full of blue skies and clichés. Where, one wonders, is the cow muck, the fog, the rusty junk in the hedgerows? Why do the cows in the brochures look so clean, the sheep so white, the village greens so perfect? This is not the real countryside, although perhaps it is a close approximation to what a London commuter would like it to be. Wearisome, too, is the way in which tourist brochures quote the writers and poets of the past in their sales pitch.

OPPOSITE: *Old brickworks at Peak, with alum shale cliffs behind*

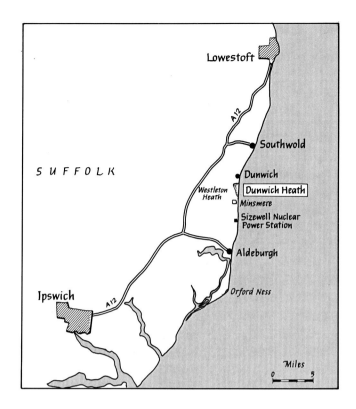

On reflection, though, I think they are wise to do so, as there is little point in tourist information centres trying to do what Shakespeare or Wordsworth have already done much better.

However, it is not simply a matter of expediency. Our appreciation of many a landscape – whether it be a valley, a wood or a stretch of coast – is enriched by its literary and artistic associations. We associate Fingal's Cave with Mendelssohn, the cliffs to the west of Dover with Shakespeare, Dedham Vale with Constable, Haworth Moor with the Brontës. To desecrate these landscapes would be an affront to art as well as nature. The Trust has never bought a piece of landscape simply because someone has written about it or painted it; but no one can deny that our enjoyment and understanding of many places are enhanced by the ways in which they have been seen and depicted in the past. The pleasures these landscapes give us are both actual and – thanks to the poets and painters – vicarious.

The novels of Leo Walmsley, many of them describing life in Bay Town at the turn of the century, were popular in their day, but Robin Hood's Bay is better known for its fossils than its literature. As far as I know it has inspired little in the way of poetry. The same cannot be said of Dunwich. In his introduction to *Dunwich: Time, Wind and Sea, Poems 1173–1981*, Ormande Pickard, the curator of the local museum, writes: 'It must be, to say the least, unusual for a remote village of no more than 120 inhabitants to have a literature as does the coastal village of Dunwich . . . ' Of particular note in this anthology is a poem by Algernon Charles Swinburne, 'By the North Sea', and an essay by Henry James, who wrote this of Dunwich towards the end of the last century:

> I defy anyone, at desolate, exquisite Dunwich, to be disappointed in anything. The minor key is struck here with a felicity that leaves no sigh to be breathed, no loss to be suffered; a month in the place is a real education to the patient, the inner vision . . . Dunwich is not even the ghost of its dead self; almost all you can say of it is that it consists of the mere letters of its old name. The coast, up and down, for miles, has been, for more centuries than I presume to count, gnawed away by the sea. All the grossness of its positive life is now at the bottom of the German Ocean, which moves for ever, like a ruminating beast, an insatiable, indefatigable lip. Few things are so melancholy – and so redeemed from mere ugliness by sadness – as this long artificial straightness that the monster has impartially maintained. If at low tide you walk the shore, the cliffs, of little height, show you a defence picked as bare as a bone; and you can say nothing kinder of the general humility and general sweetness of the land than that this sawlike action gives it, for the fancy, an interest, a sort of mystery, that more than makes up for what it may have surrendered. It stretched, within historic times, out into towns and promontories for which there is now no more to show than the empty eye-holes of a skull; and half the effect of the whole thing, half the secret of the impression, and what I may really call, I think, the source of the distinction, is the very visibility of the mutilation. Such at any rate is the case for a mind that can properly brood. There is a presence in what is missing – there is history in there being so little. It is so little, today, that every item of the handful counts.

There can be few images more poignant than the one contained in a little picture pack which I bought in Dunwich Museum. It is entitled 'All Saints Church, Dunwich, Suffolk, 1750 to 1919'. A lithograph of 1750 shows the church intact. It is not a pretty church: the tower is squat and the nave abnormally long, rendering the building slug-like. The next painting, depicting the church twenty-six years later, shows the roof in a state of collapse and the elaborate stonework of the tower in the first stages of decay. Then we move into the age of photography. By 1886 the cliff, hitherto unseen, had taken the far end of the nave; by 1909 half the nave had gone; and by 1919 all that was left was one wall of the tower teetering on the edge of the cliff. Nothing remains now apart from the odd gravestone.

*Greyfriars Priory, Dunwich*

Medieval Dunwich was one of the great ports of the east coast, possessing, in the thirteenth century, as many galleys as London. My guidebook claims that at that time Dunwich was able to send eighty ships to help the king, although it fails to say why he needed ships and against whom. Dunwich was not only a boat-building and fishing centre but a great trading port too. By the fourteenth century, however, the harbour was beginning to silt up and soon afterwards the sea began to nibble away at the streets and houses. Scarcely a relic of these times remains today; even the dead were exhumed by the elements then washed out to sea.

Stand on the low cliffs near Dunwich and observe the line of the coast: to the north, at a distance of three miles or so, you will see the red roofs of decorous, elegant, old-fashioned Southwold; to the south, about five miles away, the coast is rudely interrupted by Sizewell nuclear power station. One is struck, as James was, by 'this long artificial straightness'. As he said, every item of the handful counts, the two biggest items, at the time of his visit, being All Saints Church, which had yet to topple over the cliffs, and the ruins of Greyfriars Priory, which, happily, had been built on higher ground some

*Sizewell nuclear power station*

distance to the west of the medieval town. Perhaps the Franciscans who founded it in the early thirteenth century were possessed of a degree of prescience lacking in the rest of the populace. Today these ruins are the only substantial reminder of old Dunwich. They sit a little distance back from the cliffs, surrounded by vegetable plots and weedy fields grazed by sheep and ponies. Ancient ivies clamber over the refectory's pointillist patchwork of knapped flint, brick and sandstone.

I came here one October evening an hour before dusk. The impression was one of studied neglect: a drowsy peace had settled over the ruins, the only sounds being the champing of ponies and the listless droning of bees. The hour which remained before nightfall was more than enough to see the rest of Dunwich. It is charming in an inconsequential way. It consists of a row of brick houses, a nineteenth-century church in whose yard stand the ruins of the church of an old leper hospital, a pub, a fish and chip shack, a small museum and a shingle spit on to which the fishing boats are winched. Otherwise Dunwich is largely fresh air and memories.

*

Jack Docwra has a ditch named after him on the borders of Dunwich Heath. It is good to know that his name will be remembered long after he and all who know him have gone, for Docwra, working at first unpaid for Dunwich Town Trust, and later as the National Trust warden, has done as much as anyone for the conservation of the heath. At one time the Sandlings Heathlands stretched from Ipswich up to Lowestoft, a distance of some twenty miles. Over the years they have gradually been reclaimed for farming and forestry and only about 5 per cent of the original now survives. Dunwich is undoubtedly the best piece of heath left in this part of East Anglia.

I went to see Docwra at his house in the village of Westleton. He reminded me of J. B. Priestley's assertion: 'The East Anglian is a solid man. Lots of beef and beer, tempered with east wind, have gone to the making of him.' Docwra is soft-spoken and heavy-built, and he exemplifies all that is best in the older generation of Trust wardens. Born and brought up in Southwold, most of his working life had been spent in or around Dunwich. The majority of wardens recruited by the Trust nowadays have diplomas and degrees in subjects such as biology or conservation. Docwra's knowledge of the countryside was gathered through outdoor labour rather than indoor study. Before and after the Second World War he had a variety of jobs: he ran a milk round for many years; he also dealt in game and poultry. A true countryman, he possessed the practical skills of estate management and a keen understanding of nature. Though retired now – it was the new warden, Simon Moss, who showed me round the heath – Docwra still puts in time as an honorary warden at the Nature Conservancy Council's Westleton Heath. He has also been responsible for putting up the natural-history displays at Dunwich Museum. He is renowned for his skill at mending the bones of injured birds and before I left him he showed me the hawks and owls in the ramshackle aviaries in his back garden. Common birds were as solicitously cared for as the rare: there were pigeons here as well as barn owls and a lanner falcon.

Dunwich Heath had been in the ownership of Dunwich Town Trust for about two centuries when it approached the National Trust in 1965 with a view to selling the property. The Town Trust had found the heath increasingly difficult to manage; as it allowed caravanning it was liable to incur extensive obligations under the Caravan Act of 1960. In 1967 the baked-bean people H. J. Heinz and Co. Ltd bought the 214-acre heath for £6,500, and the following year presented it to the National Trust along with an endowment of £5,500 for its management. This was the first of a number of acquisitions which Heinz made for Enterprise Neptune.

During the First World War the heath was used as an Army training

*Birch trees at Dunwich*

ground; in the next war it was the site of a large radar station. 'The heath was a shambles when I started looking after it for the Town Trust in 1959,' recalled Docwra. 'There were bomb craters, bits of the radar station lying around and barbed wire everywhere.' At one time the Army used to fire live ammunition from Westleton Heath to what has now become the Royal Society for the Protection of Birds' Minsmere bird reserve. The 'shorts' used to drop on Dunwich Heath and after the Trust took it over bomb-disposal squads removed 500 live missiles.

The early years were traumatic. 'Six months after the opening ceremony we had a disastrous fire,' said Docwra. 'It burnt off about fifty acres of heath and nearly set fire to the warden's house at Minsmere.' There were ten fire engines on the scene and no water. As a precaution against future fires Docwra set about the digging of a ditch: it would provide water for the fire engines if there was another fire, and it would also act as a firebreak. Docwra's Ditch is a remarkable feature. Six feet deep, six feet wide and about half a mile long, it snakes along the southern boundary of the heath. In 1975 it was stocked with 350 mirror carp and ten tench. Some of the fish now weigh well over ten pounds. Fishing the ditch is ridiculously cheap: currently 50p for a day ticket, or £5 for the year. Moss and I wandered along its length on a bright and nippy autumn day. The heath was a mottled confection of russets and faded greens; the trunks of the silver birch stood out against a blue sky. Down in the ditch the water was covered by a thin veneer of American pondweed, a plant which Moss, with the help of regular work parties, does his best to keep at bay.

*Docwra's Ditch, Dunwich Heath*

Kingfishers are among the birds which feed there, and otters come over from Minsmere to prey on the fish.

Dunwich Heath, along with the Minsmere Marshes, has been classified by the Nature Conservancy Council as a Grade I Site of Special Scientific Interest. The main habitat – as one would expect – is heathland. This is dominated by ling, the common variety of heather, intermingled with which are gorse, bell heather and cross-leaved heath. There is also about a mile of foreshore and cliff – the latter supports a colony of sand martins – and dotted among the heath are patches of scrub and bracken. One of the warden's tasks is to keep the scrub under control. If heathland is to remain as such it must be burnt, grazed or cut; left to its own devices it will revert to scrub and woodland, in which case many of its characteristic birds and plants will disappear. Dunwich Heath attracts a large population of nightjars, a nationally rare and declining species. Other birds which depend on heathland for their survival, and which are to be found here, are wheatear, whinchat and stonechat. One of the rarer plants is the Dunwich rose, which is said to have been introduced here during medieval times by monks from Dunwich.

In the old days the Freemen of Dunwich could graze their sheep on the heath and cut the bracken. This helped to limit the spread of scrub, as did the grazing of rabbits, vast numbers of which lived here in the days before myxomatosis. There are still plenty of rabbits but stern measures are required to keep the scrub at bay. The practical business of maintaining the heathland is largely confined to the winter months, though Moss has groups of workers cutting the bracken and pulling up silver-birch saplings in the summer too.

'Heathland wardens,' said Moss, who had come to Dunwich two years earlier from Cannock Chase, 'generally have to spend much more time looking after visitors than managing the heath itself, especially in summer.' Some 50,000 people visit Dunwich Heath every year. 'On a good Sunday,' he said when we reached the carpark overlooking the beach, 'it's like Blackpool down here.' In the mid-1970s Docwra once counted 1,070 cars parked on the heath. When he first started work there were no parking restrictions: people could drive their cars deep into the heath and park where they wished. The Trust banned overnight caravanning and over the years Docwra restricted where the cars could go. This improved the appearance of the place; it also gave the vegetation a chance to recover from the erosion. Erosion, of course, has been one of the Trust's main concerns and within six years of taking over the heath more than 1,500 tons of soil were imported to stabilise and revegetate the cliff.

*

*Clifftop grave, Dunwich*

In some places the Trust is having to put up a fierce fight to save the coastline. Among its adversaries are government departments, private developers and landowners, and many wardens and land agents find themselves locked in perennial struggle against one foe or another. The wardens at Robin Hood's Bay and Dunwich lead a relatively struggle-free existence, but this is not to say that their tasks are easy. Wardening has never been a nine-to-five job. 'I never once failed to go down to the heath to check up after dark,' recalled Docwra. 'From Easter till the end of October I worked seven days a week. You see, it never was a job to me; it was a way of life.' Moss feels much the same about wardening, although he said that he would rather be called a 'ranger' than a 'warden'. Neither term seems satisfactory as neither hints at the variety of skills which are required. There was a time when wardens were concerned with estate management and little else; it is said that they did pretty much what the land agent, to whom they were expected to doff their caps, told them to do. However, things have changed over the past decade or so. 'From the mid-1970s onwards,' explained a land agent in the West Country, 'the Trust became aware of the need to look in greater detail at the biological and archaeological importance of its holdings, and consequently there has been a significant shift in the types of warden it has been recruiting. They must have exceptional physical skills as well as a good eye for landscape. Many have diplomas or degrees, but they need more than a knowledge of wildlife: they must be good diplomats and many have to handle large workforces.'

At Robin Hood's Bay Mel Cunningham was in charge of three MSC teams employing thirty people. He was also in charge of the Trust shop and the letting of a holiday cottage, in addition to which he had to devote a good chunk of his time to discussing the management of the Trust's estate with the tenant farmers. He had even gone into partnership with one of them, setting up a flock of sheep to graze the clifftop grasslands. 'We're lucky here,' he conceded, 'we don't have many conflicts between the visitors and farmers, and nor is there much conflict between farming activities and the preservation of the landscape.'

Moss was fortunate in that he had taken over a property which had been expertly run by his predecessor, Jack Docwra. However, like Cunningham, he had a wide range of responsibilities, and these were about to increase. When I visited Dunwich in the autumn the row of coastguard cottages overlooking the sea was boarded up. Over the winter the Trust was going to renovate them. One cottage was to be converted into living quarters for Moss and his family; the others were going to be turned into holiday flats, a shop, tea-rooms and an information centre. Moss will continue to look after the heath's wildlife, but increasingly he will find his job one of business management. It all seems a far cry from the days, not so long ago, when Docwra had to provide his own tractor.

# 2

# *Corrugated Coastline*

A<small>T TIMES THE</small> West Cornish landscape looked autumnal, mellow and welcoming; at times, cadaverous and wretchedly bleak. I arrived at St Ives during a violent storm: the sky bruised and funereal; the sea the colour of iodine. Next day dawn broke with a slushy sweet-pea haziness, the clouds tinged pink, pale blue and dove grey. Throughout the morning the clouds dispersed, only to return later, spitting irascibly, in malevolent gangs.

This is a peculiar world, full of contrast and drama. The Penwith Peninsula – the rectangular block of land which stretches from the River Hayle to Land's End – combines a North Country toughness with a Mediterranean sky and a mildish climate. It is wilder and more overtly rural than almost anywhere else in southern England, yet there are settlements here whose appearance – and history – is overwhelmingly industrial. You are constantly aware of an elemental simplicity – the very nakedness of the granitic landscape is almost shocking – yet some of the villages are as quaint as any in Dorset.

Over a third of Cornwall's 330 miles of convoluted coastline now belongs to the National Trust, which means that about a fifth of all the coastline acquired by the Trust in England, Wales and Northern Ireland is to be found here. It would have taken weeks to get around all the Neptune properties in the county, so I confined myself to the short stretch of coast which lies between St Ives and Land's End.

'Wild donkeys will not drag me into St Ives in the summer,' wrote Gerald Priestland in his book *West of Hayle River*. During the high season the town is over-run by tourists, and it is easy to see why. A jumble of narrow streets slithers down the steep hillside towards a pair of small bays, dividing which is a promontory on whose grassy knoll sits an old chapel. There are fine views over roofs, spires and sea; there is a charming railway station; and there are still a few old fishermen knocking around the pubs beside the harbour. St Ives

OPPOSITE: *Cape Cornwall – 'the connoisseur's Land's End'*

35

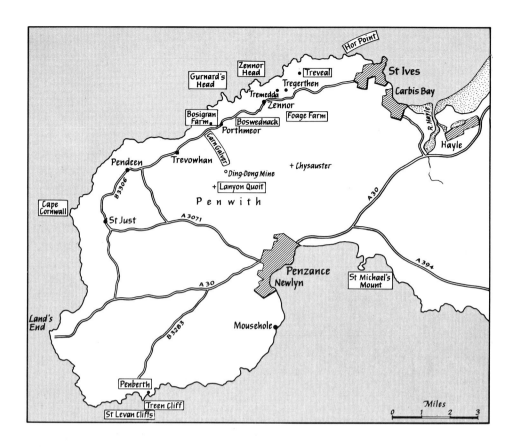

has the quintessential feel of an English seaside town; it is, as Virginia Woolf wrote, 'a windy, noisy, fishy, vociferous, narrow-streeted town; the colour of a mussel or a limpet; like a bunch of rough shellfish, oysters or mussels, all crowded together'.

As it happens, no writer has done for Penwith what Hardy did for Dorset or Priestley for Yorkshire: rather, it has been the artists and sculptors who have made the most of it. Barbara Hepworth came here in 1939 and 'gradually discovered the remarkable pagan landscape' between St Ives and Land's End. 'Here in Cornwall,' she wrote, 'I have a background which links with Yorkshire in the natural shape of stone structure and fertility, and it links with Italy because of the intensity of light and colour.' Even if you do nothing else in St Ives, you should visit Hepworth's studio, which is now a museum administered by the Tate Gallery. The sculptures in the garden live easily with the trees and shrubs that surround them. Hepworth was a member of an artists' colony which included the potter Bernard Leach and dozens of painters. Some, like Peter Lanyon, were home-bred; others, like Naum Gabo and Hepworth's husband, Ben Nicholson, came and went; and a few came and settled. Most notable among the latter is the artist and critic Patrick Heron, like Hepworth an immigrant from Yorkshire.

Since 1955 Heron has lived in Eagles Nest, a large, mostly Victorian house

*Patrick Heron*

which overlooks the sea a few miles to the west of St Ives. The house is set in a garden famous for its azaleas and camellias and it commands a magnificent view over a plateau of land which is meshed with stone 'hedges', some of which date back to the Bronze Age. At the centre of this granite web squats a huddle of grey farm buildings. Katherine Mansfield and D. H. Lawrence lived here during the First World War (Lawrence and his German wife were driven out on the suspicion that they were spies), and later the cottages were rented to Virginia Woolf. The grasslands beyond fade into cliffs which fall sheer into the frothy sea.

At first sight, the landscape of West Penwith appears so robust that one imagines it to be indestructible. However, had it not been for the activities of Enterprise Neptune, and the tireless campaigning of men like Heron, it would have been much despoiled. Heron is possessed of a grace and charm which

*Zennor church town*

seem distinctly old-fashioned, yet when he talks of those who threaten this stretch of coast his language is intemperate and unprintable. Since he settled here with his late wife Delia he has fought over a dozen campaigns, sometimes alone, sometimes in partnership with the Trust. His opponents have included mining companies, property developers and the Admiralty. 'Although there's a feeling of tremendous space,' said Heron, 'the landscape is really minuscule. Even the smallest of changes stands out a mile.' One of his perennial fears has been that the road which links St Ives to St Just might one day be widened or straightened out. 'It's a sort of pleasure road,' he said. 'You couldn't design a finer one if you tried.'

Penwith's history is etched on the landscape, rather than buried beneath it. Beside the coast road, or at least never far from it, you will come across mushroom-shaped stone quoits, relics of the late Stone Age, across Bronze Age field systems, across Iron Age forts, across the remains of farmsteads dating back to the time of the Roman occupation, and, perhaps most impressive of all, across the ruins of a tin industry which pre-dated Christianity and was still flourishing within living memory. From Heron's house the road wiggles its way westward through rugged countryside and places with names like Zennor, Boswednack, Porthmeor, Morvah and Bojewyan. Zennor is known, somewhat ambitiously, as a 'church town'. It consists of a small church built out of huge blocks of granite, a pub called the Tinners Arms, a tiny museum, a smattering of houses, and an old Non-conformist chapel now devoted to the manufacture of pine furniture. Many of the hamlets further along the road are little more than farms now, though a century or more ago they supported sizeable communities whose prosperity was based on the Cornish trinity of tin, pilchards and land. When the pilchard shoals arrived in late summer men dropped their picks and ploughs and went fishing; otherwise they divided their time between their smallholdings and the tin mines. Presumably it was the rigours of daily life which inspired the poem on William Champen's stone in Zennor Church:

> Hope, fear, false joy and trouble,
> Are those four winds which daily toss this bubble,
> His breath's a vapour and his life's a span,
> 'Tis glorious misery to be born a man.

Only one mine still operates in Penwith – the Geevor works sprawl seaward from Pendeen – but you are seldom out of sight of old chimneys and engine houses. From time to time you will catch glimpses of Ding-Dong mine, which juts like a broken tooth from the moorland horizon, and some ten minutes' drive from Zennor you will come across Carn Galver, which is owned by the Trust. As W. G. Hoskins wrote in *The Making of the English Landscape*, Cornwall provides 'the most appealing of all industrial landscapes of England, in no way ugly but indeed possessing a profound melancholy beauty'.

The winning of tin has influenced the character of towns like Pendeen and St Just every bit as irrevocably as it has shaped the landscape. 'I must restrain myself from being unkind,' wrote Gerald Priestland of St Just. 'St Just is no St Ives, but it is not that bad.' In fact, it is very good indeed; not pretty, certainly, but solid, masculine and unaffected. With its vast chapel, its rows of brick terraces and its drably grand public buildings, it reminded me of the small mining towns near Mansfield or Sunderland. There are conspicuously few bed-and-breakfasts and a great many pubs. One day I lunched with Jon Brookes, the Trust's warden, at the Star Inn: low ceilings, a coal fire, and a pub draw whose prizes included a big pasty, a sack of onions and some hair gel. There was no nonsense about scampi-in-a-basket either; we washed down brick-size lumps of Cheddar with good beer. St Just was said to be a wild place on Friday and Saturday nights after the pubs had closed, and I imagine D. H. Lawrence would have felt at home here. It seems fitting that England should come to an end – Cape Cornwall and Land's End lie only a short distance to the west – with such a tough little town.

Over most of England the landscapes we see are largely the product of human activities during the last couple of centuries; contemporary man has either razed the creations of those who came before, or buried them beneath soil and concrete. To get at the past one must dig for it. Penwith is different. 'The landscape you see here,' explained Peter Herring, an archaeologist working for the County Council, 'is pretty much as it was when it was laid out during later prehistoric times.' This was the period which began around 500BC and ended in AD400.

Herring and I began a tour of Penwith at Chysauster, Cornwall's best-preserved settlement of the Romano–British period, built around the first century AD and now looked after by English Heritage. There are eight ruined dwellings – known as courtyard houses – loosely arranged along a street. Each consists of a series of enclosures around a central yard. The enclosures are about thirty yards across, massive-walled, and cellular in design. The roofs have collapsed and the walls are topped by thickets of gorse and heather. The people of Chysauster were farmers. Each house had a small byre and a separate room in which butter and milk were kept. The land outside the village was both grazed and tilled, and above the settlement there were, until recently, good remains of a rectilinear field system which dated back to the Dark Ages. These were largely destroyed by the owner in 1983.

From Chysauster we made our way down to the coast at Carn Galver, where, within the space of a ten-minute walk, we touched upon, and walked over, the relics of human activity stretching back to the Bronze Age. Between here and St Ives, a distance of some eight miles, most of the coast, and much of the land behind it, is owned by the Trust. The 500-acre block of land round the old mine workings at Carn Galver was bought in 1978 with Enterprise Neptune funds and bequests. There are magnificent cliffs below the mine –

*The cliffs at Bosigran*

Sherpa Tensing is one of the many famous climbers who trained here – and the land sweeps up sharply to the hill of Carn Galver, at 816 feet the second highest point in Penwith.

The most striking feature is the mine itself, or at least what remains of it. The two gaunt buildings beside the road – a pumping-engine house with a chimney, and the old winding-engine house – have recently been repointed. There is a difficult balance to be struck between retaining the romance of a ruin and making the structure safe, and here the mason has been somewhat over-generous with the mortar. Below the buildings the ground is scarred by the remains of processing floors and small reservoirs which used to supply water to the mill further down. Ore from the mine was brought to the mill by mule trains and dumped on a platform; here it was broken up by children and bonneted women armed with hammers and known as bal-maidens. Once the ore had been broken up it was sent down a chute to be crushed by heavy mechanical hammers in the stamping sheds. The crushed ore was mixed with water and the resulting sludge was channelled into stone-lined vessels called buddles, traces of which can still be seen. Once the tin had settled out it was taken to the calcining plant, where impurities like arsenic were burnt off; then it was smelted and made ready for export.

*Looking north from the summit of Carn Galver*

A little way beyond the stamping sheds the heath and bracken cease and high cliffs plummet into the sea. A century ago these cliffs would have been the haunt of Cornish choughs. The choughs, like the miners, have gone, but ravens still croak over the ruins and we saw a buzzard as we made our way up to Bosigran Castle. Little remains of the Iron Age fortifications, but the views alone are worth the climb. Looking towards St Ives we could see the jagged promontories of Porthmeor Point and Gurnard's Head, both of which belong to the Trust. Above Porthmeor village there was a field of oat stooks, this being one of the few places in England where farmers still use old-fashioned binders. Not far from here, and hidden away in dense scrub, are the relics of a settlement similar to Chysauster.

From the castle one gets a clear picture of how the old farms are organised in this part of Cornwall. Each consists of a strip of land running from the moors down to the sea. On the high ground there is a large expanse of rough, unenclosed moorland; below this the moorland is enclosed and known as 'croft'; then come the enclosed pastures which are either grazed or cut for hay or silage. Finally, there is a mottled patch of land where heath, scrub, rush valleys and pastures are muddled together behind the cliffs. Each of these strips, or tenements, was developed during the Dark Ages; though patterns of ownership and use have changed over the centuries, the field boundaries are little altered. Bosigran Farm is particularly fine: 'one of the best-preserved prehistoric landscapes', according to Herring. Some of the hedges date back to the Bronze Age.

Cornish hedges are massive affairs, as much as six feet thick and sometimes as high as a man. They generally consist of two walls of stone separated by an infill of rubble and soil. In sheltered areas the stone is clothed by a thick mat of vegetation, but here, along the exposed and treeless north coast, the granite remains naked. These walls were created by farmers clearing stones from the land in order to cultivate it. They are, in effect, stone rubbish tips, and the unique character of the Cornish landscape owes as much to their existence as it does to the relics of the mining industry.

Imagine, if you can, how this stretch of coast must have been midway through the last century. Such was Cornwall's importance in the tin trade that twelve countries had vice-consuls based in Penzance. The pumping houses and chimneys still visible are but a fraction of what existed then. The air would have been filled with smoke and perpetual noise; between the hamlets and mines would have moved a constant stream of trade and people. By the end of the last century Cornwall was running out of both tin and pilchards: mines closed; the fishing industry declined; thousands emigrated. A century ago the hamlet of Treveal supported eighty people and boasted its own cobbler's shop. Now it is a single farm and home to just two families, one being the Trust warden's. The same thing – the metamorphosis of hamlet into farmstead – happened all along the coast. The land continued to be farmed – it was good dairy country – but the patterns of ownership gradually changed as smallholdings were amalgamated to make larger farms.

The National Trust now owns some 2,300 acres of land between St Ives and Land's End and it has covenants over a further 900 acres. The Trust made six separate acquisitions between 1938 and 1980, since when it has made a further sixteen. It is just as well that the Trust has stepped up its programme of acquisition: although Penwith is virtually bereft of industry, it has come under increasing threat from a whole range of activities.

That my time passed so enjoyably in Cornwall had much to do with the company I kept. I owe Giles Clotworthy, the Trust's Regional Public Affairs Manager (RPAM), and Peter Mansfield, the managing agent, a considerable debt of gratitude, for the days I spent with them proved both enjoyable and enlightening. I had already heard about Clotworthy. He was said to be one of the most effective RPAMs working for the Trust – he has been responsible for producing a staggering quantity of well-illustrated booklets about Trust properties in Cornwall – and he was evidently one of those people who once met was always remembered. I first came across him at Lanhydrock, the Trust's regional office near Bodmin, and he looked very much as the general public might expect a Trust employee to look. Unashamedly rural in dress and attitude, he was a man of considerable wit and charm. We lunched well at Lanhydrock House restaurant with Peter Mansfield, then retired to Clotworthy's office to discuss how I should spend the week. Our conversations were periodically interrupted by the flatulent rumblings of his two black labradors.

*Giles Clotworthy and Rupert*

Mansfield, the senior of the Trust's three land agents in Cornwall, took a degree in law, then trained as a chartered surveyor. He joined the Trust in 1974, since when he has seen enormous changes in the way it operates. 'Not many years before I was interviewed,' he recalled, 'I would have been asked, "Can you afford to work for us?"' In those days the people who worked for the Trust were poorly paid and many had private incomes; it was, in a sense, a gentleman's vocation. Although land agents are better paid now than they used to be, their salaries remain modest. 'I see myself as a professional enthusiast,' said Mansfield. 'Working for the Trust is really a cause.' The land agent's job in Penwith is onerous. Mansfield is responsible for co-ordinating the work of the Trust's specialist staff; he oversees the running of all the Trust properties to the west of Truro; he assesses for acquisition any land which comes on the market; he must ensure that the conservation of landscape and buildings doesn't prevent tenant farmers from making a living any more than it has to; and he must spend much time convincing the local communities that the Trust's activities are in their best interests.

Mansfield and I met one morning at Treveal, and from there we journeyed westward in the company of Jon Brookes. 'When we took over Treveal in 1982,' explained Mansfield, 'we thought long and hard about its future.' With only seventy farming acres and eighty acres of cliff the property wasn't a viable farming unit: 'We didn't want a tenant to come in and have to squeeze the juice out of every acre to make a living.' So the Trust decided to use the farm buildings as the warden's headquarters and rent the land out to adjoining family farms. A public meeting was held in Zennor to discuss the Trust's plans, and according to Mansfield, 'All hell broke loose – I was nearly eviscerated by the Women's Institute.' The Women's Institute and others, already worried about the amount of land owned by the Trust in Zennor parish, claimed that the traditional patterns of land ownership were being broken up. They were forgetting that a century ago Treveal was farmed as five units not one. This episode shows how awkward the Trust's life can be; both land agents and wardens require considerable skills of diplomacy.

Having listened to both Mansfield and Patrick Heron discuss the various activities which had threatened the Penwith coast, it came as something of a surprise to find it largely unspoilt still. Mansfield took up the story in 1957, which was the year when St Ives Council cooked up a plan to use Hor Point as a rubbish tip. The day before the Council met to decide on whether or not to

OVERLEAF: *St Ives*

exercise its right of compulsory purchase, the farmer who owned the land sold it to the Trust for £5: the Trust declared Hor Point inalienable and it was saved. Heron alluded to this, then settled down to describe the battle in the 1960s to save Carnelloe, a coastal farm a little way to the west of Zennor.

'This was when I first went into action,' recalled Heron. 'I heard that a miner who'd returned from Malaya wanted to mine tin and build masses of houses at Carnelloe, so I downed tools for nine months to try and stop him. At that time conservation didn't exist as a word, so drumming up support was none too easy.' Heron enlisted the help of the Trust, the local MP, many of the people of Zennor, and dozens of VIPs, among them John Betjeman, Edith Evans and Benjamin Britten. There was a public inquiry, and although the inspector ruled against the objectors, the minister ruled in their favour. After this the miner put in a more modest application to the County Council. He was granted permission to prospect for minerals, and subsequently he sold his rights to a Canadian mining company. Eventually, the *Guardian* ran an editorial railing against the spectre of Carnelloe being developed. 'It was only then,' said Heron, 'that the threat disappeared.'

It was around this time that Tregerthen Farm, the retreat of Lawrence, Mansfield and Woolf, came on to the market, and it soon became known that a London property dealer wished to buy it and build a holiday development. Heron, a neighbouring farmer, Mrs Griggs, and the Trust put up the money to buy it themselves. Mrs Griggs took the farmhouse and surrounding fields, while Heron bought the land behind Eagles Nest. The Trust acquired the cliffs, and it was given covenants over the rest of the farm.

Once the mining interests had been vanquished a further threat arose in the formidable shape of the Admiralty. One day Michael Trinick, then the Trust's Regional Director, informed Heron that the naval base at Culdrose had applied for a 'planning clearance order' over 350 acres of hill land behind Eagles Nest. Trinick and Heron had become firm friends during the Carnelloe affair, and the Regional Director now persuaded Heron to mount another campaign, this time to thwart the Admiralty in its plans to use the Zennor area for troop landings and training. 'The effects would have been devastating,' explained Heron. 'I made a lot of fuss and we managed to get the national press on our side.' As soon as the Admiralty realised that Heron had launched a campaign, Eagles Nest was buzzed by helicopters. 'Some came in the morning,' he recalled, 'then again later in the day.' The Admiralty, incidentally, claimed that all the relevant landowners had been consulted, which was untrue. Anyway, the proposal to use the area for troop landings was dropped.

*The ancient landscape of West Penwith*

Over the years the Trust gradually built up its holdings round Zennor and elsewhere in Cornwall, and Trinick earned the nickname 'King Neptune'. Indeed, he did much to initiate the Trust's policy of buying coastland 'one farm deep' or 'to the skyline'. Although there were few dramas during the 1970s to match those of the previous decade, this was none the less a tricky period, for other, more insidious pressures threatened the coast. The conservation ethic was becoming more deeply embedded in the national psyche, but at the same time farmers were coming under increasing pressure to work their land more intensively.

This had traditionally been a good dairying area, and ever since the railways had reached western Cornwall during the last century Penwith's farmers had exported the milk from their Guernsey herds eastwards. Since the last war there have been dramatic changes in farming practices, and these have made themselves felt even in the more remote parts of the country. During the 1960s the Milk Marketing Board began to collect milk in bulk tankers; roadside churn-stands became things of the past. Many of the farms in Penwith couldn't be reached by tankers, and farmers moved out of milk and into beef. Bullocks are a good deal more frisky and adventurous than cows and the stone hedges have suffered as a result.

Over the past couple of decades farmers throughout the country have forsaken the traditional mowing of meadows for hay and turned instead to the production of silage, which requires larger and more cumbersome machinery. Hedges are viewed as an impediment and some farmers have been eager to disband them, thus creating larger fields and gaining land into the bargain. 'The people of Penwith used to live very simple lives,' said Mansfield, 'and indeed many still do. But the recent college generation of farmers tends to have the same consumer aspirations as you and I, and consequently they need to increase their income from the land.'

Where the Trust owns land it can prescribe the farming practices of the tenants. But where it has been given restrictive covenants over land, problems frequently arise. A covenant is an agreement made between the owner and the Trust. Its purpose is to ensure that the former, and whoever owns the land in times to come, will do nothing which is prejudicial to the appearance of the landscape. The Trust has powers, as a last resort, to take the landowner to court if he or she breaches the agreement (though in practice it very rarely has to). Much of the covenanted land round Zennor came from Mrs Griggs. She had the satisfaction of knowing that after her death those who took over her farms would not be able to do anything drastic to them. Subsequent owners of covenanted land are often less sympathetic.

While some farmers, and especially those affected by covenants, view the Trust with scepticism, and sometimes animosity, others have benefited greatly from its activities in West Cornwall. Two examples will suffice. One Penwith farmer wished to hand his farm over to his son, but he had no home to which he could retire. The Trust stepped in: it bought the seaward edge of the farm and took covenants over the rest. This enabled the farmer to buy a retirement home, and it has ensured the land's future conservation. Further west there were two tenanted farms owned by one family. The family decided to sell up and the tenants were given first option to buy. Lacking the capital, they were unable to do so. However, the Trust accepted the offer of one tenant to resell the cliff land, and this provided the shortfall required to buy the farm. The Trust's action thus helped one family to remain on its farm.

The Trust's efforts to conserve the traditional landscape of West Penwith have been bolstered in recent years by the intervention of the Ministry of Agriculture (MAFF). MAFF has identified twelve Environmentally Sensitive Areas (ESAs) in England and Wales, one of which is Penwith (the others being in the Pennine Dales, the Peak District, the Norfolk Broads, the East Anglian Brecks, the Suffolk River Valleys, the Test Valley, the South Downs, the Somerset Levels, the Shropshire Borders, the Cambrian Mountains and the Llŷn Peninsula). Each of these areas possesses an outstanding landscape whose conservation depends on farmers resisting the urge to adopt intensive methods of cultivation and husbandry. Farmers in the Penwith ESA who are willing to be party to the scheme are paid £24 per acre each year, in return for which they must agree to look after their heaths, hedges, ancient monuments and so forth. 'This scheme has been a brilliant success,' said Mansfield. 'It's a very important cushion for the farmers, and in Penwith they've taken their responsibilities seriously. They're putting more effort into looking after their hedges – which is a major expense – and they're not just flying off to Ibiza with the money they get.' The West Penwith ESA covers an area of some 17,000 acres. The Trust owns 1,750 acres within the ESA and has covenants over a further 850.

Autumn in Penwith is a misanthrope's dream: you can walk for hours without seeing a soul. The sense of quiet and desolation would be absolute were it not for the almost constant presence of naval helicopters, which are forever whirring over the countryside. It would be churlish to suggest that Penwith's air space should be inviolate, not least because many of the helicopters are Sea Kings used in sea-rescue operations. But there are other species of helicopter too, and one wonders whether all the low flying is strictly

*Lanyon Quoit*

necessary. Obviously, the Navy cannot be expected to pussy-foot around the countryside, but there are times when its behaviour seems distinctly cavalier.

Heron is particularly aggrieved about the fact that the Culdrose naval base periodically unleashes small groups of trainees on the moors around Zennor. He feels that the Trust, which has covenants over his land, should prevent these incursions. But the Trust does not view such training as a problem, partly because the numbers involved are small, and partly because the trainees behave little differently from civilian outward-bound groups. Heron has done a great deal for the conservation of West Penwith and it is a shame that he and the Trust fell out over this issue. In fact the whole saga highlights one of the weaknesses of restrictive covenants. The Trust can only object if the land-owner does something – or allows something to happen – which is detrimental to the landscape. This, in the Trust's view, wasn't and isn't.

If people are suspicious about naval activities – and intentions – it is not altogether surprising. Several years ago Des Hannigan, a local journalist, made a curious discovery on the Penwith moors. He found numbers painted in road-white paint on rocks and ancient monuments. Hannigan has the qualities of a Renaissance man: he spent many years as a fisherman before turning to journalism. He is also a climber and local historian. His powers of mimicry are enviable and he managed to make the numbers story sound much funnier than it really was. 'Eventually I managed to track down twenty-one numbers daubed on ancient monuments and rocks,' he said, 'and I ran a piece in several local papers about "Bronze Age Bingo". Of course, there was nothing mysterious about the numbers; it was quite obvious who was doing it.' The numbers were being used as orienteering markers by Culdrose trainees, and they had been painted on to the rocks and monuments by military personnel who were probably not based at Culdrose. This gave the Culdrose authorities dubious justification for saying that although they used the numbers they hadn't 'actually' put them there. This sort of desecration is guaranteed to antagonise anyone who cares about the countryside.

There is something charmingly pointless about the pilgrimage to Land's End, but if you are spending time in Penwith you may as well go and peer over the edge of the cliffs; more than half a million others do every year. Even men of great intelligence have taken a childish delight at seeing England come to a full stop. Here is Daniel Defoe, who travelled to Cornwall in the early 1700s:

> . . . being resolved to see the very extremity of it, I set foot into the sea, as it were, beyond the farthest inch of dry land west, as I had done before near the town of Dover, at the foot of the rocks of the South-Foreland in Kent, which, I think, is the farthest point east in a line; and as I had done, also, at Leostoff in Suffolk, which is another promontory on the eastern coast, and is reckoned the farthest eastward of the island in general . . .

Defoe was so preoccupied with his toe-danglings, and the prospect of repeating the exercise at 'John a Grot's', that he neglected to tell the reader what Land's End was like, although he did describe how on his approach he saw 'great numbers of that famous kind of crow, which is known by the name of the Cornish cough, or chough, so the country people call them'.

By all accounts Land's End was a very scruffy place before the developer Peter de Savary and his company got hold of it in November 1987. It boasted a hotel, a few curio shops, a mass of eroded footpaths and a very good view. Land Leisure paid £6.7 million for Land's End and spent £4 million smartening the place up over the winter. The result is a glitzy series of buildings which house, among other things, shops, restaurants, craft displays, an interpretation centre and 'the legendary Last Labyrinth – a sensational and enchanting experience'. After a while you get used to the hype in this 'land of legend and laughter', as one leaflet describes Cornwall. There are some impressive exhibits in the interpretation centre covering farming, fishing, mining and so forth, but there is plenty of whimsy about such things as pirates and smugglers. Cornwall here is rendered twee, folksy and romantic. Presumably there is a demand for this sort of stuff: the countryside made safe, simple and pretty, as it is in margarine advertisements.

Over the past couple of years de Savary's outfits have taken Cornwall by storm. Highland Participants bought Falmouth Docks in 1987. Once moribund, the docks are now booming; the workforce has doubled and house prices have shot up. Then in summer 1988 de Savary bought Hayle Harbour, across the estuary from St Ives. Initially it was rumoured that his company intended to build a £250 million all-weather leisure complex which would provide 3,000 jobs. 'Not too many years from now,' said Robin Linfield, who manages the Falmouth operation, 'there'll be the Channel Tunnel and a direct rail link from Paris to Hayle. At the moment Hayle's just a shanty town with lovely beaches, but Peter thinks it's got great potential.' *Hayle vous souhaite les bonnes vacances!* It is a curious thought. The idea of a leisure complex has not been abandoned, but de Savary subsequently announced that his first move would be to build 800–1,000 new houses at Hayle.

Feelings in the area about the new-look Land's End are mixed. There are those who applaud any venture which brings work and money into this economically depressed area; and Land's End does. And there are those who detest it. 'A small unpleasant-looking hotel is one thing,' said Heron. 'A big money-making complex quite another. It totally vulgarises the coast.' Had the Trust bought Land's End in 1981, when Charles Neave-Hill put it on the market, there would have been changes too, though of a different nature from those brought about by Land Leisure. (The Trust put in a bid of £1·5 million, but someone else offered almost double that.) 'If we'd got it,' said Clotworthy, 'we'd have invited the world's press and blown up most of the buildings.'

Mansfield was wary of passing public judgement on the Land's End developments, but he, like most people in Cornwall, was impressed by the thorough way in which de Savary had gone about things. 'His PR is absolutely brilliant,' said Mansfield. 'He's very responsive to local opinion, and what he's set out to do he's done well.' Linfield thought that one of the cleverest things de Savary had done was to give everyone within ten miles of Land's End a free entry pass. 'PR is very important,' he said. 'We spend half our lives just talking to MPs, councillors, in fact to everybody – we try to take them along with our plans.'

De Savary is eager to court the conservation lobby. He has hired David Bellamy's firm of consultants to look after the wildlife interests of Land's End, and local schoolchildren are involved in a scheme to revegetate the cliffs with Cornish wildflowers. De Savary has also given a chunk of the bird-rich mudflats at Hayle to the Royal Society for the Protection of Birds. This is more than just good PR.

My feelings about Land's End are ambivalent. I found the new developments aesthetically unobjectionable – the addition of a few more buildings hasn't prejudicially affected the landscape; and if de Savary is helping to shorten the dole queues (unemployment in West Cornwall is approaching 20 per cent), then so much the better. My reservations are more to do with the effects which leisure-cum-interpretation centres have on the atmosphere and spirit of the countryside than with the physical nature of the beasts themselves. The problem is that they tend to negate the coast's greatest attractions: the wildness, the sense of space, and indeed the knowledge that to get the best out of it you must abandon your car and walk. The real joy of the countryside lies in personal discovery.

It remains to be seen whether de Savary will get planning permission for his leisure centre at Hayle. 'If it comes off,' said one worried local, 'we'll have de Savary and his pleasure grounds at both ends of Penwith.' Then it might just be a matter of time before the theme-park tentacles wrapped themselves round the coast road and the remoter areas inland. Suggestions that one day Chinook helicopters will cart sightseers from Land's End to Hayle, and that the Council will widen the coast road to cater for the increase in bus traffic, may not be that far-fetched. De Savary is no philanthropist; he is spending vast amounts of money and he expects to recoup it. The countryside may end up paying.

People are attracted to Land's End more by its geographical fame than by its landscape. Though there is little wrong with the latter, it is not in the same league as Cape Cornwall – or 'the connoisseur's Land's End', as Peter Mansfield called it – which was bought by H. J. Heinz and Co. Ltd and given to the Trust in 1987. Mrs Thatcher received the deeds from Heinz, thus putting her government's stamp of approval on the idea of private sponsorship.

Cape Cornwall juts out to sea four miles as the gull flies to the north of Land's End. I went there twice and both times it was virtually deserted. You go down a lane past a field with a tiny ruined chapel, then climb up the flanks of the promontory to an old chimney, the culmination of a flue which once

served an engine at the foot of the hill. The draught provided by the chimney was so vigorous that the boiler was repeatedly burnt out and another chimney had to be built further down the slope. Luckily, this one was left where it stood. It is a beautiful chimney, and so much a part of the landscape that its removal would be an act of emasculation. Bedded into its granite base is a small plaque the shape of the label on a tin of Heinz baked beans. The views, both out to sea and back down the coast, are stupendous. There are no cafés, thank God; no signposts telling you how far it is to Australia; no shops selling sea-shells or scented soap or Portmeirion china.

Penwith seems to attract people from Yorkshire: Hepworth and Heron both came from there, and so did the cleaning lady in my hotel. The latter said that she was one of hundreds who had come south for seasonal work and settled permanently. If you come from Yorkshire, and particularly from those parts of the Pennines built out of millstone grit, you will probably feel at home here. Crudely speaking, Penwith is like an ironed-out version of the West Riding. It differs chiefly in terms of its climate, which is better, its towns, which are fewer and smaller, its air, which is cleaner, and its views, which are inferior. By this I do not mean to suggest that the landscape is any less lovely in Penwith than in Yorkshire, but simply that it is less easily observed. The heaving topography of the Pennines enables the walker to climb high above the valleys; from some hills the panorama takes in not just one valley, but several, and you see the countryside much as the curlews and plovers do. From the top of Carn Galver there are good views, but you don't get the same bird's-eye feel as in the Pennines. There is a simple remedy for this, and it is to be found at the Land's End Aerodrome outside St Just. After lunch at the Star Inn, Jon Brookes and I made our way there and bought half an hour's worth of flying.

Everything about the aerodrome is enchanting. Even if you have no intention of flying, it is worth coming for the homemade cakes in the Choxaway Café. The girl behind the Westwards Airways counter sold us a ticket, gave us a Westwards Airways biro and told us how much she loved the job. She was on a government youth-training scheme. After a short wait she led us on to the grass airstrip to a four-seater Cesna Reims Rocket. It looked like a Ford Anglia with wings and its standards of comfort were similar. Once we'd been strapped in, the girl asked us to 'lip-read' an information leaflet which had red crosses through pictures of false teeth and spectacles. The pilot

OPPOSITE: *Priest's Cove, Cape Cornwall*

*A stream running beneath the cliffs at Bosigran*

said that he would point out the landmarks, but with Brookes in the back seat there was no need.

Brookes would have figured more prominently here had he been working longer in Penwith. Having spent six years as warden of Box Hill, a recreation area popular with walkers, Hell's Angels and all sorts in Surrey, he and his family had moved to Treveal in early summer and he was still getting to know the area, for which he had already developed a deep affection. He was one of the new breed of Trust wardens: confident, outgoing, undeferential. Had I not learnt otherwise, I would have said, from what I saw now, that Brookes had led a life of hedonism on leaving school. He hadn't: he'd joined the Navy when he was sixteen; more predictably, he'd hated it. He had trained as an engineer at Culdrose, and later he had taken a four-year extramural course in ecology and conservation at London University.

After a teeth-chattering take-off, we flew over Cape Cornwall and headed north-east past Pendeen. The sea below Geevor mine was a rusty red. A few minutes later we passed Bosigran, then in quick succession came Gurnard's Head, Zennor Head, Treveal and Hor Point, on which, mercifully, there was no rubbish tip. St Ives from the air looked precisely as Woolf had described it, though from 1,000 feet the houses were more like barnacles than mussels or oysters. Once over St Ives we wheeled sharply south towards St Michael's Mount, then headed back to St Just along the south coast. This is an altogether gentler world: much of the land is cultivated, the granite hedges are submerged beneath thickets of scrub, and although there are cliffs they are modest compared to those on the north and west coasts. There are two towns of significance – Penzance and the thriving fishing port of Newlyn – and several small fishing villages, one of which, Penberth, is owned by the Trust.

Today the sky seemed preternaturally blue; the land below, strangely soft, its colour and texture lichenous. We flew over mineheads, harbours, cliffs, chimneys, ragged farms, small fields, villages, moors. Here was a landscape full of complexity, with its fair share of scruffiness and dereliction: a far cry from the 'designer countryside' of theme parks and margarine ads.

# 3

# *Far From the Madding Crowd*

HE ISLE OF PURBECK is not an isle at all, but a rectangular peninsula, some ten miles long by seven wide. Roughly speaking, it encompasses all the land to the east of a line between Lulworth Cove and the small town of Wareham. It is bounded on three sides by water. To the north lies Poole Harbour, beyond which are the towns of Poole and Bournemouth. Purbeck's eastern shores comprise the dunes and sands of Studland Beach, the chalk promontory of Old Harry, the resort of Swanage, and the bays of Swanage and Durlston. Then at Durlston Head the coast turns west and progresses in a spectacular series of undulations and indentations towards St Aldhelm's Head, Kimmeridge Bay and Lulworth Cove.

No other area of comparable size in Britain boasts as many plant and animal species as Purbeck. That nature's cup runneth over is almost entirely a reflection of Purbeck's geology, which, even to the untutored eye, is staggering in its diversity. There are two great ridges, the longer of which is chalk and runs from just north of Swanage to Lulworth Cove. It is interrupted midway by a narrow ravine in which stand the ruins of Corfe Castle. Where uncultivated the chalk downland is profusely carpeted with orchids, vetches and dozens of other flowers which thrive in the springy sheep-grazed turf. The other ridge provides the much-quarried cliffscape of marble and limestone between Durlston Head and Gad Cliff. Overlying the chalk there are wide expanses of sands and gravels whose acid soils support a type of heathland peculiar to this part of the world; it is here that one finds such rarities as the Dartford warbler, the smooth snake and the sand lizard. And for those plants which find the chalk too rich in lime, and the gravels and sands too acid for their taste, there are the neutral clays.

It is some indication of Purbeck's importance for wildlife conservation that it possesses three National Nature Reserves, a bird reserve owned by the

OPPOSITE: *Eastington Farm*

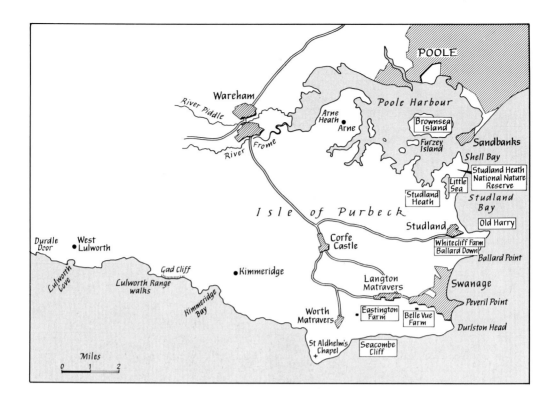

Royal Society for the Protection of Birds, and twenty Sites of Special Scientific Interest (SSSIs). Indeed, one committee which made recommendations to government about which areas might be declared National Parks included Purbeck on its shortlist. Purbeck was not chosen – nor was any other area in lowland England – though later it was designated an Area of Outstanding Natural Beauty (AONB). Not that this means very much. Although planning controls are stricter within AONBs than in non-designated countryside, they do not provide the degree of protection afforded to land within National Parks. Fortunately, however, over 7,000 acres of Purbeck are now in the ownership of the National Trust, whose largest holdings are at Studland and Corfe Castle, both of which were part of the 16,000-acre estate left to the Trust by Ralph Bankes in 1982. The Trust has also acquired, sometimes with the help of Enterprise Neptune funds, small blocks of coastal cliff and farmland at Belle Vue, Whitecliff and Ballard Down.

'The villages through Wessex,' wrote the poet Geoffrey Grigson in his guide to the area, 'do not often quarrel with their landscape.' And neither do the towns. Corfe, the old capital of Purbeck, is especially striking with its ruined castle looming above the mellow roofs of the main square. It is almost too perfect: the sort of thing a Victorian Romantic like Ruskin might have dreamt up. Swanage, in contrast, possesses little of architectural merit, yet there can be few more agreeable seaside resorts in England. This is where I began my

*Punch and Judy,*
*Swanage*

travels in Dorset, and I urge anyone who wishes to acquaint themselves with Purbeck to spend their nights here and their days walking the coast. I made several journeys to Purbeck, the first in the company of friends at the tail-end of October. We arrived one Friday night, installed ourselves in one of Swanage's many bed-and-breakfasts, then set off for an evening on the town. We forwent the entertainments at the theatre and the cinema – *Macbeth* in one, *The Jungle Book* in the other – and headed for the pubs, which were healthily packed. After closing time we wandered along the seafront. Gangs of teenage boys loitered with their girlfriends in the bus shelters; the odd drunk staggered against the stiff breeze; and far along the beach a crowd had gathered round the coastguard to observe the flounderings of a flashy yacht. Three men were doing their best to prevent it breaking up on the beach.

Swanage is used to such dramas: the previous week another yacht had broken in two when washed ashore by a storm. As we arrived on the scene the coastguard was explaining that there was nothing he could do; he said the police were scouring Purbeck's pubs for the yacht's owner. The girlfriend of one of the rescuers foolishly wondered aloud whether her man had earned salvage rights. We polished off a bottle of fizzy wine and listened to the slurping of the waves. It was a balmy night, warm and clear with a three-quarter moon. Away to our left stretched the chalk cliffs beneath the whaleback of Ballard Down; to our right was the town centre, beyond which was the modest harbour and pencil-sharp Peveril Point.

It was the small things in Swanage which caught the eye: the neat rows of wooden beach huts; a column topped with cannon balls commemorating a Saxon naval defeat; a clock tower with oriental pretensions; the notice which read 'Lost Children Here Please'. I met several people who told me that Swanage was dying, that many hotels had closed and that the number of visitors was declining. They said that the resort no longer had the amenities the youth of today demands: the amusement arcades were too old-fashioned and there weren't enough discos. Swanage certainly is old-fashioned, but that is precisely its charm. There is even a chemist's which doesn't sell Tampax or contraceptives. That alone endears me to the place.

The next morning we armed ourselves with Rodney Legg's *Purbeck Walks*. Mr Legg is an industry. He seems to have written about everything in Dorset: ghosts, smugglers, quarries, churches, wildlife, fossils, Lawrence of Arabia; the list is endless. We began with walk number six, 'Westward from Kimmeridge (5 miles)'. The path headed inland from Kimmeridge Bay to Kimmeridge village (there was a Legg buried in the churchyard), then along the chalk ridge to Gad Cliff and down to the sea again. The countryside looked soft, velvety and indescribably lovely. The large fields below the ridge had been harrowed to a fine tilth and they were a creamy brown, like milk chocolate. There was little in the way of woodland apart from the odd copse: most of the trees were shorn by the winds and leafless, but here and there explosions of green signalled the presence of holm oak and holly. Perched on Kimmeridge Bay's western cliffs was Clavel Tower, a circular, colonnaded folly built by a vicar in 1831. Equally curious, at least in this setting, was BP's nodding donkey see-sawing oil to the surface at the other side of the bay.

If you glanced at an Ordnance Survey map you might suppose that the coasts of Purbeck and Penwith were similar, with their long stretches of cliff interspersed with small bays and beaches. But they could hardly be more different. The Penwith coast has an intensely wild, chaotic feel to it, while the Dorset coast is less rugged, more curvaceous and in many ways much grander. It is also more varied: in places the cliffs are monumental and sheer; in places modest and reclining. There are golden cliffs, white cliffs, black cliffs – in fact cliffs of almost every colour you care to think of.

This is essentially a walkers' coast, and one of the few places west of Durlston Head which can be reached by car is Lulworth Cove. It shows. The village of Lulworth has been entirely given over to tourism, and whatever character it may once have had has been ruined by coaches, cafés and carparks. Lulworth's popularity is understandable: as Grigson wrote, the cove is 'exaggeratedly curious and exquisite'. However, once you get to the

*St Aldhelm's Head, looking east*

*St Aldhelm's Chapel*

far side the crowds begin to thin out, and we had the petrified forest inside the Lulworth Ranges almost to ourselves. There were wheatears messing around on the gorse, jackdaws on the cliffs, and shags out at sea.

The last walk we did that weekend – number twelve in Mr Legg's book: 'Seacombe and Chapman's Pool (6 miles)' – was probably the finest. It had everything: the Square and Compasses at Worth Matravers, ammonites, quarries, downland, heaving cliffs, an isolated chapel and a remarkable view west from St Aldhelm's Head. It even had graffiti, both contemporary and ancient. Painted on a pillar in the limestone quarry at Seacombe was the suggestion 'Bloody tourists sod off', and scratched on the central pillar of St Aldhelm's Chapel were the initials of scores of men and women going back 300 years and more.

A week later I returned to this bit of coast with two archaeologists: Dr David Thackray, the Trust's Chief Archaeological Adviser, and Martin Papworth, who was carrying out a survey of the Bankes Estate for the Trust. We began the day at Eastington Farm, a Trust property which runs down to the coast at Seacombe Cliff. It is always good to be with people like Thackray and Papworth, for they can read a landscape much as a pianist does a musical score. 'This is a massively worked landscape,' explained Thackray as we made our way towards the sea. 'All these humps and holes – this limestone country has been farmed and quarried for hundreds, even thousands of years.'

The landscape we observed looked much as it must have done in the eleventh century, when the compilers of the 'Domesday Book' were tramping round the country and noting down who owned what and where. There would have been roughly the same amount of tree cover then as now, which is to say not much.

During medieval times rabbits were an important source of protein and a little way below Eastington Farm we came across an artificial rabbit warren – in appearance not unlike a long barrow – which prompted Thackray to reflect on the work of the Trust. 'One of the great things about the Trust,' he began, 'is its ability to conserve whole landscapes, not just individual sites. Here, for example, we've got a farm, a medieval field system, old parish boundaries, warrens, quarries . . . The range of stuff the Trust has is enormous. We've got Iron Age hill forts, neolithic cave dwellings, royal castles, lots of vernacular buildings . . . ' And the range continues to expand for the simple reason that the commonplace, given time, often becomes unusual, and therefore worthy of the Trust's consideration. Churn-stands are now being conserved; and so are Second World War pill-boxes. 'Even rusty, corrugated-iron roofs might be thought of as vernacular,' suggested Thackray, not entirely tongue-in-cheek. As it happens, the presence or absence of roofs determines which department within the Trust looks after a building. 'If it's got a roof, the Historic Buildings Department looks after it,' explained Thackray, 'and if it hasn't, we do.'

I asked Thackray whether he thought the Trust's archaeological work was underfunded. 'Well,' he replied cautiously, 'it would be nice if they put more money into it – we're certainly understaffed.' At present the annual cost of archaeological survey work comes to about £100,000, with each of the four members of the survey team covering, on average, 6,500 acres a year. 'The way we're going,' said Thackray, 'this programme will take us well into the next century. Obviously, for every 30,000 acres of new land which the Trust acquires you can add another year to the survey work. But the Trust is getting there. Ten years ago it had only one person working on its archaeology. Now there are six of us, in addition to which we hire others on short-term contracts. Things have definitely improved.'

Inevitably, with so few people looking after (or at least investigating) the 40,000-odd sites of archaeological interest on Trust properties, the advisers cannot afford to specialise in any one historical period. Thackray described himself as 'more of an architectural historian than an Iron Age-barrow chap', his speciality being Anglo-Saxon archaeology, art and literature. In practice, he has to advise the Trust on how to conserve everything from pre-Christian burial sites to twentieth-century coastal defences. Thackray's job entails much travel and by the time we reached Seacombe quarries he was musing on the pleasures of a sedentary life. 'I sometimes think I'd like to be a warden,' he said. 'It would be very rewarding to get to know one area intimately.' I think he genuinely meant it, and on that day I felt much the same myself: it was warm and sunny and more like May than November; larks were singing and bees were buzzing around the late-flowering harebells.

The Seacombe quarries were opened up around 1700 and abandoned in the 1930s. The quarry workers carved the Portland limestone out of the cliff, working their way in from the side and progressing a good distance under the hill. The quarry roofs are supported by thick pillars around which the men worked. 'They're very architectural,' remarked Thackray, 'much like a church.' Inside the air was still and catacomb-cool. The quarries' only occupants are bats; visitors are few and, I gather, foolish: there are frequent roof-falls and the gallery floor is covered with debris.

The rocks and sediments of Purbeck have been exploited for thousands of years. 'Apart from working the land,' wrote Grigson,

> working the stone is the oldest and most enduring of the Wessex industries; and stone is not the only substance which has been exploited in this geological museum. Kimmeridge shale has been dug for marling the land. The dark brown bituminous stone known as 'Kimmeridge Coal' has been mined along the sea ledges below Kimmeridge and made into cups and bowls and ornaments as far back as Roman and prehistoric times. The clays . . . are made into bricks and tiles; shale oil has been extracted – with little profit – around Kimmeridge . . . In the Isle of Purbeck, if you stand on the hill by Grange Arch, or on the jutting hill of Corfe Castle, you can look northwards over the heaths where the Dorset ball-clays are mined, valuable pure clays carried here by an ancient river and formed of the decomposed granite of Devonshire . . . Gravel and sand in these days of concrete are another valuable commodity of Wessex . . .

Grigson's guide to Wessex – long out of print, sadly – was published in 1951, since when large clay-mining works have been opened up near the Royal Society for the Protection of Birds' reserve at Arne. More significantly still, in 1973 British Gas discovered beneath Purbeck what is thought to be the largest onshore oil field in Western Europe. At present BP oversees the extraction of 10,300 barrels of oil a day at Wytch Farm. Plans are now afoot to open up new well sites on Furzey Island in Poole Harbour; yields of oil are expected to rise six-fold, those of gas thirty-fold. So far BP has gone out of its way to minimise the visual and ecological impact of its operations, but environmentalists are understandably concerned about the scale of industrial development on and around the Isle of Purbeck.

Preservation, at its best, is not simply a matter of protecting landscapes, buildings or artefacts from physical despoilation. 'One of the things we're trying to do at Corfe Castle,' said Thackray, 'is to preserve the atmosphere of romance.' Atmosphere, he conceded, was hard to define; at Corfe, it meant looking after the ruins in such a way that they might capture the imagination of today's visitor just as they did the imagination of the Victorians. On the cover of the Trust guidebook, written by Thackray, is a watercolour of the castle by J. M. W. Turner. It is a wishy-washy painting, but it does hint at the Arcadian spirit of the place: a shepherd and his sheep relax in the shadow of the craggy ruins. There are no shepherds grazing the castle grounds today, but the Trust is doing its best to prevent the ruins deteriorating further without making it look like a restoration job. Old man's beard clambers over the walls by the gatehouse, and summer visitors will see on the castle mound a variety of colourful flowers such as bee orchid, common spotted orchid, horseshoe vetch and yellow rattle. Thackray has even arranged for some of the late-Victorian restoration work to be undone. Turner, one feels, would approve.

The castle's history has been long and eventful. It is said that Edward the Martyr was killed here in the tenth century. In the eleventh century it became a royal stronghold and remained one until Tudor times. King John was particularly fond of Corfe and he brought his court here for several months each year. During his reign the 'Gloriette' was built, and this is where he had his state rooms. Towards the end of the sixteenth century Queen Elizabeth I sold the castle to Sir Christopher Hatton, the Lord Chancellor. Then in 1635 it was bought by Sir John Bankes, and it remained in the hands of the Bankes family until the Trust took over the estate in 1982.

Corfe Castle plugged the gap in the Purbeck Hills, the chalk ridge running from Ballard Down to Lulworth, and it had two functions: its occupants could prevent people entering south-east Purbeck, or they could stop people leaving. This, at least, was the theory. However, as Thackray remarked as we clambered up to the keep, 'Castles are curious things – they're very much statements of magnificence.' To historians the castle is probably most famous for the role it played in the Civil War, when it was heroically defended for Charles I by Dame Mary Bankes and the villagers during the siege of 1643. A further siege three years later would probably have failed too had it not been for the treachery of one of the Royalist officers at Corfe: he let some of the

*Corfe Castle*

other side in and the castle was finally taken. 'It wouldn't have mattered a hoot if Dame Mary had stayed,' explained Thackray, 'but it became symbolically important to the Parliamentary forces that she didn't.' Once the castle had been taken, the Parliamentarians, aided by sappers from Lulworth, tried to knock it down.

It is the product of this vandalism that one sees today. Although the Parliamentary forces set about the task of demolition with verve, lighting fires beneath the walls and packing holes with gunpowder, substantial sections of the castle and its walls withstood the onslaught. The inner portcullis split down the middle, one half dropping some ten feet below the other. The outer defences were much diminished by the demolition, but over a dozen towers remain, seldom upright and some leaning out so far that one expects them to tumble down the hillside any minute. 'When the Trust acquired the castle,' said Thackray, 'we realised that a major consolidation programme was needed.' One of the first tasks involved the removal of a ramp of soil by the curtain wall. Much to Thackray's astonishment, the workmen unearthed a staircase and discovered two massive blocks of masonry, the remains of the old guardroom ceiling. The consolidation work is complemented each year by an annual dig to discover more about the castle and its history.

Many castles, whether ruined or intact, are cold and unwelcoming places; sometimes they are plain ugly. Corfe is dramatic without being forbidding; its hard edges have been tempered by time, weather and neglect and there is an organic feel about the ruins. During 1988 over 160,000 people visited the castle; there must be many days in summer when it seems over-run – its atmosphere, as Thackray put it, 'being one of visitors'. I am glad I was there late in the year; it was closed, deserted and utterly enchanting. Plumes of grey smoke rose from the chimneys below and the rolling countryside beyond was bathed in the bright, hazy light of a November sun.

The land agent responsible for looking after Trust property in this part of Dorset is Tim Moore. In addition to managing the Bankes Estate, he oversees the management of Brownsea Island in Poole Harbour and the small blocks of coastline acquired through Enterprise Neptune. The Bankes Estate presents Moore with some peculiar difficulties as the Trust, under the conditions laid down by Ralph Bankes in his bequest, must run the estate as a self-financing venture. 'At the moment,' said Moore, 'we have about five million pounds' worth of outstanding repairs to do.' The largest drain on the estate's resources is Kingston Lacy House, which was built for a former Ralph after the destruction of Corfe Castle. This magnificent classical building, much altered by Sir Charles Barry in the 1830s, was in a far worse state of disrepair than the Trust realised when it was offered the estate. 'We thought we'd need about £1 million to restore the house,' explained Moore, 'but the costs have been astronomically higher than expected and we've spent £2·8 million.'

The restoration and maintenance of vernacular buildings – cottages, farms, barns and the like – has also been 'hellishly expensive'. All the rent from the tenants of farmland and buildings goes straight into repairs, but there is still a tremendous shortfall. Fortunately, the Trust is able to raise capital by selling off some of the less outstanding parts of the property. (Badbury Rings, Corfe Castle, Kingston Lacy and the coastal land in Purbeck have been declared inalienable; in other words, they cannot be taken from the Trust, except by Act of Parliament, nor can the Trust dispose of any part of them.) Moore expects the Trust to sell a number of outlying cottages, and some of the farmland north of Wimborne will come to the Trust's financial aid.

Management of the coastal properties in Purbeck presents less of a financial headache. The running costs at Studland are high – in the region of £120,000 a year – but the Trust charges for car parking and the property just about pays its own way. What Moore called 'the countryside coast', such as one finds round Worth Matravers, needs little other than a bit of footpath maintenance and the erection of the odd sign. A good indication of how much it costs to run this sort of coast comes from Cornwall. The Trust estimated that recurring expenditure for 1989 for its West Penwith properties would be £108,000. Recurring income, deriving from rents and so forth, was expected to be £58,000, thus leaving a net deficit of £50,000. Obviously non-recurring costs – incurred by such things as building projects – vary from year to year.

Building projects, it seems, were very much in the minds of the Bankes family in the early years of this century. In the Trust's office near Wimborne there is a stack of tattered old posters advertising 'Studland Bay Freehold Building Estate'. Moore thought that this was probably the doing of Ralph Bankes's mother, who was 'a great old go-getter'. Fortunately, the plans to develop Studland came to nothing, and it still looks pretty much as it appears in the poster's eleven photographs, under which, printed in bold type, is a list of its virtues:

FINE SANDY BEACH, safe for Bathing.
PURE WATER from New Waterworks.
NEW PIER is being arranged for.
GOLF LINKS & CLUB already started.
GRAVELLY SOIL and PINE WOODS.
GRAND SCENERY & DRIVES & SHELTERED WALKS on Beach, Heath and Downs.
THE PLACE for the BOTANIST, GEOLOGIST and ENTOMOLOGIST.

The photographs on the poster encapsulate nicely the character of Studland. There are three of thatched cottages buried in thick woodland; two of fishing boats and the long sandy beach; two of the chalk cliffs and the off-shore stacks of Old Harry and Old Harry's Wife; one of Studland Manor Hotel; and two of Studland's exquisite Norman church. There is also a photo of the Agglestone, a huge, 400-ton block of sandstone on the heath behind the village. In those days it looked like a mushroom; now it is toppled on one side.

The 2,500 acres of land owned by the Trust at Studland are of interest not only to botanists, geologists and entomologists, but also to ornithologists and the vast number of people who come every year to swim, sunbathe and fraternise. Approximately 1,500 acres are jointly managed as a National Nature Reserve (NNR) by the Trust and the government's Nature Conservancy Council (NCC). Studland Heath NNR was first leased to the NCC

*Geoff Hann*                    *Studland Beach, with Ballard Down beyond*

in 1962 and it is considered to be of international importance. It contains a wide range of habitats – woodland, heathland, freshwater, boggy ground and sand dunes – and consequently it supports a rich flora and fauna, including all six British reptiles, a large overwintering population of wildfowl and many rare plants, one of which, the Dorset heath (*Erica ciliaris*), is found only on Purbeck and in the Pyrenees.

Four hundred years ago there were no sand dunes here. Then gradually sand began to accrete at both ends of the bay. By midway through the last century the southern block of dunes had developed a spit which ran parallel to the northern block; some time after 1850 the two blocks coalesced and a body of water which had formerly been an arm of the sea became landlocked. Little Sea, which falls within the reserve, gradually lost its salinity and is now freshwater. The dunes have continued to expand at a surprisingly fast rate, the Ordnance Survey finding in 1959 that the high-water mark had moved fifty yards out to sea in a mere five years.

Before I met Geoff Hann, the Trust's head warden at Studland, it had never occurred to me that beaches needed much looking after. I imagined the warden's job to consist largely of taking the gate fees at the carparks, doing a bit of restoration work on the dunes, and getting rid of the litter. There was, I discovered, a lot more to it than that.

Studland's popularity is understandable: it is probably the finest beach in southern England. It is three and a half miles long and one of the few east-facing – and therefore sheltered – beaches of any size along this part of the coast. Somewhere in the region of 1 million people come here every year. There are four main carparks, and two overspills, with a maximum capacity of 3,700 cars. On busy days during the summer 1,000 or more additional cars park along the road which leads to the Sandbanks Ferry. 'When Studland belonged to the Bankes family, management was very low-key,' explained Hann, who has been at Studland since 1966. During Ralph Bankes's time there were just two of them looking after the carparks and the beach, but within six months of the Trust taking over Hann was appointed head warden for Purbeck and he now has four full-time wardens under him as well as many seasonal workers. His job is a peculiar one, for he is as much policeman as conservationist.

Studland has been what Hann described as 'an unofficial nudist area' since just after the last war, and now it attracts up to 3,000 nudists on a sunny summer's day. 'It used to be mostly men,' said Hann, 'but now we're getting more and more families.' If the nudists did nothing other than expose themselves to the elements there would be no problem. However, a good deal of soliciting and sex goes on among the gays – 'On a good day, we get about 600 homosexuals,' said Hann – and one of the wardens' tasks is to try and make sure that such activities are not brazenly conducted within view of other members of the public. Hann stressed that this has nothing to do with prejudice against homosexuality; indeed, if he finds any heterosexual couples misbehaving he ejects them from the beach too. The gays tend to congregate in the dunes between Little Sea and the beach. 'We walk through the area along the footpaths,' said Hann, 'just as any unsuspecting family might. We don't go searching for activity, and if the homosexuals were huddling behind trees the case wouldn't stand up in court.' When Hann and his assistants come across men indulging in illegal sexual acts, they arrest them and hand them over to the police.

Of equal if not greater concern is the way in which Studland attracts peeping Toms and flashers. 'We're very worried about the exhibitionists,' said Hann. 'So far, we've never managed to catch them.' Other nudist beaches in Britain – Hann cited Brighton and Formby – also attract homosexuals and peeping Toms. Hann thought the presence of sand dunes had something to do with it. I asked him whether he found the job of arresting miscreants un-nerving. 'No,' he replied, 'I'm an ex-copper, so it doesn't worry me.' Once a warden was threatened with a knife, but most people go quietly when they are arrested. Moore told me of an occasion when a group of Hell's Angels turned up on a bank holiday, got drunk and began breaking up beach huts to make a barbecue. 'There was no sense in Geoff Hann confronting them,' he said, 'but he did keep an eye on them to make sure things didn't get too out of hand.' Evidently, some local people were upset that the Trust didn't deal firmly with the vandals. This sounds like bar-room bravura.

There used to be a problem with people tearing around the dunes and beach on trail bikes, but Hann soon scotched it by arresting everyone he caught – he has a bike too – and prosecuting them. Another menace came from jet-skis – an aquatic form of motorbike – but in 1989 the Trust banned people from launching them at Studland Beach. Something else which the Trust would like to stop is dogs defecating on the beach. Bournemouth, Poole and Swanage have all banned dogs from their beaches during the summer months, but the Trust cannot do this as there are public rights of way at Studland. 'We're particularly concerned about the health risk,' said Moore. There is a worm found in dog faeces that transmits the parasite *Toxocara canis*, which is now known to be a cause of blindness in children. 'I wouldn't want to ban dogs,' said Hann, who exercises his own on the beach, 'but we're considering getting people to keep their animals on a lead and take the messes away with them.' Presumably, the day will come when all dog owners have to carry a pooper-scooper.

The cost of looking after Studland comes to much more than the wardens' wages. Disposal of litter – there are at least four tons to be got rid of each week in summer – costs between £6–8,000 a year, in addition to which there is the expense of maintaining vehicles and buildings, and sometimes of buying new ones (a new lavatory block has just set the Trust back £50,000). The parking charge of £1.50 struck me, at first, as being rather stiff. But £1.50 is buying you more than a space for your car. It pays for the beach to be kept clean, for reasonable standards of decency to prevail, for the retrieval of your children, should you lose them, and for such facilities as public lavatories. And, when you consider that the average length of stay is six hours, it seems even cheaper: £1.50 wouldn't even buy an hour's worth of parking in central London.

After leaving Hann's office at Marine Terrace I walked along the sheet-white cliffs to Old Harry. It was late afternoon and the rain had cleared; the sky was a pale blue and the sea a milky green. Gulls and oystercatchers were feeding on the ploughed fields below King Barrow, a large Bronze Age burial mound. Had I come in summer I could doubtless have eulogised about the wealth of flowers along the clifftops, about the seabirds breeding on Old Harry and on the other splinters of rock rising from the sea beside this

curiously indented coastline, and possibly about the views across Studland Bay to Bournemouth. But it was cold and I was eager to set off for London before nightfall, so as soon as I reached Old Harry I turned and made my way back to the village.

Perhaps I would have viewed Studland somewhat differently had I had the good sense to read Rodney Legg's *National Trust Dorset* before going there, rather than after. The area is not without its literary associations (I don't suppose anywhere is), and Legg records that the ashes of H. G. Wells, 'the radical author and futurist', were scattered in the sea near Old Harry. More intriguing still were the activities of another radical. At Cliff End, writes Legg, 'a promising 38-year-old mathematician named Bertrand Russell first went to bed with Lady Ottoline Morrell, the wife of Liberal MP Philip Morrell, during the Easter of 1911. The affair lasted until 1916 when Russell was thrown out of Trinity College for his opposition to the Great War.'

'Other countries change in miles and leagues,' wrote the rural essayist H. J. Massingham, 'ours changes in furlongs.' This is particularly true of Dorset. To get the real flavour of it one should travel by foot or on horseback; then one could smell the countryside and study it with the attention it deserves. Reading Defoe's account, written during the 1720s, of his journey from Wareham to Lyme Regis, I am struck by the poverty of experience which car travel engenders. On his way across the county Defoe stopped at inns, conversed with peasants and gentlemen, observed the state of towns and farmland, and meditated on everything from the colour of Purbeck marble to the size of mackerel, which were sold at Bridport for one hundred a penny. The car traveller could never come up with observations such as this: 'The grass, or herbage of these downs is full of the sweetest, and the most aromatic plants, such as nourish the sheep to a strange degree, and the sheep's dung again nourishes that herbage to a strange degree; so that the valleys are rendered extremely fruitful, by the washing of the water in hasty showers from these hills.'

Defoe was writing here of the downs round Dorchester, which supported, he was told, a flock of 600,000 sheep. 'I do not affirm it to be true,' he wrote, 'but when I viewed the country round, I confess I could not but incline to believe it.' Until not long ago the chalk downland in Dorset did support a vast flock of sheep, but numbers have declined dramatically over the past century,

OPPOSITE: *Cliffs and pinnacles around Old Harry*

from a quarter of a million in the 1880s to less than 50,000 in 1950. I saw few sheep as I made my way towards the west of the county, and indeed the amount of permanent pasture is but a fraction of what it used to be, most of it having been ploughed up and converted to arable land.

Arable cropping and commercial forestry have also put paid to most of Dorset's heathland. In Defoe's day a solid block of heath stretched almost uninterrupted from Dorchester to the New Forest. It was largely intact fifty years ago, but today only isolated fragments remain. Egdon Heath, wrote Hardy in *The Return of the Native*, had 'a Face upon which Time makes but little impression'. The Forestry Commission and the Common Agricultural Policy have succeeded where Time failed.

One cannot but reflect with sadness on the way in which economic expediency and greed have chipped away at the heaths and downs. Their loss seems particularly futile as one of the main problems for European agriculture today is over-production: the heaths and downs have gone, and there is no bringing them back. Admittedly, laudable attempts are being made to turn cultivated fields into chalk grassland, but these are ferociously expensive and always small scale. The Trust is doing this on Ballard Down, but with costs running at around £500 an acre there is a limit to the amount of restoration that can be done.

Writing of the changes in Dorset during the first half of this century, Massingham declared how it broke his heart to see the way in which the 'sweet diversity' of the countryside was being ironed out. He wrote beautifully of the dying art of flax growing – flax and hemp provided the raw materials for Bridport's rope industry – and of such things as the skills required in milling corn and making cider. However, Massingham's writings, like those

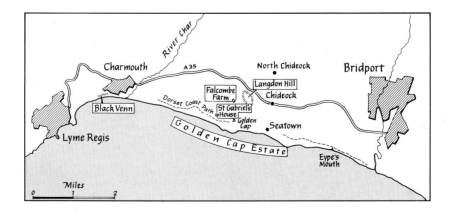

of many other commentators on rural life, are filled with nostalgia, of which we should beware. Like Cobbett, and for that matter Thomas Hardy, he seemed to be mourning a golden age which coincided with his youth. Even Defoe, that most practical of men, wrote of 'the injury of time' and of 'time the great devourer'. I raise this issue because there is a tendency among all of us to romanticise the past. We should remember that many of the jobs which farmers once had to perform were back-breaking and tedious in the extreme.

Even so, I wholly subscribe to Massingham's love of diversity and his abhorrence of all which serves to reduce it. And it is diversity – of landscape, wildlife and artefact – which the Trust seeks to preserve by acquiring land along the coast. Twentieth-century man has ironed out much of the variation in the landscape, yet there is still plenty to marvel at as one travels the length of Dorset, even if one does so by car. The countryside in Purbeck and round Dorchester is broad, rolling and voluptuous; gradually, as one moves westward, it becomes more intimate, more Celtic in feel.

The Trust owns over 2,000 acres of land, strung along about seven miles of coast, between the village of Eype and the Devon border. Dominating this stretch are the magnificent cliffs of Golden Cap, at 618 feet the highest in the south of England. Behind the cliffs the land falls back towards Filcombe Farm, which was where I met the warden. George Elliott, a bearded, animated man in his mid-forties, had been working for the Trust at Golden Cap for five years. Earlier in his life he had managed farms in Shropshire and Hampshire, worked as a shepherd in Scotland, and helped run a holiday park in Devon. He had about him the air of competence which comes with experience. 'I'm involved in everything on the estate,' he announced without exaggeration. 'I deal with tenants' problems, poachers, fence repairs, forestry, building maintenance, the lot.'

Most of the Trust's holding at Golden Cap is accommodation land – land without buildings which is let to nearby farms – and only two of the fifteen tenants have farms proper, renting both buildings and land. 'We couldn't wish for a better crew,' said Elliott. Fortunately for the Trust, the land is unsuitable for arable farming. It is steep and hilly, and the soil is poor and flinty. The farmers make a living from sheep, beef and dairy cattle, and most of the fields are down to grass. 'The public tend to think that conservation looks after itself,' said Elliott, 'but it doesn't. All the countryside round here is man-manipulated and a huge amount of management is needed to keep it as it is.' Not only must the fields be grazed or cut, but the hedges must be laid and trimmed, and twenty miles of public footpath and over 200 stiles must be maintained. All of which costs money and needs manpower.

*Golden Cap, looking up from the shore below Seatown*

In fact manpower was very much on Elliott's mind when I arrived and he immediately expressed his satisfaction with the Employment Training (ET) scheme, which had recently superseded the Manpower Services Commission (MSC) schemes. 'We're getting three times more work out of them under ET and it's twice the quality,' he said. In the past, if Elliott was unhappy with the work done by MSC teams he had to inform the land agent, who then had to make an approach to the local MSC office. 'Now I can sack them myself,' he said. 'You used to get people just hanging around chatting and smoking – it was like the lower fifth form. And we once got through five leaders in a single year.' Elliott said that he now had an excellent man – a former gamekeeper – in charge of the ET team. During my travels I heard plenty of grumbling about MSC schemes, and complaints about the standard of work were doubtless justified in some instances. But it should be stressed that overall the Trust has benefited enormously from the MSC programme, and I saw dozens of examples of work which would never have been done had the Trust not been able to employ what virtually amounted to free labour. The key to success, apparently, lies in good leadership.

Much of Elliott's work is directly or indirectly concerned with the visiting public. 'The numbers coming have increased by leaps and bounds over the last five years,' he said. Golden Cap is within driving distance of London, but it also attracts people from further afield – Elliott had recently been visited by a 'Chinese gentleman' who wanted to see how the Trust managed its open spaces. He even gets people walking up to Golden Cap at three o'clock in the morning. Some of them go to listen to the church bells; some to watch badgers; and some for reasons best known to themselves.

We climbed up to Golden Cap midway through the afternoon, stopping frequently for Elliott to point out features of interest: a badger set in the banks beneath a straggly hawthorn hedge; the old London to Exeter coach road, a mere cart-track which until 1840 had been the main route to the West Country; and the eroded path up to the summit. This path takes up a good deal of Elliott's time. Each year some six tons of hard-core are carried up the hill and bedded into the path in an attempt to stabilise it.

The views from the top of Golden Cap are magnificent. To the east the land drops away sharply down to the village of Seatown, then the cliffs rise again and curve southward. Golden Cap gets its name from the band of green sandstone which glistens like gold in the sun, and the same band runs across the cliffs to the east of Seatown. Above the sandstone is a thin layer of cherty soil, and below a massive bed of grey Blue Lias clay. Behind Seatown there is a fertile bowl of cultivated land, most of which grows corn, then the land rises again to culminate in a heath- and gorse-covered ridge.

Looking westward across the great bay towards Lyme Regis and Devon, the views are equally imposing. Golden Cap falls steeply and messily seaward, the Blue Lias clay cascading away from the undercliff like a lava flow. 'The cliffs are always on the move,' explained Elliott. During the spring and winter, or whenever the weather is damp, the clay is so mobile that it is dangerous to walk over it. At the foot of Golden Cap, near a small woodland, is the derelict chapel of St Gabriel's, beyond which the land undulates gently west. First come the cliffs of Cain's Folly, then those of Black Venn, and finally Lyme Regis. Behind the cliffs is a network of small fields, dotted among which are small farmsteads. From a botanical point of view, these flower-rich meadows are among the finest the Trust owns. Mixed in with the meadows are small woods, thick hedgerows, patches of grass heath and small ponds and flushes. Among the rare and unusual plants to be found here are adder's-tongue fern,

*Golden Cap seen from Ridge Cliff, with Seatown below*

green-winged orchid, autumn lady's-tresses, corky-fruited water dropwort and pepper saxifrage.

The Trust refers to its property here as the Golden Cap Estate. This is misleading, for it suggests that the 2,000-odd acres of land came in one lump, much as the Bankes Estate did in east Dorset. This is not the case at all. The Trust gradually built up its coastal holdings here by buying land as it became available. The individual acquisitions were often very small. For example, Enterprise Neptune funds bought forty-nine acres at Black Venn in 1966. A further fifteen acres of Black Venn were acquired two years later. An eight-acre col between Golden Cap and Langdon Hill, known as the Saddle, was also purchased in 1968. Ten years later the Trust paid for the 26-acre summit of Golden Cap. And so it goes on: sometimes the Trust bought a field, or perhaps a field and an orchard and a slice of cliff; sometimes it bought a whole farm.

Many people within the Trust think of the Golden Cap Estate as Enterprise Neptune's flagship. One can see why. The first acquisitions were made soon after the launch of Neptune, and most of the land has been bought with money raised by the appeal. It has been a slow process, but the plans to bring as much of this coastline as possible into Trust ownership have been entirely successful. Furthermore, the Trust has acquired not only the cliffs and clifftops but much of the farmland behind, thus ensuring that this whole mellow, majestic landscape is conserved for all time.

# 4

# White Cliffs and Black Deeds

'I MUST GET from this Dover, as fast as I can,' wrote William Cobbett in *Rural Rides*. I felt much the same myself after a few days in the place; nor was I filled with much enthusiasm for the surrounding country-side. It may be that I chose a bad time of year to visit east Kent: wherever I went a grey, wintry mist clung to the white cliffs and grey towns. Or perhaps I had been spoilt by my recent visits to the Dorset coast, which is incomparably superior.

Each year some 14 million people pass through Dover on their way to the Continent. The vast majority head straight for the docks, climb on a ferry and settle down to their sausage and chips or croissant having seen little or nothing of the town itself. In a few years' time, when the Channel Tunnel is open for business, many of those who now use the ferries may decide to go beneath the sea rather than upon it. Dover will lose some of its trade and its citizens are understandably concerned about the effects which the tunnel will have on the local economy. Consequently, the District Council is busy promoting the town as a tourist resort. The idea is that you and I should come to Dover for no other reason than pleasure. This, according to the Council's 1989 holiday guide, is what we will find:

> The famous White Cliffs of Dover stand majestically overlooking the English Channel: a symbol of the nation's strength against old enemies and a welcoming sight for those returning to home shores. Beyond the gleaming façade lies a landscape of timeless beauty, steeped in history. Here is the unspoilt Kentish countryside; here is a coastline of variety and excitement; here is the history and tradition of Dover, Deal and Sandwich; here is the warmest of welcomes. Here is White Cliffs Country.

Hyperbole is the stock in trade of tourist brochures, but this verges on the mendacious. Certainly, there are white cliffs both to the east and west of

OPPOSITE: *South Foreland Lighthouse, near St Margaret's-at-Cliffe*

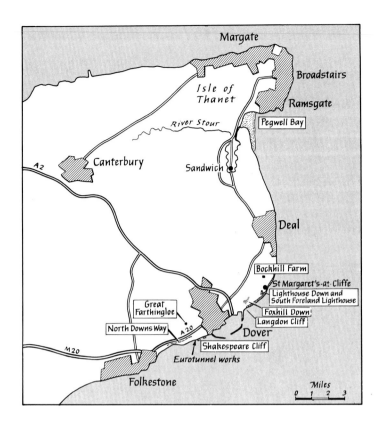

Dover, but there is precious little in the way of unspoilt countryside behind them. Indeed, one of the few decent stretches of hinterland – the dry valley which runs from Folkestone to Dover – is likely to be ruined by the building of a new road. Presumably it was across this valley that Edgar led the blind Gloucester, to be followed later by King Lear, on the way to what is now known as Shakespeare Cliff. This was where Gloucester attempted – and failed – to commit suicide, egged on by Edgar's description of the view:

> How fearful
> And dizzy 'tis to cast one's eyes so low!
> The crows and choughs that wing the midway air
> Show scarce so gross as beetles; half way down
> Hangs one that gathers samphire, dreadful trade!

Well, it is a very long time since there were choughs in Kent, and I doubt whether anyone has gathered samphire on these cliffs within living memory. 'The fishermen that walk upon the beach/Appear like mice,' continued Edgar. There are no fishermen here today, and indeed there is no beach; instead walkers on the North Downs Way look down on a monumental industrial site. It is here that the tunnel-lining segments await despatch, surrounded by gigantic cranes, huge hoppers and dozens of Portakabins. Between the site and the cliffs is the railway line linking Dover to Folkestone; and beyond are the lagoons in which the muck dredged out of the tunnel is being dumped. The Channel Tunnel is one of the most ambitious engineering projects of all time. It is also one of the most disruptive.

The National Trust does not own many properties along the Kent coast. Apart from the cliffs around Dover, its only other coastal holding is at Pegwell Bay on the Isle of Thanet. The reason why the Trust owns so little is simple: there is little worth owning. Much of the coast, especially along the northern shores of the county, is unattractive and spoilt, and Kent has nothing to compare with the ancient ports of Rye and Winchelsea in neighbouring Sussex. The further east one goes the grimmer Kent becomes. Would that I could have spent time in the area around Tenterden, which is known as the Garden of England. Central Kent is intimate, verdant and pretty, whereas the countryside further east, and especially beyond the North Downs, is dull and depressing.

The Isle of Thanet, the low-lying triangle of land in Kent's north-east corner, is renowned for its fertility and its holiday resorts. When Cobbett visited the area in the 1820s he marvelled at the fine crops of corn and lucerne, but he didn't stay long. Margate, he wrote, 'is so thickly settled with stick-jobbing cuckolds, at this time of year, that, having no fancy to get their horns stuck into me, I turned away to my left when I got within half a mile of the town'. I went into Margate one morning and left promptly. Being winter, the town was half-deserted and the seafront looked tacky and garish. Perhaps the town would liven up at Christmas: Gary Glitter was billed to appear at one of the clifftop lidos.

Margate and Ramsgate, the one facing north, the other south, used to be separate towns but now they are glued together by industrial estates and suburbia. Sandwiched between the two, and facing east from the bulge of Thanet, is Broadstairs, a narrow-streeted town whose beach is overlooked by Bleak House, which was where Dickens wrote *David Copperfield*. The Kent coast has attracted an uncommonly talented procession of writers over the last century or two: Dickens at Broadstairs, Noël Coward and Ian Fleming at St Margaret's Bay, and Joseph Conrad a little way inland from Dover.

After Ramsgate comes Pegwell Bay, a large chunk of which is owned by the Trust. This is where the Saxons, led by Hengist and Horsa, are supposed to have landed in AD449; and St Augustine, who came on a proselytising mission, is thought to have landed at the same place in AD597. The marshes and mudflats are famous for their bird life and part of the bay is leased by the Trust to the Kent County Naturalists' Trust. I have seen photographs of this place which endow it with a forlorn beauty. The camera deceives: Pegwell Bay reminded me of those great, muddy expanses of shabby estuarine land to the east of the Thames Barrier. Way offshore I could see bait-diggers searching in the mud and flocks of waders rising and falling like swirls of grey confetti. Behind me were the immense cooling towers of Richborough power station. The noise of traffic along the A256 was continuous and irritating.

South of Richborough, and beside the River Stour, comes a thin ribbon of industrial development bordered by fields of cabbage and corn. There is a large Audi–VW car yard, a waste-disposal site, a drugs factory, a pyro-technics factory, a Little Chef and a sign which says 'Welcome to the Isle of Thanet for Leisure and Pleasure'. After this – in other words, as you move away from the Isle of Thanet – things improve considerably: first comes Sandwich, then Deal. Between the two is a signpost which reads 'Ham Sandwich', Ham being a small village. Cobbett said that Deal was a villainous place, 'full of filthy people'. It is now stately and sedate – the antithesis of Margate in fact – and it overlooks a fine stretch of shingle coast.

The economy of east Kent has long been based on the disparate trinity of agriculture, seaside tourism and coal mining. Until about fifteen years ago the largest employer in the area was the National Coal Board, but at the time of

*Bleak House and Broadstairs*

my visit there was only one colliery in operation, and that was about to close. Unemployment on the Isle of Thanet climbed well above 20 per cent in the mid-1980s, though it has since fallen somewhat. The region's biggest employer now is the port of Dover: some 8,000 people work for Sealink and P&O, and about 1,000 are employed by Dover Harbour Board. A further 2,000 or so people have found work with the companies building the tunnel. Keith Southey, Dover Harbour Board's public relations officer, told me that it was hard to say how much trade Dover was likely to lose as a result of the tunnel. 'Originally, there was a feeling of great pessimism,' he said, 'but now we're more confident that there will still be a healthy ferry business in the future.' However, the Board has decided that it must diversify its interests. 'We're keen to plug tourism,' explained Southey. 'Dover is very rich in its heritage.'

In 1988 the Council announced its plans to build a £13,750,000 heritage centre, which will be known as 'The White Cliffs Experience'. It hopes to attract 300,000 visitors a year and thus offset some of the trade losses which the tunnel is expected to cause. For those interested in military history the area has much to offer, and fortifications of one sort or another can be seen all along the coast. Most prominent are the castles. There is a magnificent one dominating Dover – the first fortress here was built during the Iron Age; and there are others, built by Henry VIII, at Deal and Walmer. The latter is the official residence of the Lord Warden of the Cinque Ports, a post held by the Queen Mother at present. The Cinque Ports – Sandwich, Dover, Hythe, Romney and Hastings – were granted various privileges, such as freedom from taxes, by a series of royal charters (the first was given in 1278), in return for which they agreed to defend the coast and provide ships to fight for the Crown against the French and other enemies.

Cobbett's reason for fleeing Dover had nothing to do with the town itself, which was very clean and had 'less blackguard people in it than I ever observed in any sea-port before'. No, what appalled him were the defences on the hills, and in particular the trenches, caverns and bomb-proof shelters behind Shakespeare Cliff. Cobbett was incensed by the vast expenditure entailed in digging 'these horrible holes' and by their geographical location: if the French wished to invade, he suggested, they would have the good sense to land somewhere flat – Romney Marsh, for instance, or perhaps on the shingle beaches near Deal, which was where Caesar is thought to have entered Britain. Cobbett was also disgusted by the cowardly nature of the holes, which he claimed were 'the only set of fortifications in the world ever framed for mere *hiding*'.

*Shakespeare Cliff and the Channel Tunnel workings*

Getting on to the land behind Shakespeare Cliff is not as simple as it used to be because Transmanche-Link (TML), the contractor employed to construct the tunnel, has taken most of it over. Public access is now limited to the North Downs Way, a long-distance footpath which runs along the cliffs from Capel-le-Ferne, on the outskirts of Folkestone, to Dover. However, employees of the Trust are allowed to drive across TML land and save themselves a lengthy hike. And that was how I got there in the company of James Cooper, the land agent responsible for managing the Trust's clifftop properties around Dover. The Great Farthingloe property, running up to – but excluding – Shakespeare Cliff, covers seventy-eight acres. The Trust bought sixty-seven acres from the Ministry of Defence in 1979 and it leases a further eleven acres from British Rail, which owns the cliffs and clifftops.

Cooper is a tall, easy-going, affable man in his thirties. Having trained as a chartered surveyor at Cirencester, he worked in private practice, then wandered round India for a while before joining the Trust in Cornwall. One of two land agents in Kent and East Sussex, he is responsible for looking after roughly half of the 7,500 acres owned by the Trust in the region. Working in Kent, he explained, was very different from working in Cornwall: 'It's like living in a greenhouse here – we've got a huge membership in the south-east and people are watching what we do all the time. As soon as you do anything wrong, letters come streaming in.' However, Cooper enjoyed the variety of his work. 'One day I'll be discussing the conservation of an old tapestry in a country house; another I'll be looking at a farm-drainage scheme, or a footpath on the White Cliffs; and the next I might be trying to buy some land.' He has some fifty people working on the properties he looks after. Among them are Chartwell, Winston Churchill's home, and the George Inn, a galleried coaching inn near Guy's Hospital in south-east London.

Cooper, his dog and I left the car near a Ministry of Defence firing range and headed for the cliffs. At the edge we gazed down, like Edgar, 'from the dread summit of this chalky bourn'. Some 400 feet below were the tunnel workings, known as the lower site; behind us, in the shallow floor of a dry valley, was a great expanse of tarmac and temporary buildings, this being known as the upper site. The two sites are linked by an adit which was built in the early 1970s before Harold Wilson's government withdrew its funding for an earlier tunnel scheme. 'It's amazing how fast they move,' said Cooper. 'Every time I come here something new has happened.'

There are several concrete battery observation posts on the clifftop, about which the Trust's 1981 management plan drily commented, 'It is considered that the fortifications along this length of coast are of interest as an example of the fire-control systems employed in the coastal defences at the time (1939–45).' At the time of my visit Eurotunnel was thinking of setting up a display in one of the posts to explain to walkers what was happening below. This would be a very simple affair, and nothing like the Eurotunnel exhibition centre beside the M20 on the way into Folkestone.

Much of the land behind the cliffs is classified as a Grade 1 Site of Special Scientific Interest and the Trust's Round Down is as fine an example of unimproved chalk grassland as one could wish to find. 'Given the full weight of Parliament behind the Channel Tunnel Act, our approach here,' explained Cooper, 'had to be one of damage limitation.' The Trust never contemplated using the weapon of inalienability as it knew, when it acquired the land in 1979, that there were already plans for an extension of the A20 London to Dover road, and possibly for the construction of a Channel Tunnel. Fortunately, Eurotunnel has been keen to work with the Trust, rather than against it, and dealings between the two have been reasonably amicable. Under the Channel Tunnel Act, Eurotunnel compulsorily purchased a small amount of land belonging to the Trust, and by further agreement two cottages on the Old Folkestone Road. The Trust's tenant had to move out and she now lives in a bungalow, bought with the proceeds of the sale, in St Margaret's Bay. I doubt whether there are many landlords who would go to such trouble.

The idea of creating a fixed link between England and France is far from new. As long ago as 1751 Nicholas Desmeret, a French farmer, wrote a tract advocating that either a bridge or a tunnel should be built. Half a century later Napoleon Bonaparte toyed with the idea of a tunnel, and many people will be familiar with the delightful plans proposed by the engineer Mathieu-Favier. Horsedrawn carriages were to trot along a tunnel on the sea-bed; illumination was to be provided by candlelight, ventilation by means of flues poking up, periscope-like, to the surface. In 1880 a scheme to build a rail link under the Channel led to tunnel-boring near Calais and Dover. Both sides got about a mile in before work was halted. Further attempts at tunnel construction have been made since then, the last being abandoned in 1974.

Eleven years later the French and British governments invited proposals to build and operate a fixed link. In 1986 a scheme designed by Eurotunnel, a private-sector Anglo–French consortium, was chosen, and the consortium was given a 55-year concession to build and operate the tunnel. The cost of the project was originally estimated to be around £6 billion; it has risen dramatically since then. The opening date for the tunnel has been set for summer 1993. Simply put, the scheme consists of two rail tunnels bored through a bed of chalk beneath the sea. Between these two tunnels, and joined to them by frequent cross-passages, there will be a smaller tunnel which will provide ventilation and enable maintenance work to be carried out. Access to the tunnels will be at Folkestone and Calais. Passenger and freight trains will run between Britain and the Continent, in addition to which there will be a shuttle service for vehicles between Folkestone and Calais. At peak times the shuttle trains are expected to leave every twelve minutes and the journey from one terminal to the other should take no more than thirty-five minutes.

Image is everything nowadays and Eurotunnel has made as much mileage as possible out of some small wildlife rescue operations, such as the trans-location of over 400 newts from a pond which was in the way of the workings to a safe site elsewhere. Eurotunnel may have altered some of its plans to suit, among other things, great-crested newts and late spider orchids, but the tunnel workings are inevitably having an impact on the appearance of the landscape, particularly at the terminal site behind Folkestone, at Shakespeare Cliff, and on the hill west of Dover where a thousand or so miners are housed in a prefab village which looks like a Soviet gulag. It is hard to imagine what

Great Farthingloe will be like in a few years' time. Before long the lower site will start rising from the sea as the tunnel spoil is piled into the artificial lagoons. It has been suggested that this will eventually be grassed over for use as a 'recreation area'. Cooper scoffed at the idea. 'Who on earth,' he demanded, 'would want to use a spoil heap divided from the mainland by a railway line as a recreation area?'

The Trust is very worried about the effects which the new transport system built to serve the tunnel – and especially British Rail's high-speed rail link from London to the coast – will have on the landscape. At the time of my visit British Rail was still in the process of deciding which of four possible routes the new rail line should take. Suffice it to say that the whole business has been handled supremely undemocratically. With government support, British Rail can use the Private Act system to circumvent the planning procedures which determine the actions of most other industries. There will be no public inquiries, many people will lose their homes, and substantial tracts of countryside will be wrecked.

I was astonished to read in a Eurotunnel handout that its campaign to get the high-speed link had 'met enthusiastic support in Kent'. This was nonsense. There was massive opposition throughout the county, and indeed beyond as well: British Rail eventually announced that it would spend £500 million on environmental 'improvements'. Intriguingly, the government had recently shown an uncharacteristic interest in a whole gamut of environmental issues: such things as acid rain, ozone depletion and marine pollution were no longer dismissed as minor problems unworthy of ministerial concern. Mrs Thatcher had turned 'green' and the environmental lobby was viewing her conversion with a mixture of scepticism and hope.

There is, needless to say, plenty of support for the tunnel in places like Ashford and Folkestone, where the economic benefits of construction are considerable. Over a period of five years unemployment in Ashford, a small industrial town in central Kent, has fallen from 14 per cent to under 6 per cent; and in 1987 house prices in Ashford rose by a third. This boom can be largely attributed to the tunnel construction and the arrival of the M20 motorway. A large number of jobs has been created in Dover by the tunnel workings, but the future there is not so rosy: many of these jobs will go once the work is complete, and the tunnel will lead to a decline in the numbers of people coming to Dover to take cross-Channel ferries. The Council hopes to offset these losses in trade by attracting people to the new heritage centre, and it has been a keen promoter of the Department of Transport's plan to build a new trunk road along the Old Folkestone Road dry valley.

Looking back from the cliffs at Great Farthingloe, Cooper pointed out the planned route for the new A20. 'It will have a devastating impact,' he said, 'it will absolutely ruin the valley.' For much of its length the road will travel through an open, rolling landscape. It will be impossible to screen it effectively and the valley's pleasing atmosphere of rurality will be shattered, both by the visual impact of the road and by the noise of traffic travelling along it. The Trust has known ever since it bought land at Great Farthingloe that a road might go though here. However, the original proposal for improvements to the A20 assumed that there would be no tunnel and that there would be what planners call 'an ever-increasing demand for vehicular capacity' between Folkestone and Dover. Indeed in May 1985 Mrs Lynda Chalker of the Department of Transport commented: 'It is an expensive scheme . . . which could well be difficult to justify for traffic that would continue travelling between Folkestone and Dover if a Channel fixed link were provided.'

However, in January 1987 the Department of Transport published draft orders announcing plans for a new dual carriageway to replace the existing A20 east of Folkestone. The National Trust was one of many environmental organisations which opposed the Department of Transport's plans at a public inquiry held in the spring of 1988. The Trust never really held out much hope of stopping the new road or of getting it diverted along a less destructive route. Most people are convinced that the road will be built, not because there is any real need for it, but because it is a government sop to the town (or, at least, to the Council) of Dover. The road, it is thought, will go some way towards compensating for the raw deal which Dover is getting from the tunnel. Incidentally, the final cost to the Trust of being represented at the inquiry came to £54,597.81. One might ask why the Trust bothered spending so much money if it didn't think it had a chance of getting the road re-routed. The answer is simple: non-opposition to the Department of Transport's plans would have been construed as a form of approval.

One man who views the prospect of the Channel Tunnel with approval and relish is Sidney Hopper, the Trust's warden at Bockhill Farm, a 275-acre chunk of land east of St Margaret's Bay. 'The tunnel's an excellent thing for our children and for their children,' he announced as we wandered over the farm, adding, by way of explanation, 'I'm an Aquarian, which means I'm fifty

OPPOSITE: *Second World War defences, St Margaret's Bay*

*The cliffs at Bockhill Farm*

years ahead of my time!' Hopper was born in the area in the 1920s and apart from a spell in Lincolnshire, where he worked in the police force, he has spent most of his life in and around St Margaret's Bay. Garrulous, energetic and exhaustively knowledgeable about every aspect of local life, Hopper gives the impression of someone who is wholly satisfied with his lot.

The cliffs to the east of Dover are much more interesting and varied than those to the west. The most spectacular are the ones which separate Bockhill Farm from the sea: these are pure white, vertical and over 300 feet high.

Hopper is particularly proud of the network of footpaths which he has created: there are now some sixteen miles of these criss-crossing the arable fields. 'They are a labour of love,' he said. During the summer months he spends much of his time walking behind a mowing machine. Hopper is also a great tree-planter. In the six weeks before Christmas he was planning to plant 600 hawthorn bushes; the year before he had planted over 2,000 on his own. 'You've got to love your work,' he explained.

Bockhill Farm was bought by the Trust with money raised by the White Cliffs of Dover Appeal, which was launched in 1974 under Enterprise Neptune. The target of £500,000 was quickly reached, and the appeal has been used to buy over 430 acres of land and some four miles of coastline. When I saw Cooper in late 1988 the fund residue stood at £640,000. That it had grown rather than diminished was a reflection of two things: an astute investment policy and the inability of the Trust to spend the money as freely as it would wish. The fund was set up in such a way that it can only be used to acquire land and buildings; it cannot be used for the management or improvement of existing properties.

Bockhill cost the Trust £216,000; five years later, in 1979, the Trust paid £25,000 for a mile of clifftop land at Great Farthingloe. The White Cliffs of Dover Appeal funds were also used to buy eighteen acres at Foxhill Down, and the Trust has been given ten acres at Lighthouse Down, thirty-five acres at Langdon Cliffs and eleven acres at Kingsdown Leas. Cooper was now contemplating with some excitement the possibility that one day the Trust might be able to bring under its protection all the land between Dover and St Margaret's Bay.

The view from the top of Foxhill Down, which lies behind Langdon Cliffs, is curious and compelling. On a clear day you can see France, but the real attractions for the third of a million people who come here each year are more immediate. Below the cliffs are Dover's eastern docks. 'It is a sort of Toytown,' suggested Cooper: the articulated lorries looked like Dinky toys and the ferries like boats in a child's bath. On the far side of the docks is the seafront, with its scruffy rows of Regency-style houses and hotels, a dirty white like the cliffs, and the monstrous wall of the Gateway Flats. Allow your eye to drift inland and it will flicker across some hideous modern buildings before coming to rest on the windswept battlements of the castle. Beyond the town is Shakespeare Cliff and, in the far distance, way past unseen Folkestone, the land sweeps out to Dungeness and its nuclear power station. Finally, if you turn your back on the sea you have the concave dishes of Dover's satellite communication base.

*Eastern Docks, Dover, seen from Langdon Cliff*

The cliffs here have been heavily worked and if you peer over the edge from the Trust's viewing point for disabled visitors you can see the hewn-out ledge along which the old Dover to Sandwich railway used to run. The land behind supports a mix of scrub, grassland and concrete. In the 1780s a prison was built here by convicts awaiting shipment to Australia. The base of the governor's house can still be seen – it is used as a carpark now – and scattered among the bushes are the ruins of the old prison walls. Shortly after the First World War Langdon Prison was declared unfit for human habitation and it closed down in 1925.

With Langdon Cliffs in Trust ownership there is now no danger of Dover spreading any further eastward. It is a fascinating but awkward area of land for the Trust to manage, and I imagine that the previous owners, Dover District Council and the Ministry of Defence, were glad to be rid of it. 'Before we took over last spring,' explained Cooper, 'this was an appalling place for vandalism.' However, a summer warden was employed and the incidence of car break-ins was reduced dramatically. The Trust has also made an effort to tidy the place up, and the public lavatories are cleaned four or five times a day in summer, instead of infrequently, as before. There are now plans to modernise the distinctly unsightly ice-cream kiosk beside the carpark: one half will continue selling refreshments, the other will house a small display about the area and its wildlife.

Before Cooper and I parted company he took me to see South Foreland Lighthouse, which Trinity House, the organisation responsible for navigation

*Machinery that turned the lantern,*
*South Foreland Lighthouse*

*Sidney Hopper at Bockhill Farm*

aids in England and Wales, had recently put on the market. The Trust already
owned Lighthouse Down and it was keen to get the lighthouse as well. 'There
are several reasons why I'd like us to buy it,' explained Cooper. 'It's a
fascinating building for one thing, with its turn-of-the-century fittings; and
it's a very important feature in the coastal landscape.' The lighthouse was
built in 1843 and it was from here that Marconi sent his first radio signals in
1898. Ninety years later it was closed down and put on the market. Sale was to
be by private tender and the Trust decided to offer Trinity House around
£300,000. One of the problems for Cooper and the Trust was working out
how much the lighthouse was worth on a sealed-tender system. They seem to
have got their sums right as the Trust's offer was accepted and the lighthouse
is now open to the public during the summer months.

# 5

# *Tales of the Unexpected*

F EW PLACES can be so little understood, and so unfairly perceived, as Northern Ireland is by those who haven't been there. This was my first visit to Ireland north of the border and I arrived in Belfast, on a grey morning in early April, with a ragbag of ill-assorted fears and prejudices. The English have been moaning about the Irish problem – which is to say the British problem – for over four centuries. Prejudice has probably been bred into us, and it is certainly reinforced by the coverage, in newspapers and on television, of the present troubles: virtually everything we hear about Northern Ireland is gruesome, and consequently one anticipates the worst.

I expected Belfast to be a vast, scruffy city full of poor architecture: something like Birmingham with the added ingredient of sectarian violence. And I expected the countryside to be dull and unkempt: a place of low fertility, high rainfall and morose farmers. I was surprised to find that Belfast is quite a small city, in places prosperous, girded about by good-looking hills: there is a lot more to it than ghettoes. But it was the countryside which really shook me: there are great stretches along the coast which far surpass in grandeur and beauty most of what can be found in Britain. It is true that there are few pretty villages in Northern Ireland, but then the same can be said for most of Scotland. Soon after I arrived I found myself walking down a hill around midnight in a southern suburb: the city below was a constellation of lights, compact, quiet and superficially unmenacing. It reminded me of the West Riding towns where I was brought up; and indeed, Belfast has much in common with the industrial north of England: it is a solid place with its fair share of handsome buildings, one of which, the Crown Liquor Saloon, was acquired by the National Trust in 1978.

I had come to Belfast with a friend, a native of the town whose family still lived there. This was good for my confidence – in Belfast it helps to have an insider explain the city's geography and interpret the country's peculiarities –

OPPOSITE: *Murlough Bay and Fair Head*

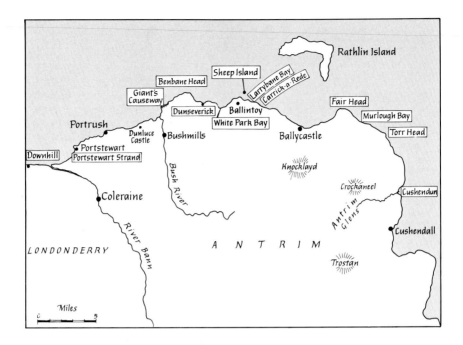

but bad for my constitution: this is the home of serious drinking and huge breakfasts. Our first stop of consequence was the Crown on Great Victoria Street. Again, I found myself thinking of northern England: Great Victoria Street has that incongruous mix of ornate Victoriana and down-at-heel post-modernism that one finds in places such as Liverpool and Newcastle. Along the street from the Crown is the eye-catching Opera House, built during the last century, while opposite is the appallingly ugly Europa Hotel, which is said to be the most bombed building in Western Europe.

By six o'clock in the evening the Crown was already packed. John Betjeman described this old gin palace as a 'many-coloured cavern'. This is an understatement. Built in the 1890s, the Crown is a monument to the Victorian predilection for the florid and gaudy. It comes as no surprise to learn that many of the craftsmen employed in its making had come to Belfast to decorate and embellish the newly built Catholic churches. With its rich mix of brass, granite and oak, with its painted glass, gilded mirrors and ornate tiling, the Crown has a thoroughly Catholic feel to it. There are griffins, eagles and lions on the partitions between the snugs; there are gas lamps hanging from the stucco ceiling; and there are waiters dressed in black and white, as waiters should be. The Crown is run for the Trust by Bass Ireland and I imagine it is one of the Trust's most popular properties: it is undoubtedly one of its oddest, but then there is a lot that is odd about Ireland.

The following morning we made our way south to Newcastle. Within half an hour of leaving Belfast we were in sight of the Mourne mountains. The countryside looked magnificent, all brilliant light and primary colours. The upper reaches of the Mournes were white with snow; below, thick hedges of yellow gorse cast a riotous grid across the green fields. Hawthorn and horse chestnut were breaking into leaf; blackthorn and apple were already in full blossom. There were scattered clumps of primroses, celandines and violets beside a mountain stream. A few rhododendrons had burst into red and purple flower, but we were a bit early for the full works.

I was struck by many things, among them the beauty of the mountains and the coast, the drabness of the small towns and villages, and the dreadful *hacienda*-style modern bungalows littered willy-nilly across the landscape. As someone from the Trust remarked, you can tell where the Belfast bourgeoisie go for their holidays – the Costa del Sol. A further element of ugliness stems from the sectarian troubles, and to a stranger it all seems vaguely ludicrous. Even in the smallest village the police barracks – and they are called barracks, not stations – are surrounded by floodlights and fortifications. More macabre still are the territorial markings of the different factions. The Irish flag flutters above the townhall in Hilltown, a town with Republican sympathies not far from the border. In Loyalist areas, and especially in the poorer parts, the kerbstones are painted red, white and blue; and then there are the flags, sometimes the Union Jack, sometimes the Red Hand of Ulster. Once you have mastered the acronyms – IRA, INLA, UDA, UVF and so forth – you can generally work out from the graffiti whether you are in a Loyalist or a Republican area. My companion was able to enlighten me about other references which I found obscure: 'Ulster Says No' referred to the Anglo–Irish Agreement; 'Remember 1690' to the Battle of the Boyne, where William of Orange defeated James II.

The next day we headed north, through Ballymena and Ballymoney and on to the Antrim coast. Around midday we arrived at Bushmills, home of the famous whiskey distillery, and searched for a pub: it was Sunday, this was the land of evangelical Presbyterians and Bushmills was dry for the sabbath. And so, it seemed, were the towns of Portstewart and Portrush. It was raining hard: a grey sea faded into a grey sky; the streets were grey and the towns looked mean and miserable. In Portrush we watched a flag-bearing band assemble outside the Orange Hall; passing cars were checked by the RUC. Then we headed back along the coast, past the magnificent ruins of Dunluce Castle, through Bushmills and on to Ballycastle. We ate lunch at the Antrim Arms, donned our waterproofs and made for Murlough Bay. By the time we arrived the clouds had begun to lift and a watery sun breathed soft colours into the landscape. Soon we could make out the low outline of Rathlin Island, which lay a few miles to the north, and before long we could see over to Scotland and the Mull of Kintyre.

At the north end of Murlough Bay a great jangle of black boulders separated the sea from the vast basalt cliffs of Fair Head. Within minutes of arriving we saw a peregrine, a pair of buzzards, a pair of choughs and a raven. We made our way down to the foot of the cliffs, peered into the entrance of an old coal mine, then tramped down to the shore. Above the lichen-encrusted boulders were the ruins of miners' cottages. Oystercatchers piped on the jagged shoreline, eiders bobbed in the waves and a gannet plunged for fish further out to sea.

The Trust owns a big wedge of land, over 1,000 acres altogether, stretching from Fair Head to Ruebane Point and encompassing all of Murlough Bay and most of the land beneath the cliffs behind. The diversity of the landscape is astonishing. The black volcanic basalts of Fair Head contrast with the white limestone cliffs which ring the bay. While Fair Head and Ruebane Point, the latter composed of a hard schist, jut aggressively out to sea, the bowl of land behind the bay is altogether more soft and subtle. There are steep fields grazed by sheep and suckler beef and some good patches of woodland: birch, beech, ash, rowan. The woods had a blurred, out-of-focus look about them, the trees almost in leaf but not quite. Dotted around the bay are reminders of an industrial past: coal mines and derelict cottages below Fair Head and some handsome lime kilns to the south. Midway across the bay, and commanding

*Mosses and lichens,*
*Murlough Bay*

fine views in all directions, are the ruins of Drumnakill Church. There is still some praying done in the bay, though not here. Sir Roger Casement's memorial, halfway up the hill behind, has apparently become something of a shrine. Casement was brought up in the Antrim Glens as a Protestant and Unionist. He worked for many years for the British Foreign Office before espousing the cause of a United Ireland. He was hanged as a traitor at Pentonville Prison in 1916.

Along the fifty-odd miles of coastline between Magilligan Point in the west and Cushendall in the east the Trust has over a dozen properties. It owns sand dunes and estuarine mudflats at Portstewart Strand and Bar Mouth; it owns magnificent sandy beaches at White Park Bay and Cushendun; in the Giant's Causeway it possesses one of the great geological oddities of the world; and at Downhill and Cushendun the Trust has inherited some unusual buildings. Indeed, the attraction of this coastline stems partly from its variety: like a good stew, it contains a little bit of everything.

Midway between the mouth of the River Bann and Magilligan Point, in the County of Londonderry, are the remains of Downhill demesne, the eighteenth-century creation of Frederick Augustus Hervey. Hervey was Bishop of Derry and Earl of Bristol, and consequently he was known as the Earl-Bishop. One of the reasons he chose Downhill as the site for a vast country house was because it possessed certain features which were thought to render it sublime. 'The qualities of the sublime,' wrote Peter Rankin in an article about Downhill, 'included obscurity, which induced a sense of terror; power, the power of nature untamed, that left man isolated and insecure in a landscape that dwarfed him to insignificance; privations, such as solitude and emptiness, which were sublime because they were terrible; and vastness, heights that towered above the onlooker and depths that opened out below, which created a sense of infinity that filled the mind with awe.'

Set back from the sea-cliffs and surrounded by grass fields are the remains of the country house. Judging from old drawings and photographs, Downhill Castle was angular and ill-proportioned. From a distance the shored-up ruins look like an abandoned barracks; and indeed the castle did serve as a barracks during the last war. In contrast, the small temple perched above the cliffs is a building of astounding beauty. Elsewhere on the demesne there is a ramshackle walled garden, within which is a fine dovecote and an ice house. There is also a storm-damaged mausoleum and a wooded valley, at the entrance to which is Bishop's Gate, whose small lodge is now the home of Jan Eccles, the Trust's warden.

*Jan Eccles in her garden at Downhill*

I approached Bishop's Gate through the Black Glen. It was raining hard and from the floor of the wood rose the pungent smell of garlic. Miss Eccles had spent the morning in the garden, undeterred by the rain. I arrived as she was having lunch and she invited me to join her. Miss Eccles was brought up in Sligo, on the west coast of the Republic. She mentioned that she was already a young woman at the time of the first Irish troubles, which put her somewhere in her eighties. She neither looked nor acted her age, and she was scornful about the photograph of herself on a bicycle on one of the display boards in the temple. 'I might be antique,' she said, 'but I'm not dead yet.' Miss Eccles still rides her bike, works all hours of day and smokes a pipe.

Miss Eccles came to Downhill at the invitation of Lord Antrim in 1962. The Mussenden Temple had been given to the Trust in 1949, along with covenants over thirteen acres round it, and in 1962, with the help of the Ulster Land Fund, the Trust bought Bishop's Gate lodge and a further eighteen acres of land. Downhill Castle and the mausoleum were acquired in 1980. When Miss Eccles arrived the lodge was derelict and the valley behind overgrown. Lord Antrim, then the chairman of the Trust's Northern Ireland Committee, and later chairman of the National Trust itself, had the lodge re-roofed. Miss Eccles moved in and over the next ten years she cleared away the scrub in the valley and created the garden. She retired in 1972. 'I hated retirement,' she recalled, 'so I came back after five years.'

Until recently Miss Eccles had been responsible for looking after everything at Downhill. Much to her chagrin, she has now been relieved of some of her duties, but she continues to tend the garden. 'I've built it up with the help of visitors,' she said. 'Lots of people bring me plants and in that way the garden has grown.' She was particularly pleased with some *Metasequoia* trees which were just about to come into leaf. She explained that a long time ago seeds and pollen found on the north coast had been identified by Kew Gardens as being from *Metasequoia glyptostroboides*, a tree thought to be extinct. Then in 1941 living specimens of this tree were found in Tibet, since when it has been introduced to many parts of Europe. Miss Eccles had planted some here and they were thriving.

Standing on a grass bank behind the lodge is a headless statue which once stood on the mausoleum erected in 1779 in memory of the Earl-Bishop's elder brother George. George was blown off the mausoleum during a storm in 1839. 'I'm still searching for his head,' said Miss Eccles. Head-hunting has already proved a worthwhile business: 'One night I went into the rose garden with a torch and I found twelve heads.' These were Roman copies of famous Greek statues. At one time they adorned the castle; now they can be seen in the crypt below the temple. Miss Eccles also mentioned that she had been out at night looking for the ghost of a butler. The Earl-Bishop is said to have murdered the servant by throwing him down a well.

The Earl-Bishop was a quixotic character: literate, well-travelled, liberal, eccentric. He built three great mansions – the finest being at Ickworth in Suffolk, also owned by the Trust – and collected many works of art. Though a Protestant, he allowed Catholics to hold services in his temple and he introduced an Act into the Irish Parliament which enabled Catholics to remain loyal, in a spiritual sense, to the Papacy. Work on the castle began in the 1770s and continued for over a decade. The Earl-Bishop lived here on and off during the 1780s but eventually he lost interest in Downhill and turned his attention to building projects elsewhere. The landscape around the castle remains bleak, so presumably his ambitious planting schemes were not a success. 'Downhill is becoming Elegance itself,' he wrote in 1785 in a letter to his daughter, '300,000 Trees without Doors upon all the banks & upon all the Rocks, & almost as many pictures & Statues within Doors counts very well.' There is nothing elegant about the castle today. 'It used to be a lovely, picturesque ruin,' said Miss Eccles. The recent restoration work may have made the structure safe; it certainly hasn't improved its looks. Both castle and temple had been daubed with Protestant paramilitary graffiti just before my visit. The Earl-Bishop would have been disgusted.

The temple, which the Earl-Bishop dedicated to his cousin Mrs Frideswide Mussenden, is one of the loveliest buildings imaginable, its design being based on the Temple of Vesta at Tivoli. Above the door is the Earl-Bishop's coat of

*The Mussenden Temple, Downhill*

arms, and carved into the golden stonework beneath the dome is a quotation from Lucretius which, in translation, reads as follows:

> 'Tis pleasant, safely to behold from shore
> The rolling ship, and hear the tempest roar.

Very apt, for the temple is provocatively perched, as though challenging the elements, on the edge of the cliffs. The views from inside are magnificent: there is the churning sea below, and off to the west miles of empty sand. In the distance are the hills of Donegal, while close by, and immediately below, runs

*Nesting fulmars at Benbane Head*

the railway line which links Coleraine and Derry. The Earl-Bishop used the temple as a library and one can imagine him periodically glancing up from some learned treatise of the day to observe the passing of peregrines and choughs.

One bird the Earl-Bishop is unlikely to have seen is the fulmar petrel, which is now a common sight all the way along this coast. In 1921 only one pair of fulmars bred on the north coast of Ireland, but the fulmar has recently expanded its range and it is now thriving: there are somewhere in the region of

4,000 pairs nesting on the Antrim cliffs. The coast is also notable for peregrines, buzzards and ravens, all of which are doing well. Unfortunately, the chough has become progressively rarer, and there are now only ten pairs left in Northern Ireland: five on Rathlin Island, the rest on the mainland. The 'improvement' of the coastal grasslands has contributed to the birds' decline. Many pastures have been reseeded, and nearly all are treated now with artificial fertilisers; consequently, they are floristically poor and support few insects, the fodder of the chough.

Since the last war many of the greatest threats to wildlife have come from changes in farming practices. This has been especially the case in lowland Britain – one thinks, for example, of the loss of heathland in Dorset, the ploughing up of herb-rich meadows, the destruction of hedgerows – but there have been changes too on the poorer, marginal lands. Throughout Britain and Ireland stock farmers have sought to increase the productivity of their grasslands. Traditional hay-meadows spattered with dozens of wildflowers – orchids, buttercups, crane's-bill, vetches – are now a thing of the past, and anyone who imagines Northern Ireland to be an outpost of old-fashioned farm practices will be disappointed. The difference between the old pastures and the new 'improved' variety can be clearly seen behind Fair Head. The Trust's unfertilised land has a mottled, shaggy look about it, while the drained and reseeded fields of a neighbouring farmer are a brilliant green. The former supports a wealth of wildflowers and insects, while the latter, whose sole purpose is the production of vast quantities of protoplasm, is as sterile as concrete as far as wildlife is concerned.

For centuries Antrim's farmers have taken sand from the beaches. In the old days this presented no problems: the farmer would come down to the beach with horse, cart and shovel and take enough for his own domestic purposes. Sand was used as bedding for cattle and perhaps to fill in holes in the land. Unfortunately, the scale of sand removal has increased dramatically and the Trust is seriously concerned about the effects on some of its beaches. Christine Nevin, the warden in charge of Portstewart Strand, considers this one of the main threats to the survival of the dunes and beach.

Nevin took me round the Trust holdings at Portstewart and Bar Mouth one grim, rainy morning. Under these conditions it was hard to imagine why Portstewart Strand should be so popular with summer tourists: on a good day 1,000 cars are parked along the beach. The Trust owns 185 acres of duneland and it leases the beach from the oddly named The Honorable, The Irish Society. Nevin said that there might be a problem with cars compacting the sand, but there was no hard evidence for this. The visitors leave vast

*White Park Bay, looking west*

quantities of litter – indeed the Irish are disgracefully complacent about their
waste – but Nevin was more concerned about the farmers than the tourists.
'I reckon there's easily ten tons of sand going off the beach each week,' she
said. The farmers preferred dry sand, so they tended to take it from the base of
the dunes. They were not coming with a shovel and cart as their forebears did,
but with a JCB and trailers. 'When I first came here,' said Nevin – she had
arrived eighteen months earlier – 'I tried to talk to the farmers but they either
ignored me or they were abusive. They say they have a right to dig sand, but
no one has ever come up with evidence of this in writing.'

   Jim Wells, the Trust's Information and Education Officer for the north
coast, took me to two other sites where sand extraction is worrying the Trust:
White Park Bay and Cushendun. 'I came to White Park Bay two weeks ago
and there was a JCB and seven tractors and trailers,' he said. 'Over the Easter
weekend they took about 400 tons of sand.' Local farmers believe they have a

right to take sand; but if such a right exists, then the sand taken would be for agricultural use only. The quantities involved are so vast that it seems probable that some are selling the sand to builders. This they deny. According to Wells, the farmers' answer to any objections goes as follows. First, they say it is their right and no one is going to deprive them of it. And second, they say that there is no problem, for the sea is replacing the sand they take. Unfortunately, this is not the case.

While I was on the north coast the local paper, the *Chronicle*, featured on its front page the findings of a study on coastal erosion commissioned by the Department of the Environment for Northern Ireland and undertaken by Drs Bill Carter and Darius Bartlett, two geomorphologists at the University of Ulster, Coleraine. The report begins with a brief summary of man's impact on the Antrim coast. During neolithic times there was small-scale fishing and flint-collecting, but it wasn't until the Middle Ages that human activities really made much impression on the coast: marram grass was gathered for thatch, warrens were established on the dunes, seaweed was collected for iodine extraction, and small harbours and jetties were built. The scale of human interference has inevitably increased during the last two centuries: villages have grown into towns; rivers have been dredged; sand dunes have been turned into golf courses. Erosion is a natural process but the report makes it clear that certain activities along the Antrim coast are speeding up the rates of erosion and threatening the survival of some of the beaches. Since 1960 over 50,000 tons of sand have been removed from White Park Bay by farmers. So far there is no evidence that the beach has decreased in size, but the authors point out that the supply of sand along the coast is finite. 'This means that the sea won't replace what is taken by the farmers,' said Wells. 'One day we may see the taking of the piece of sand that breaks the camel's back.' Erosion as a result of sand removal is occurring on a major scale at White Park Bay, Cushendun and Glenarm, and to a lesser extent, according to Carter and Bartlett, at Ballycastle and Portstewart.

The dunes at Portstewart form a wedge between the sea and the River Bann. We walked across them and Nevin pointed to the patches of buckthorn introduced early this century to stabilise five acres of dunes. After myxomatosis reduced the rabbit population in the 1950s the buckthorn spread rapidly and it now covers twenty-five acres. 'It's very invasive and controlling it is a problem,' explained Nevin. 'But it does at least provide cover for badgers and foxes and a nesting site for birds.' Linnet, willow warbler and reed bunting are among the birds that breed in the scrub.

We returned again to the problem of erosion, one cause of which, the dredger *The Bar Maid*, was making its way down the river and out to sea. The mouth of the River Bann is constrained by two long walls, known as moles. The first phase in their construction took place in the 1880s, the second in the 1930s. These were part of a navigation improvement scheme designed to encourage larger ships to make their way up the tidal Bann to the harbour at Coleraine. In 1976 the harbour authority bought a dredger and this has been in operation ever since, scouring sand from the river bottom and dumping it out at sea. Some of the dunes inside the estuary are crumbling away; it seems probable that dredging is the cause as it removes sand from the system on a permanent basis and alters the current patterns within the estuary and along the coast. Erosion round the base of the moles is such that there are now fears of their being breached.

I had never seen so many old people's homes as there were along the North Antrim coast. Portstewart supports a large population of retired people and attracts what is known as a 'genteel clientele' during the summer months. Portrush is more garish, and probably more fun. Its centre is dominated by amusement arcades and various places devoted to relieving visitors of their money; its bungalowed outskirts coalesce with vast caravan parks; and the seafront is lined with Regency-style guest houses, guttering awry, paintwork peeling.

Tourism has a long history in these parts, and for over two centuries people have been coming up to the north coast to inspect the Giant's Causeway. Dr Johnson said that it was worth seeing, but not worth going to see. This is unfair. The Giant's Causeway, a bizarre collection of some 40,000 basalt columns, is an extraordinary sight, and to my mind just as thrilling as the Pyramids of Giza, which, like the Giant's Causeway, have been declared a World Heritage Site by UNESCO. Jim Wells thought Johnson's disappointment might have stemmed from his expectation of something more substantial, having seen the paintings of the Causeway done in the 1740s by a Dublin spinster called Susanna Drury. Miss Drury submitted two views of the Causeway in a competition held by the Dublin Society. Her columns look larger than the real things, although the paintings are said by geologists to provide a good record of how the Causeway used to look (some of the stones having been pinched since then). Anyway, Miss Drury's paintings attracted much interest, both in Britain and in Europe, where etchings of them were widely circulated.

OVERLEAF: *The Giant's Causeway*

Once the coastal road from Larne opened in the 1830s, the number of visitors increased rapidly. In 1836 the Causeway Hotel was built and it still does a good trade. (During my visit a party of French people were staying there; they had come to inspect the Bushmills whiskey distillery, which had recently been bought by Pernod.) During the latter half of the last century mass tourism began to transform the settlements along the coast. In 1855 the railway arrived at Portrush, which grew to accommodate the summer influx of visitors, most of whom were working-class Protestants from Belfast. Later Portrush was to become popular with industrial workers and their families from southern Scotland. Meanwhile Ballycastle became a popular holiday resort for Catholics.

There are some marvellous photographs taken during the last century of groups of top-hatted gentlemen and lacy-frocked women posing on the stones. There was a shanty of curio stalls beside the Causeway and the tourists were waylaid by tough-looking women with bonnets and pipes and leathery skins. One means of transport, the hydro-electric tram, built in the 1880s to connect Portrush with Causeway Head, became an attraction in itself. Sadly, it was closed down after the last war, during which it had been popular with American soldiers. The views from the tram must have been stupendous, especially where it passed the ruins of Dunluce Castle. There is a very good story about the fate of the cooks at the castle. After eating their first course one evening, the king and his court waited a long time for the next to arrive. Growing impatient, the king went to see what had happened, only to find that the kitchen had tumbled off the cliff, and with it six of his staff.

In 1896 the Causeway was fenced off and visitors had to pay an entry charge. This remained in force until 1961, which was when it was acquired by the National Trust. The Trust took down the fences, ousted the traders, cleared away the stalls, and improved the paths down to the Causeway. At the top of the hill, and set back from the Causeway Hotel, is Moyle District Council's visitor centre, built at a cost of £850,000 and opened in 1986. The Trust leases space within the centre and this was where I met Jim Wells. Every year some 300,000 people come here. 'About the only country we're waiting on is Albania,' said Wells. Over the Easter weekend, the Giant's Causeway had been visited by people of sixteen different nationalities, including a party of Nigerians and two Japanese girls whom the staff had spotted walking gingerly along the clifftop on the wrong side of the safety fence: the girls had

OPPOSITE: *Basalt columns, Giant's Causeway*

never seen sheep before and they were frightened of being savaged by them.

Approximately half the visitors to the Causeway are Northern Irish and about 15 per cent come from Great Britain. The rest include Swedes, Dutch, Americans, French and virtually everyone else, Albanians excepted. According to Wells, most of the non-Irish visitors stay in County Donegal, in the Republic. Many people are frightened of staying the night in Northern Ireland, hence the rush of buses back to the Republic before nightfall. The centre houses an attractive exhibition about the Causeway Coast, its people and wildlife. It is a tasteful and relatively inobtrusive building: the opposite, in fact, of the buildings at Land's End. Thank goodness the Trust owns the Causeway and not some theme-park entrepreneur.

The Giant's Causeway gets its name from legend, its creation being attributed to the giant Finn McCool. McCool, goes the story, built the Causeway so that he could cross the sea to Scotland to fight a rival. And indeed basalt columns similar to those at the Causeway can be seen at Fingal's Cave on the island of Staffa, a few miles off Mull. The igneous rocks along the Antrim coast were laid down between 55 and 60 million years ago. In geological terms, the events which created the great basalt plateau in Antrim are considered recent. Volcanic eruptions pierced the layer of chalk and the spreading lava solidified to form the lower basalts, the upper layers of which gradually weathered to become the red 'interbasaltic beds'. You can see this iron-rich seam snaking its way along the coast, midway up the cliffs, to the east of the Giant's Causeway. After a period of relative calm there were further bursts of volcanic activity. These gave rise to the middle basalts and the Giant's Causeway. On cooling, the lava fractured into long columns. Vertical contraction also took place and the columns have a jointed appearance. Approximately half are hexagonal, the remainder possessing between four and nine sides apiece.

I went down to the Causeway twice, both times a little before dusk. On the first evening it was cold and bright; on the second damp and grey. This is a landscape which wears the weather like a model: it looks good in anything. The Giant's Causeway is but a minor embellishment in a coast already made extraordinary by its jutting headlands, its rich colours, its deep-set bays.

The National Trust owns some eleven miles of coastline immediately to the east of the Giant's Causeway. Once past Dunseverick Castle, of which little remains, basalt gives way to cliffs of limestone. White Park Bay is especially lovely with its crescent of rough grassland between the white sands of the beach and the white cliffs behind. The Trust's coastal path ceases at Ballintoy Harbour, which is well worth visiting for a number of reasons. For one thing,

*The 'Professor's' house, Ballintoy Harbour*

there is a building of profound eccentricity on the way down to the harbour. It is the creation of someone who calls himself 'professor', to which the local population have added their own prefix. The house looks like a Braque painting. It is a conglomeration of cubes, boxes, lozenges and columns, most of them made out of concrete and breeze blocks, some with windows, many sprouting little forests of reinforced steel rods. There is a number beside the door – forty-nine, I think – though it is hard to see why the house should require a number as it stands alone. Above the door there are plastercast heads of a minotaur and a unicorn.

That anyone should be able to build such a house says a lot about the planning controls, or lack of them, in Northern Ireland. Responsibility for planning does not rest with local authorities, as it does in Great Britain, but with the Department of the Environment for Northern Ireland. According to Anthony Lord, the Trust's Regional Director in Northern Ireland, 'It's all been going badly wrong since the Cockroft Report of the mid-1970s, which virtually said that a man has a right to build a house on what he owns.' The vast majority of applications for planning permission are recommended for approval by local authority councillors, who are much influenced by their constituents. The owner of the house in Ballintoy might claim his creation to be a work of art; the same certainly couldn't be said for most of the new bungalows one sees here.

Northern Ireland has an old-fashioned feel about it. The villages still have proper village stores; the public houses tend to be of the spit-and-sawdust variety; most people still go to church (of one sort or another); and there is a tremendous amount of snogging done in carparks. All this is charming, and much like England was thirty years ago. However, the sooner the planning system is modernised the better: the *laissez-faire* approach is wrecking the countryside. So far the north coast has not suffered too much, but in the hills near Belfast and in the countryside round Strangford Lough the situation has become critical.

Whatever one thinks about the professor's aesthetic sensibilities, one cannot but admire his choice of site. The views from his house are stunning. Just offshore is Sheep Island, which supports eleven species of breeding seabird: four species of auk, four species of gull, fulmar, shag and cormorant. The latter, of which there are 400 pairs, are the cause of some controversy. 'The problem,' explained Wells, 'is that the cormorants have developed a taste for salmon and every morning they fly over to the River Bush and gorge themselves.' Needless to say, this goes down badly with local fishing interests. 'So far we've resisted the calls for a cull,' said Wells. 'Our view is that we should find a way of scaring the cormorants away from the salmon grounds without actually killing them.'

A little way to the east of Ballintoy is a stretch of coastline almost as celebrated as the Giant's Causeway. The Trust bought the island of Carrick-a-Rede and the associated mainland in 1967 with the help of Enterprise Neptune funds. Eleven years later, again with Neptune funds, the Trust acquired fifty-eight acres of land to the west of Carrick-a-Rede, including the quarry of Larrybane. I came here first on a Sunday evening. We parked in the lee of the great lime kiln below the main road, then walked along the clifftop path to Carrick-a-Rede, stopping periodically to lean over the cliffs. At one point a peregrine flew out from beneath us. We watched the straight-winged fulmars gliding past, and far below flocks of kittiwakes swirled above the surface of the sea. By the time we reached the island we had been overtaken by a party of jaunty young men: ruddy-faced, country types wearing spivvy suits and fancy

*Gypsy caravans, Larrybane Quarry*

shoes. Swaggering along behind them was a bevy of young girls. With their mini-skirts, high-heeled shoes and skimpy tops, they looked as though they were off to a disco. The men made some good jokes at our expense, some of them generously offering us the services of the girls at £1.75 each.

We assumed this was a school party; probably from the Republic, if their accents were anything to go by. But there was no school bus in the carpark; instead, there were a couple of brand-new Volvos, a brand-new Mercedes and a brand-new Suzuki Patrol. These were gypsies, not schoolchildren, and when I returned with Wells we drove down to Larrybane Quarry, where they were temporarily encamped. There were about twenty vehicles (mostly Volvos and mostly new) and a dozen or so sparkling caravans. These gypsies made their money by selling carpets, laying tarmac and dealing in antiques: business was obviously thriving. They had been thrown out of Ballycastle earlier in the week, and the Trust was now hoping that the police would shift them out of the quarry. It was impossible not to admire them.

Since the Trust took over Larrybane Quarry it has cleaned the site up. All the old buildings have been removed, with the exception of the quarry office, which has been converted into an information centre. Wells thought that the quarry had spoilt this part of the coast, and no doubt he was right when he said that planning permission for quarrying in an area like this would never be granted nowadays. But quarries are fascinating places and after a few years nature softens the hard edges. This quarry is especially interesting as it provided both a black dolerite – an igneous rock – and a hard white chalk. The dolerite was used for building, while the chalk was used to make fertiliser and cement.

*An artist's impression of the swing bridge at Carrick-a-Rede*

There are two salmon fisheries on the coast here: one off Larrybane Head, the other off the island of Carrick-a-Rede. It is the latter which attracts more interest, probably because its setting is so dramatic. The fish are netted as they migrate from the North Atlantic to their spawning grounds in the Antrim rivers, in particular the Bush and the Bann. Carrick-a-Rede is Gaelic for 'rock in the road', the road being the one followed by the salmon, and there has been a salmon fishery here for several hundred years. The island is separated from the mainland by a deep chasm some sixty feet across. At the beginning of the fishing season the local fishermen sling a rope bridge across the chasm and those who are brave or foolish enough can make the short trip across the 75-foot drop over to the island. The bridge goes up in April and comes down in September. 'It is entirely functional,' said Wells, 'and it's up to the salmon fishermen, not us, to put it up.'

The small town of Ballycastle, a few miles to the east of Carrick-a-Rede, signals the beginning of a new world, for here the inland plains merge with the mountains of north-east Antrim, and Protestants give way to Catholics. Ballycastle is a small, unpretentious town with a pleasant main street running from the market place down to the harbour. Apparently there used to be a good hotel down by the harbour, but the IRA blew it up a long time ago. This leaves the visitor with the choice of the Antrim Arms or one of the many bed-and-breakfasts. The Antrim Arms is not recommended on grounds of comfort, but it is full of character. The beds have linen sheets and the old enamel baths are the size of cattle troughs. The barman left at around one o'clock in the morning and asked us to turn the lights out and lock up when we went to bed. It was that sort of a place: nobody slept there except the guests.

The population of Ballycastle is around 6,000, Catholics and Protestants being here in roughly equal numbers. To the west the villages and towns are solidly Protestant; to the east, in the Antrim Glens, solidly Catholic – indeed, they are 'very Sinn Fein' as someone in the Antrim Arms put it. I was told on various occasions by people who worked for the Trust that I shouldn't dwell on the sectarian divisions in Northern Ireland: the Trust was not a political organisation; those who worked for it were chosen for their skills and aptitude, their religious background being irrelevant. But the religious map of Northern Ireland does have significance for the Trust, as a Catholic in the Antrim Arms pointed out. 'I think the Trust do a very good job,' he began, 'because they protect all the old stuff, whether it's great Protestant houses or mean little cottages which Catholic peasants lived in. But the problem is that nearly all the farmers on the poor land are Catholics – the Protestants took the good land – and many of them resent the Trust, although often for the wrong reasons.' He said that the farmers saw the Trust as an English-based and Protestant organisation. I met others who expressed more strongly the antagonism towards the Trust. 'Let's face it,' said one person, 'many of the tenant farmers loathe and despise the Trust.'

'We're not an English organisation,' said Anthony Lord, the Regional Director, when I saw him later in the week. 'Obviously, our headquarters are in London, and most of our funds come from there, but all the people serving on our Regional Committee come from Northern Ireland, as do an increasing number of our staff.' Lord pointed out that all the wardens along the north coast were Northern Irish. 'These wardens are making a colossal difference,' he said. 'After a while the Trust becomes the person working on the ground. I do think things will get easier . . . ' Lord felt that some of the resentment towards the Trust in north-east Antrim stemmed from the fact that it is a large landowner.

A brief wander round Ballycastle and you soon realise that the town is economically depressed. Dozens of buildings are empty and there is little in the way of industry apart from a factory making pyjamas. The prosperity of this area is based on farming and tourism, and the latter has suffered considerably since the last round of troubles began some twenty years ago. At the Antrim Arms someone who worked with the Chamber of Commerce said that it had been trying to encourage foreign tourists to base themselves here for activity holidays: 'For £114 we pick them up from Belfast Airport, give them seven nights in a guest house and take them out riding, sight-seeing and so forth.' He said that a fair number of Dutch, Belgian and French tourists came here, but few people from Great Britain.

The countryside to the east of Ballycastle is grander than that to the west, and once you climb into the mountains it looks very much like the Western Highlands of Scotland. There are two roads to Cushendun. The coast road commands tremendous views across the sea to the Mull of Kintyre. Midway round is Torr Head, where the Trust owns a small bit of land. Equally impressive is the landscape along the main road, the A2, which skirts round the hill of Knocklayd, then climbs on to the peat moorland between the peaks of Carnanmore and Crockaneel. These wild, treeless hills are dissected by a series of deep and, in places, heavily wooded glens, the most northerly of which is Glendun, at whose mouth is the tiny village of Cushendun.

To the south of the river mouth there are three largish buildings, two of which are public houses, the other being an old people's home. The rest of the village lies over a small bridge. Dick Rogers described it in *Castle, Coast and Cottage*, a book dealing with all the National Trust properties in Northern Ireland:

> The Main Street is all very black and white, nineteenth-century vernacular in style, modest and quiet. Number One Main Street has been refurbished by the Trust as an information point with a tea-room and a small shop. McBride's is a decent public house and there is a post office and shop. The Cornish-style square was built by Clough Williams-Ellis in 1912, commissioned by Ronald McNeill, Baron Cushendun, and his Cornish wife, Maud. It consists of two-storeyed terraces with mansard roofs and Georgian glazing, planned symmetrically around a courtyard entered between massive gate-piers; the terraces are linked by arches at the corners. Round the turn of the road to the right, and facing the sea, are the Cornish-style Maud Cottages built by the same architect in 1925 in memory of Maud.

The Trust owns over sixty acres of land at Cushendun. Most of it was given by the Ulster Land Fund in 1954, though a further two acres of beach were bought with Enterprise Neptune funds in 1965. It is sad to have to report that the Trust's unpopularity in Cushendun is to some extent its own fault. In 1987 it paid £100,000 for the erection of a basalt breakwater which juts out to sea from the northern lip of the river mouth. It is an ugly structure and people have been quick to point out that had anyone else built it, the Trust would have been among the first to object.

The Trust decided to build this breakwater because it thought that it would help to prevent the river mouth from silting up, thus making it easier for the local fishermen to get into the harbour. In their report on coastal erosion, Bill Carter and Darius Bartlett have the following to say about the breakwater: 'This move is extraordinary in the light of the known failure of previous breakwaters to resolve the problem [of silt deposition], and has aroused vehement opposition and anger from the local population, not least of all because it was conducted without the necessary planning permission having been obtained.' Carter and Bartlett add that the breakwater has 'probably done little to maintain a clear channel for navigation . . . ideally, it should be removed'.

The grassland behind Cushendun Beach is being steadily eroded away by the sand diggers. Now it seems that the breakwater may be reducing the quantities of sand being deposited on the beach, and consequently it may be contributing towards the problem of erosion. Local fishermen claim that the breakwater has affected the run of salmon up the river. A pity, perhaps, to end on this note, for the Trust has done more than any other organisation to safeguard the North Antrim coast. Such is the scale of its involvement here that much has been missed out. I have said nothing, for example, about the dune restoration work at Portstewart, nor about the bird hide at Bar Mouth and the wintering wildfowl. Neither have I mentioned the work which has gone in to creating and maintaining the coastal footpath round Benbane Head, or the buses which the Trust lays on for disabled visitors at the Giant's Causeway. That these and many other things have gone unmentioned gives some indication of the great riches which are to be found between Downhill and Cushendun.

# 6

# A Very Peculiar Place

I KNEW NEXT TO nothing about the National Trust when I set off on this trail around the British coast: I had rarely met anyone who worked for it, and had no inkling of how it operated. Nevertheless, I had formed, in caricaturish way, a picture of the sort of person who ran the Trust and looked after its properties. I imagined him to be wealthy by birth and conservative both by nature and politics; a public-school education – possibly at Eton – would have been followed by a spell at Cambridge, or at the Royal Agricultural College, Cirencester, or perhaps in the Army. His skills would be those of estate management; he would be knowledgeable about such things as building maintenance, animal husbandry and property law. He would probably admire Wordsworth's poetry, but not Shelley's; he would be able to tell a Claude from a Turner, a Friesian from an Ayrshire; he might even speak a foreign language. Above all, he would be a gentleman.

And perhaps the Trust once was full of people like this. A few whom I met came close to this stereotype (which is in no way meant to be disparaging), but the Trust has undergone tremendous changes during recent times. For one thing it employs many more people than it did a decade or two ago. For example, when the Trust opened its office in Kent at Scotney Castle in 1974 it was staffed with four people; now there are over forty. The Trust has also taken on increasing numbers of people with specialist skills; many of them, needless to say, do not conform to the old image. 'When I started work for the Trust twenty years ago,' explained one land agent, 'I could speak for it on nearly every aspect of its work. This is no longer the case, because as the Trust has grown it has taken on more and more specialist staff.'

Based at either Queen Anne's Gate in London, or at an outpost in Cirencester, there are staff who can give advice to the regions on such things as forestry management, wildlife conservation, archaeology, the conservation of art collections and so forth. And specialist knowledge is not confined to the

OPPOSITE: *Sheep and drowned drumlins, Strangford Lough*

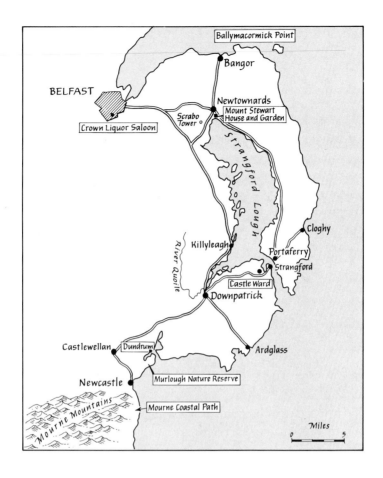

Trust's offices: many of today's younger wardens are college graduates. The three I spent time with in Northern Ireland – Christine Nevin at Portstewart, Dr Bob Brown at Strangford Lough and Jo Whatmough at Murlough – had all gained natural-science degrees at university.

According to its Articles of Association, the Trust was established for the purpose of preserving places of historic interest, fine landscapes and 'their natural aspect, features and animal and plant life'. In other words it intended, from the outset, to look after wildlife as well as buildings, and among its early acquisitions were such outstanding nature sites as Wicken Fen, Blakeney Point and the Farne Islands. Over the years the Trust acquired more and more land of nature-conservation value, and by 1977 it had become the owner of 342 Sites of Special Scientific Interest covering over 200,000 acres of land. It was thus by far the largest private owner of high-grade conservation land in Britain. This was a laudable achievement, but throughout the 1960s and 1970s the Trust was heavily criticised for failing to look after the wildlife on many of its properties. Among those who took the Trust to task were the government's Nature Conservancy Council (NCC) and voluntary bodies like the Royal Society for the Protection of Birds (RSPB) and the county naturalists' trusts.

'Fifteen years ago,' said one English warden, 'the Trust hardly knew what it had on its properties, and few of the land agents were interested in wildlife conservation.' Although some of its wardens at that time – men like Jack Docwra of Dunwich, for instance – were skilled managers of the wildlife habitats within their charge, a much greater number were not. This has all changed. Many – perhaps most – of the wardens on open land are now highly knowledgeable about wildlife, and the advisers at Cirencester, with the help of the wardens, have surveyed most of the Trust's properties and devised management plans for them.

All the same, the Trust still comes in for some stick from other conservation groups, and I came across a fair number of staff who endorsed the criticisms. It was said that the Trust was prepared to spend large sums of money on buildings and their renovation, but relatively little on active conservation management. I am not sure that this is entirely fair: for one thing, the last major acquisition of a house by the Trust was Kedleston Hall in 1986; and for another, between 1983 and 1989 in one region alone the Trust spent £600,000 on the acquisition of open space for 'pure conservation' reasons, and £1·5 million on estates where nature conservation was to be a high priority.

I also sensed a degree of disappointment, especially among the wardens, about the Trust's reluctance to make clear policy statements on key conservation issues. For example, the Trust has never made any pronouncements on the subject of the greenhouse effect and global warming. In a recent annual report Dame Jennifer Jenkins, the Trust's chairman, explained why the Trust remains mute on such issues: 'The National Trust seeks to achieve its objectives not through exhorting others to good conservation practice, but through seeking to care for its extensive estate according to the very best principles and standards.' In other words, the Trust is not a pressure group.

In Northern Ireland things are rather different. 'We've got a special dispensation to speak out on major development issues,' explained Anthony Lord, the Trust's Regional Director. I went to see Lord at the Trust's regional offices at Rowallane, half an hour or so to the south of Belfast. Earlier in the week I'd asked somebody who worked for the Trust what he was like. There was a long pause, then: 'Very nice, very subtle, very shrewd.' This seemed about right; you'd certainly have to be subtle and shrewd to survive ten years as Regional Director in Northern Ireland. Before he came here Lord had spent twenty-five years with the Trust in the Lake District. 'It was a shock to me,' he recalled, 'coming over from the Lakes and finding that the Trust had to operate without the sort of planning framework I was used to there.'

The Lake District is rather an unusual case – the National Park has its own 'special planning board' – but throughout England and Wales planning, and the protection of the countryside, is a relatively complex and sophisticated business. In Britain the government – through the NCC and the Countryside Commissions – plays an important role in the conservation of wildlife and landscape. The NCC manages around 200 nature reserves and employs over 600 people, many of whom are professional biologists. Though both the NCC and the Commissions are satellites of the Department of the Environment, they are reasonably free to make pronouncements on issues of significance to the conservation of wildlife and landscape. Indeed, in their bolder moments they are critical of other government departments (especially agriculture, forestry and transport) and they periodically lend their weight to campaigns whose purpose is to thwart government objectives. The NCC and the Commissions give financial support to a range of voluntary bodies whose activities they see as complementary to their own.

In Northern Ireland there is no NCC and no Countryside Commission. Nor are there any National Parks. Some parts of the country are classed as Areas of Outstanding Natural Beauty, but this designation is of questionable value. In so far as the government plays a role in wildlife conservation, it is through the small Countryside and Wildlife Branch of the Northern Ireland Department of the Environment. 'Ten years ago, hardly anyone in the Branch was professionally qualified,' said Lord. 'Today the staff are more professional, but come the threat of a tidal barrage, a new road or whatever, and they are squashed flat by the planners and financiers within the department.' Lord stressed that the Trust has an excellent relationship with the Countryside and Wildlife Branch, and indeed it receives considerable financial support from the Department of the Environment. Each year the Department of the Environment gives the Trust in Northern Ireland some £400,000 – which goes towards acquisitions and capital costs – in addition to which there are further grants for the management of nature reserves.

'We've got a good relationship with the Countryside and Wildlife Branch,' confirmed one warden, 'but the problem is that they can't stand up for themselves. So we have to be able to speak out on major issues.' Consequently, the Trust in Northern Ireland is more forthright in its public statements than is the Trust in England and Wales. Conservation has no voice within government; the Trust is its main spokesman without. The RSPB, with 7,000 or so members, makes a lot of noise, but it owns little land and has little clout. The Ulster Wildlife Trust has few members, hardly any land, and is struggling. This leaves the Trust, which in Ireland is commendably pugnacious.

*

An excellent example of how the Trust, with the help of other groups, is seeking to conserve Northern Ireland's wildlife comes from Strangford Lough, a vast lozenge of seawater over twenty miles long and in places five miles wide. The lough is at its narrowest where it joins the sea proper, the straits between the villages of Strangford and Portaferry being less than half a mile across. Within the lough are over 100 islands, and beside it is a diverse mix of farmland, woodland, saltmarsh and mudflat. There are several villages along its shores, one medium-sized town and two of Ireland's truly great country houses, Castle Ward and Mount Stewart, both of which are owned by the Trust.

There are as many views of Strangford Lough as there are worms in your lawn, and I recommend two in particular. You begin to get some idea of its size, and how it fits into the landscape, if you climb up to Scrabo Tower, which is perched on a hill at the north-west corner of the lough. Scrabo Tower can be seen from a great distance: it is imposing and ugly, like a space rocket built in the Scottish baronial style. It was erected in 1857 in memory of the 3rd Marquess of Londonderry, Charles William Vane. Beneath this information, which is carved in stone, is the curious observation 'Fame belongs to history, remembrance to us'. The views from here are fine. Looking back, towards the north, you can see the industrial smudge of Belfast no more than ten miles away; then immediately below, and on the northern shores of the lough, is the town of Newtownards. There is nothing here to entice the eye to linger long, and one's attention is inexorably drawn to the lough itself, which, on the day of my visit, glistened like polished pewter between the modest and undulating farmland which constrained it. This is drumlin country. These well-rounded hillocks of boulder clay are what was left behind after the recession of the glaciers at the end of the last Ice Age. They are especially fertile towards the north, where market gardening flourishes.

The other view I recommend is to be had from the Portaferry Hotel. There are two ways to get there from Scrabo: you can either drive along the eastern shore of the lough, or you can take the road due south of Scrabo to Downpatrick, turn east to the village of Strangford, then take the ferry across the neck of the lough to Portaferry. If you follow the eastern route you will enjoy good views of the lough virtually the whole way along. The road cuts a course between the shore and the drumlin farmland: small fields, high hedges. The road to the west of the lough is set some way back and you get little more than the odd glimpse of water, though there are numerous small roads leading down to the shore. When I arrived it was a lovely spring day. The blackthorn was covered with white blossom; hedges of yellow gorse stood out against the

*Strangford village*

purple-brown soil of ploughed fields; and beyond, in the far distance, traces of snow clung to the upper reaches of the Mourne mountains.

One way or the other, you will end up in the bar of the Portaferry Hotel, an attractive Georgian building at the end of a good-looking terrace along the quayside. Station yourself by a window with a plate of Strangford oysters and you can observe one of the prettiest scenes imaginable. Plying its way back and forth across 'the Narrows', between Portaferry and Strangford, is a small ferry. Such is the strength of the current here that the ferry always appears to

be heading a long way to either one side or the other of its destination, depending on whether the tide is flowing in or out. The water runs at some ten miles per hour and you can gauge its speed by watching the seagulls flow past. Bob Brown, the Trust's warden, told me how he once set off in his car after a herd of killer whales. 'They were swimming into the lough with the tide behind them,' he recalled, 'and I could only just keep up with them.'

On the western shore of the Narrows sits the village of Strangford, its pink and white houses creating a small mosaic of colour beneath the brown-green

*Castle Ward*

of some good woodland. Then in the distance, some way to the north of the village and beyond an unseen creek, perched above a grassy slope of parkland, is the gothic façade of Castle Ward, an extraordinary building which reflects the differing tastes of the couple who built it. Bernard Ward, MP for County Down from 1745–70, favoured the classical style; his wife, Lady Anne, the gothic. They came to an admirably democratic agreement and resolved to have a house whose rear half would be built in the classical style, whose front half would be gothic. I wandered round the outside of the house and then down to the water's edge before I visited Bob Brown. The countryside looked, sounded and smelt good. The rhododendrons were in bud or out; the horse chestnut was almost fully in leaf; the floor of the woodland was thick with bluebells.

An exile from England, Brown had worked in Scandinavia and the Caribbean before taking up the post as head warden of Strangford Lough in 1981. His enthusiasm is matched by his knowledge of the lough's wildlife and his ability to explain succinctly how the lough's biological systems work. With every tide some 80,000 million gallons of water are swept through the Narrows and into (or out of) the lough. The speeds of the current are at their greatest where the water enters and they gradually diminish as the water proceeds inland. 'In the Narrows,' explained Brown, 'virtually everything is swept away and the bottom consists of bare rock and huge boulders.' The nature of the bottom gradually changes as different sediments settle out. Cobbles give way to shingle, then to gravels and sand, and in the quietest reaches are to be found fine silts and mud. This succession of sediments gives rise to great biological diversity, and the lough supports some 2,000 species of marine animal. The vast majority are invertebrates, but Strangford is also noted for its fish and marine mammals.

'Not only do we have a tremendous number of species,' said Brown, 'but the actual number of individuals is also immense.' The turbulence caused by the sea flowing through such a narrow strait means that the plankton is thoroughly mixed and plenty of food reaches right down to the bottom. The availability of vast quantities of food, both animal and vegetable, is one of the reasons why the lough attracts so many birds. Strangford is particularly famous for its wintering population of wildfowl and waders. Every autumn some 15,000 pale-bellied brent geese – two-thirds of the European winter population – descend on the lough from their summer breeding grounds in Arctic Canada. Other species which arrive in large numbers include whooper and mute swan, shelduck, teal, oystercatcher, knot, curlew and redshank. Not all the birds have thrived. 'We used to get 20,000 widgeon each winter,'

ABOVE: *Brent geese over Strangford Lough*

LEFT: *Common seal at Strangford Lough*

recalled Brown, 'but now we're lucky if we scrape 1,000.' Brown thought that the decline was initially caused by shooting, but he was unsure why the widgeon population hadn't picked up in recent years.

During the summer the lough's islands provide a breeding refuge for many species of bird. Red-breasted merganser, cormorant, mallard, greylag goose and shelduck breed on the islands and around the lough shore. With its vast shoals of sand eels and safe nesting sites, the lough also supports a third of all the terns breeding in Ireland. Unfortunately, the roseate terns have failed to breed for the last few years. 'We used to have a colony of a hundred and fifty,' said Brown, 'but now there aren't that many in the whole of Ireland. They seem to be on the way out all over Europe – it's as though they're retreating from their range.'

Another creature which has suffered – both here and elsewhere in Britain – is the common seal. In 1988 a virus related to canine distemper devastated seal populations around Britain and off the shores of neighbouring countries. By August 12,000 common seals were thought to have died in the North Sea, and by December over 2,700 carcasses had been counted round the British coast, almost half coming from East Anglia. Many more would have been washed away to sea. There is still uncertainty about the causes of the epidemic, but it seems that pollution may have been a contributory factor: organochlorine insecticides and polychlorobiphenyls (PCBs) are known to reduce the immune responses of animals.

Before the virus struck, Strangford Lough was home to about 800 common and sixty grey seals; this was by far the largest colony in Northern Ireland. When I met Brown, the 1989 count had yet to be done, but he estimated that the seal population could have been halved during the previous year. He and his fellow wardens had spent many weeks catching and lifting dying and dead seals from the lough and taking them to the veterinary research laboratory in Belfast. Deaths from the virus were much lower during 1989, but the Trust will be monitoring the seal populations in its care very closely over the coming years. It is fortunate that the grey seal – which is much rarer than the common – has shown greater resistance to the virus, but the NCC has expressed fears that otters may succumb to the disease.

I asked Brown what he considered to be the main threats to the lough. 'Well,' he replied, 'there are a few very big threats, and then there is a cluster of smaller threats which, were they to happen, would cumulatively be disastrous.' In the former category comes the proposal for a tidal barrage to generate electricity. 'So far the proposal has come to nothing,' explained Brown, 'for the simple reason that it is considered uneconomic. But

economics change, and we want the barrage idea to be declared *environmentally* unacceptable.' Were a barrage to be built the tides would be reduced to a third or less of their present volume and much of the shoreline would be permanently under water: the effects on the wildlife would be catastrophic.

Brown believes that pollution levels are relatively low, but he warns against complacency. There are a few minor problems: partially treated human effluent enters the lough near the main centres of population; there is some run-off of nitrates and slurry from surrounding farmland; and the use of an antifouling paint on boats has undoubtedly been harmful to wildlife. However, the fact that oyster farming is a thriving business is an indication that the water is reasonably pure.

Plans to establish a salmon farm in the lough have been thwarted, though Brown fears that further bids to practise this highly polluting form of pisciculture will be made in the future. There are a number of problems associated with salmon farming: much of the fodder which is fed to the fish settles on the bottom together with the vast quantities of sewage produced by the fish. In calm water this leads to a process known as eutrophication, whereby the bacteria and algae which feed on the waste deplete the supply of oxygen in the water. A further threat to wildlife is posed by the cocktail of chemicals routinely sprayed over the fish to rid them of lice and parasites.

Perhaps the most serious threat to the lough's wildlife at present comes from shellfish trawling. A century and more ago a fair-sized fishing industry was based at Killyleagh, on the western shore, and at Portaferry. For one reason or another the commercial fisheries went into decline towards the end of the last century, but in recent years the queen scallop has been intensively sought after. The problem with trawling is that it churns up vast quantities of material from the lough bottom and destroys the beds of horse mussels which provide a habitat not only for the scallops but for many other creatures too. The Trust has warned the Northern Ireland Fisheries Department that trawling is causing irreversible damage. Its response, according to Brown, has been 'flippant'.

It is now over twenty years since the Trust helped to found the Strangford Lough Wildlife Scheme, whose purpose is to reconcile the needs of the wildlife with the many different human activities which take place in and around the lough. Bob Brown approvingly quoted a local observer who commented: 'Strangford Lough is an area of water totally surrounded by committees.'

OPPOSITE: *Murlough, with the Mourne mountains beyond*

*Jo Whatmough at Murlough*    *The beach at Murlough*

A bewildering array of groups representing different interests are having to come to terms with each other. Here you will find property developers, conservationists, oyster farmers, fishermen, yachting enthusiasts, wild-fowlers and farmers. 'Unfortunately,' explained Brown, 'there is nobody with teeth co-ordinating what goes on. There is a desperate need for an overall plan.' In the meantime, and until such a body and plan emerge, the Trust and other groups – for example, the Ulster Museum and the British Association for Shooting and Conservation – are doing the best they can to limit damage to the lough. The Trust has acquired control of shooting rights over 90 per cent of the shore and it owns or manages much of the shoreline and some of the land behind. Through ownership and management agreements it now controls some forty islands and in places it even owns some of the lough bed.

Before leaving Northern Ireland I paid a brief call on Jo Whatmough, who took me round the nature reserve of Murlough. Whatmough had been warden here since the Trust acquired Murlough from the Marquess of Downshire's estate in 1967. The vast dunelands at Murlough and the associated sands and tidal lagoons are magnificent, their aesthetic beauty being matched by their importance for wildlife. Many people think of nature reserves as areas of unspoilt, untouched and unmanipulated land. Occasionally they are; but the vast majority of nature reserves encompass landscapes which have been modified by human activities. The discovery of arrow-heads, rough tools and pots at Murlough indicates that the dunes here supported small populations of people during Stone Age and Bronze Age times. The dunes continued to be used during the early Christian and medieval periods. Rabbits, which were introduced to Ireland by the Normans, determined the nature of the vegetation for the next 700 years. For many centuries Murlough supported a vast warren, supplying fur to the hatters of Belfast and meat for the local markets. The introduction of myxomatosis in the 1950s led to a sharp decline in the rabbit population, and trees and shrubs began to invade the dunes as grazing pressures diminished.

Walking across the high dunes today one gets the impression of deep tranquillity, yet during this century Murlough has been heavily used by the Armed Services, both as a training area and a temporary airfield. There has also been an attempt, in one corner of the dunes, to establish a small forest. During the summer months Murlough and the adjacent sandy beaches attract tens of thousands of holiday-makers, and the Trust expends much time and energy looking after footpaths, restoring eroded dunes, and ensuring that visitors can enjoy themselves without harming the wildlife.

What struck me most, listening to Whatmough describe the dunes and their history, was the way in which they have endured centuries of human interference. Murlough has survived the activities of unsophisticated hunter-gatherers, the grazing of rabbits, the intrusion of the Army, and the presence of vast numbers of modern visitors. But these are minor threats compared to much of what is now being foisted on the countryside. If the developers and racketeers are to be kept in check, environmental concerns must be fairly represented within government. In Northern Ireland they aren't. It is plainly wrong that the task of looking after the countryside falls so heavily on the National Trust. What would have been lost were it not for the Trust does not bear thinking about.

# 7

# The Quixotic Kingdom

'HERE IS ABUNDANT business for an antiquary,' wrote Daniel Defoe of Northumberland; 'every place shows you ruined castles, Roman altars, inscriptions, monuments of battles, of heroes killed, and armies routed, and the like.' He might have added that the county also possessed a great variety of landscapes and one of the loveliest coastlines in Britain.

To the traveller going north from the mouth of the River Tyne the coast may initially appear unpromising. Tynemouth is modestly grand, but Whitley Bay is garish, and Blyth and Ashington are archaically industrial. The surrounding countryside has been transformed by coal mining, especially where the coal has been stripped off the surface. Mining has also given rise to towns and villages which chiefly consist of off-the-peg brick terracing: the Victorians may have had a taste for the gothic and the ornate, but when it came to building homes for industrial workers aesthetic considerations were far outweighed by the utilitarian. However, once past Newbiggin the traveller begins to sense that something special lies ahead. First comes the long sweep of Druridge Bay, which is then followed over the next forty miles or so by a rich mix of cliffs, sandy beaches, high dunes and jagged headlands. Every place, as Defoe remarked, seems to have a castle, though it is odd that he made no mention of the priories and churches: the coast's religious architecture, though less conspicuous than the secular, is equally memorable.

I arrived at Bamburgh towards the end of May: full summer in the south of England, late spring here. Oak and ash were in bud but not in leaf; the hawthorn hedges were festooned with white blossom and elder was coming into creamy flower. On the cliffs below Bamburgh Castle grew clumps of purple valerian, pink thrift and white campion. Fulmars squawked from their nests or wheeled above the castle walls in the company of jackdaws and swallows. On my first evening I walked out along the dunes and climbed on

OPPOSITE: *Lindisfarne Castle*

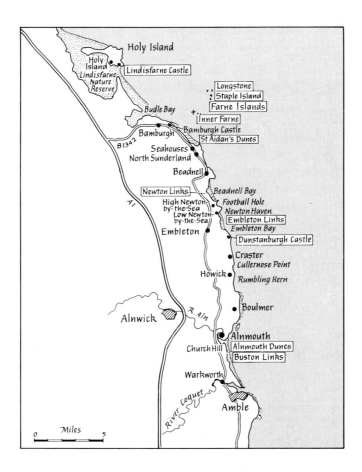

to the basalt ridge which cleaves the golf course in two. Wheatears and yellowhammers sang from the gorse; oystercatchers strutted along the fairways. In a damp ravine a sea of yellow buttercups was dotted with purple orchids and shepherd's purse.

The views from here were all-encompassing. To the north, beyond the wide sandflats of Budle Bay, was the long, low-lying expanse of Holy Island, its eastern extremity punctuated by Lindisfarne Castle, the most northerly of the National Trust's properties. To the east, just a few miles offshore, were the Farne Islands, also owned by the Trust. Then immediately to the south, between high dunes and fertile farmland, was the village of Bamburgh itself, and beyond that, though out of sight, the villages of Seahouses, Beadnell, Low Newton, Embleton and Craster.

Bamburgh Castle, the home of Lord Armstrong, is vast, heavy-walled and perfectly situated. On one side the heaving dunes drop away to a great length of sandy beach; on the other side are sheer cliffs, in the shadow of which are a war memorial and a cricket pitch. At night floodlights turn the whole structure a lurid greeny-purple; but during the daytime, whether shrouded in a grey sea-mist or basking in sunshine, it looks magnificent. It probably bears little resemblance to the original castle, which was largely destroyed by the forces of Warwick the Kingmaker in 1464. When Defoe passed this way it lay in ruins, and its restoration only began when Lord Crewe, the Bishop of Durham, bought it in the eighteenth century. The castle was later sold to the first Lord Armstrong, the inventor and armaments manufacturer who built a remarkable house at Cragside, near Rothbury, in the 1870s. The much-derided interiors of Bamburgh Castle were predominantly his doing. The present Lord Armstrong handed the Cragside Estate to the National Trust in 1979, and today he and his family live at Bamburgh.

Even without the castle Bamburgh would have much to recommend it. The stone-built houses around the triangular green – rookery at one end, horse-trough at the other – are mostly Victorian or earlier: some of them have mullioned windows; many of them do bed-and-breakfast. There are a couple of good pubs, two grocery stores and a butcher's shop. This is a proper village, too far from any town to be emasculated by commuterism, and if any proof of its vivacity was needed I found it at St Aidan's parish church the next morning. I was told that the population of Bamburgh was around 200, in which case about half turned up for communion. This, one felt, was how rural England should be: a booming sermon, an exquisite church, the sound of bells ringing across the fields, the countryside fresh and sparkling. At the end of the church's unusually long chancel is a stone reredos depicting Northumbria's saints, the best-known of whom are St Aidan, who brought Christianity from Iona and died on the spot where the church stands, and St Cuthbert, who led a hermitic life on Inner Farne.

When Aidan arrived in AD635, Bamburgh was the seat of the Northum-brian kingdom and King Oswald installed the missionary on Lindisfarne, which is now known as Holy Island. The island is approached over a long causeway which is submerged at high tide. The road follows the southern shore, skirting the vast sand and mudflats of Lindisfarne National Nature Reserve. After a couple of miles you come to the village of Holy Island, which consists of a few streets, several hotels, a couple of churches and the ruins of the old priory. Below the priory half a dozen upturned boats have been converted to storage huts.

Perched on a basalt dyke a little way to the east of the village, across a small bay backed by fields of grass and wheat, is Lindisfarne Castle. It began life in the sixteenth century, some 500 years after the founding of the priory. The castle's history was largely uneventful; it was never laid waste, except by time, and when Edward Hudson, the owner and founder of *Country Life*, bought it from the Crown in 1901 it was little more than a squalid ruin. The castle was

*Gertrude Jekyll's garden*

fastidiously converted – restored would be the wrong word, for it bears no
resemblance, save from the outside, to a military building – by a great friend
of Hudson's, the architect Edwin Lutyens. In 1921 Hudson sold the building
to Sir Edward de Stein, who in 1944 gave it to the Trust, though he remained
its tenant until his death in 1968. It is now one of the most popular Trust
properties, and indeed the numbers visiting it every year give rise to some
concern: they may not damage the fabric of the building, but they certainly
affect its atmosphere – and its furnishings.

I came to see David Robinson, the Trust's administrator, during a weekday
morning, when the castle was closed to all except school parties. Robinson
and his wife have been living here for five years and they obviously love it,
though they view the rise in visitors with trepidation. In 1980 around 40,000

people visited the castle; by 1987 the figure had risen to 55,000 and in 1988 it climbed to over 70,000. One can see the attraction, for it is a most curious place set in idyllic surroundings.

I found Lutyens's refurbishment a bit too precious and too studied, as though he had designed it for public consumption rather than private comfort. But perhaps this is churlish, for the castle is quite unlike any other building – and its eccentricity fascinates and often pleases. From the outside it appears tiny – and indeed it would almost fit into Bamburgh's Great Hall – but inside it is surprisingly spacious. There is some fine oak furniture and each room has its own peculiar character and charm. Not everyone who stayed here liked it, including Lutyens's wife, and Lytton Strachey said that it was 'very dark, with nowhere to sit, and nothing but stone under, over and round you, which produces a depressing effect'. Lutyens, however, considered it 'the greatest success' and Hudson was also pleased with it, though he spent much more money on its conversion than he had intended. Incidentally, Lutyens removed a balustrade from the castle ramp, which undoubtedly improved the overall appearance, giving it a Camelot-like quality. Unfortunately, the Health and Safety Executive has now told the Trust that a wall of sorts must be reinstated. This may well spoil the look of the castle.

I particularly liked the walled garden, which sits a couple of hundred yards away across a field grazed by sheep. John Owen, who looks after the garden, says that it is not a success, at least not by the standards of Miss Gertrude Jekyll, who designed it. For one thing, Lutyens's attempt to meddle with perspective misfired. The walls are of varying height and angled in such a way that from the castle the garden should appear larger than it is. But Lutyens got his geometry wrong and the illusion fails. However, the garden's real problem is the weather. 'It's incredibly difficult to grow many of the plants Miss Jekyll wanted,' explained Owen. 'One day in six we have gale-force winds. It can be very cold in winter, and plants like hollyhocks and lavender simply shouldn't be here.' All the same, the Trust has done its best to re-create Miss Jekyll's garden, and the setting is superb. Owen said the garden would be at its most colourful in August; he also said I did well to avoid the crowds which that month would bring. It is sad to report that the garden has frequently suffered from thievery. 'People pick plants and uproot them under our noses,' said Owen, 'and some members of the Trust seem to think that that's their right.'

Peter Hawkey, the Trust's warden for the Farne Islands nature reserve, is a big, fit-looking man a few years away from retirement. He came to the Farnes in 1970, since when he has seen changes not only in the fortunes of the islands' bird life, but also in public attitudes towards nature. 'Not all that long ago,' he said, 'if you wandered around the countryside with a pair of binoculars you were likely to get arrested as a peeping Tom.' We spent the afternoon sailing out to the islands in the company of a large party of primary schoolchildren, a small group of old ladies, and half a dozen serious birdwatchers.

When Hawkey came to the Farnes, they received about 9,000 visitors a year; three years later they attracted over 50,000. 'In the 1960s,' explained Hawkey, 'natural-history programmes on television undoubtedly got people interested in birdwatching. Then there was the fact that people had more leisure time, and of course the motorways made the north-east more accessible to people from Yorkshire and the south.' There was no permanent staff when Hawkey arrived, though during the breeding season the Trust employed temporary wardens. Indeed even before the islands were bought by public subscription and given to the Trust in 1925, the owner had a couple of men keeping an eye on the birds during the summer. Hawkey now has two full-time assistants and nine seasonal wardens. He lives on the mainland at Seahouses, while the seasonal wardens – young men recently out of school or college – sleep and eat in the pele tower on Inner Farne. 'In the old days,' said Hawkey, 'it was all very informal and people could land where they liked.

*Peter Hawkey*

Soon after I arrived we decided we had to do something to control the numbers, so we set up a licensing system for the boats.' The Trust has given licences to eight boats – all run by local fishing families – and a maximum of 450 people can visit the islands in the morning, and the same number in the afternoon, weather permitting. Access is restricted to two islands, Staple and Inner Farne, the former being open to the public in the morning, the latter in the afternoon.

In Britain much of our wildlife is discreet, both in appearance and demeanour: many mammals are nocturnal, and many birds are so humble and retiring that the chances of seeing them are slender. The Farnes are different, for here the wildlife is profuse, noisy and audacious. Well before the boat reached the islands we were surrounded by birds: puffins, aptly known as sea parrots, skimmed across the water; guillemots and shags bobbed up and down on the waves; terns, white-winged, sharp-billed and full of grace, returned to their nests, beaks clamped over silver sand-eels. Before putting in at Inner Farne we headed for the outer islands, where grey seals lounged on the rocks or swam languidly in the sea.

By the end of the last century the killing of seals for fur and blubber had reduced the population on the Farne Islands to around a hundred. However, protective measures led to a rapid increase in numbers and by 1970 there were over 7,000 grey seals on the islands. This was far too many. Death rates among the infant seals were exceptionally high and overcrowding led to aggressive behaviour among the adults. The seals were also wearing away the vegetation on some of the islands, thus depriving birds of their nesting sites. The Trust decided to reduce their number and a culling programme brought the population down to around 4,000. Hawkey believes that the population is now increasing at the rate of some 4–5 per cent a year, although the seal virus which reached the North Sea in 1988 led to a slight fall in the number of breeding cows.

Seals are highly unpopular with fishermen, who have frequently argued that their numbers should be reduced. There is little doubt that fish stocks have been depleted off the Northumbrian coast, but there is a simple reason for this: they have been overfished. It may be true that an adult seal can eat thirty pounds of fish in a day, but multiplying the seal population by thirty – as some elements within the fishing lobby do – and claiming that that is the daily poundage eaten by the seals is a nonsense. 'If there's a glut, the seals will gorge themselves,' said Hawkey, 'and if there's little food, then they'll eat very little.' Most of the fish eaten by seals are unfit for human consumption, yet when fishing interests make economic projections for the putative losses, they

*Birds of the Farnes* (left to right):
*shags; kittiwakes; puffins; shags and kittiwakes*

often multiply the seals' alleged consumption of fish by the best price of cod. This is patently unfair.

There are between fifteen and twenty-eight islands in the Farnes, depending on the state of the tides. The three largest are Inner Farne, Staple Island and Brownsman. By far the most interesting is Inner Farne, for it was here that St Cuthbert lived during the seventh century, and it was here that the monastic House of Farne was established. (St Cuthbert was probably the first person in Britain to entertain the idea of bird conservation. Eiders are called cuddy ducks in Northumberland because St Cuthbert laid down rules on the Farnes to protect the birds when nesting.) There is a small chapel, built in the fourteenth century, inside which is a fine oak screen which was taken from Durham Cathedral. An even smaller chapel beside it has been converted into an information centre, and a little way beyond is the pele tower, a fortified house typical of the Border country, built in 1500. At the other end of the island, which is to say about 100 yards away, there is a squat lighthouse.

We made our way from the jetty up the rocky slope to the chapel, protecting our heads from the terns, which greet visitors by dive-bombing them and pecking their heads. The Farnes have much in common with a Third World slum: they are noisy, squalid, and wonderfully alive. The air is heavy with the

smell of guano and the terns shriek incessantly. Every square foot seems to be occupied, if not by terns, then by puffins or eiders. The birds are fearless: terns and eiders nest right up to the footpath, and the shags and kittiwakes on the cliff ledges pay no attention to the visitors who lean over their nests. Hawkey and his colleagues recently undertook a survey of the Arctic terns in which they measured the breeding success of the birds. To their astonishment they found that those nesting close to the paths produced more fledged young than those further away. Presumably, predators keep their distance from the flow of human traffic.

The Trust's management policies have been highly successful and since Hawkey arrived the number of breeding pairs of seabird – seventeen species nest on the islands – has risen from 25,000 to over 50,000, half of which are puffins. This is about as much as the environment can stand. 'The birds are beginning to ruin their habitat,' explained Hawkey as we wandered past an area of bare soil. While eiders and terns need vegetation in which to nest, puffins lay their eggs in burrows beneath the surface. Without a veneer of vegetation the thin soils will blow away, and without vegetation the burrows are more prone to flooding when it rains. As the puffins have increased, so has the density of burrows. This has caused a decline in the growth of perennial plants, and in an attempt to save the soil the Trust has been sowing denuded areas with sea campion and a saltmarsh grass.

Prosaic matters such as this are probably of little interest to visitors, most of whom, like William Howitt, a traveller during Victorian times, are overwhelmed by the sights and smells. 'It was one of the most curious and beautiful sights that I ever saw,' wrote Howitt of Staple Island. 'They were chiefly guillemots and puffins. They seemed all to be sitting erect as close as they could crowd and waving their little dark wings as if for joy.' In those days fowlers collected vast numbers of eggs, many of which were despatched to London. 'They are used to make puddings,' wrote Howitt, 'while the eggs of the gull are boiled and eaten cold to breakfast, and are in that state considered by many wealthy families quite a luxury.'

Egg-collecting has long since ceased, but the Farnes are more important than ever for the local economy. According to Hawkey, they generate £2–3 million a year in tourist revenues. 'If it wasn't for the Farnes,' he said, 'Seahouses wouldn't be the attraction it is.' Needless to say, the importance of the Farnes cannot be measured solely in pecuniary terms: this is one of the finest seabird sanctuaries in Britain, and for many schoolchildren the islands provide the first real taste of raw nature. Inevitably, some visitors find the whole experience a bit too much: Hawkey recalls hearing one querulous woman – aggravated by the rough terrain on Staple Island – demand, 'Why doesn't the Council put a pavement down?'

By far the greatest proportion of coast identified as worthy of acquisition by Enterprise Neptune consisted of cliffs and their hinterland, and consequently I'd spent most of my time observing the sea from a great height. There had been exceptions, of course: Studland in Dorset, Murlough in County Down, and Dunwich Heath in Suffolk. But even in these places I had tended to stick to the dunes and heathland, and when I did venture down to the shore it was generally on to sand, whose wildlife can only be got at with a spade.

Along the Northumbrian coast sandy beaches alternate with rocky headlands, and by scrabbling around in the rock pools you can get glimpses of the marine world. If you spend half an hour poking about under the kelp and bladderwrack you should find a score of animals which inhabit the intertidal zone. Among the more obvious are starfish, brittle-stars, sea urchins, sea anemones, chitons, limpets, dog whelks, mussels, winkles and barnacles. With luck you will find shore and hermit crabs, perhaps some shrimps and some fish too, and under the rocks there will be a promiscuous gathering of sea worms. This is a beautiful world: colourful, delicate and constantly changing. One day the pools may be strewn with thousands of starfish, legs intertwined like lovers. The next there may be none at all.

Such is the richness of life in Newton Haven that the Trust runs it as a marine nature reserve. Dr Bob Foster-Smith, a marine biologist who lives at High Newton, has surveyed most of the coast between the Tweed and the Tyne. This, he says, is one of the best stretches, the wealth of species reflecting the great variety of physical habitats. To the north and south of Northumbria, along the coasts of Yorkshire, Durham and southern Scotland, the geological strata tend to lie near the horizontal plane, giving rise where land meets sea to wave-cut platforms and a fairly uniform environment. But in the area to the south of the Cheviots volcanic activity has tilted and contorted the rocks, which tend to dip towards the south and east. As these have eroded, the harder rocks have been left to jut into the sea in finger-like reefs. The coal measures – a multi-deckered sandwich of limestone, shale, sandstone and coal – have been augmented here by the intrusion of an igneous rock. The Great Whin Sill, which crosses Northumberland, and on which have been built parts of Hadrian's Wall and many castles, not only introduced a new geological element into the landscape, it also metamorphosed the neighbouring limestone into a marble. The sill is made of a hard, black, heavily jointed basalt, and it gives the headlands a characteristic cragginess. To the north of Newton Haven a double reef of limestone and Whin Sill juts into the sea, and

*Rock pool,*
*Low Newton*

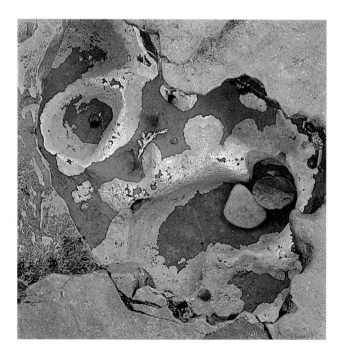

faulting has led to the pattern being repeated to the south. In between these headlands is a sheltered bay of sand. Heart urchins, normally found only in the sub-littoral zone, in other words below the low-tide mark, are here found in the intertidal zone, as are Devonshire cup coral and a rich gathering of marine worms, molluscs and crustaceans.

Anglers claim, somewhat grandly, that the right to fish at sea is enshrined in Magna Carta, and that this presupposes a right to collect bait as well. Bait-digging has become quite a problem in some parts of Britain, and all the major lugworm areas in the north-east have received the attentions of anglers. Others with little interest in fishing have also been lured down to the sands by lugworm, which they can sell for up to £12 a pound. There are various reasons why people object to bait-digging. Round Berwick and at Budle Bay bait-diggers keep large flocks of waders away from their feeding grounds; at Newton the bait-diggers have hunted out both lugworm and the highly prized razor shell, and in doing so they have trodden on and killed heart urchins and other creatures buried in the sand; at Boulmer local fishermen claim that bait-digging has eroded the beach and thus made it harder for them to launch their boats. The Trust leases the sea-bed at Newton Haven from the Crown, which gives it some control over what happens there. It has been able to limit the number of boat moorings and it has also banned bait-digging. But elsewhere conservationists have had to resort to the gentle art of persuasion in their quest to prevent people damaging the marine fauna and flora. In some ways it is easier to conserve wildlife on land, for one can buy land and, if the worst comes to the worst, put a fence round it. The sea-bed can neither be bought nor fenced.

Newton Haven lies midway between the villages of Beadnell and Craster, at the heart of an eight-mile stretch of coast which is almost entirely in the ownership of the National Trust. Twelve years ago I walked along here – from Beadnell to Newton Links, out on to the rocks at Football Hole and Newton Haven, then round Embleton Bay, up to Dunstanburgh Castle and through the fields to Craster. Little seems to have changed since then. Certainly, there are more caravans round Beadnell; the pubs have been tarted up and suffer now from the blight of piped music and electronic gambling machines; and some of the old meadows have been ploughed out. But for the most part the villages and countryside appear much as they did then. Twelve years is not long, and perhaps there is little cause for celebration, but the pace of change in the countryside has become so fast that one half-expects to find the things one has known destroyed, or abused, or simply vulgarised. These are the fears of which Philip Larkin wrote in the poem 'Going, Going':

You try to get near the sea
In summer...
                    It seems, just now,
To be happening so very fast;
Despite all the land left free
For the first time I feel somehow
That it isn't going to last,

That before I snuff it, the whole
Boiling will be bricked in
Except for the tourist parts –
First slum of Europe: a role
It won't be so hard to win,
With a cast of crooks and tarts.

And that will be England gone,
The shadows, the meadows, the lanes,
The guildhalls, the carved choirs.
There'll be books; it will linger on
In galleries; but all that remains
For us will be concrete and tyres.

Some coastal areas inspire nothing other than pessimism and regret. But Enterprise Neptune has made safe many areas which otherwise might have been 'bricked in'. Familiarity breeds affection, but this only goes part way towards explaining why I love the Northumbrian coast above all else in England. It is like a great painting, or a great piece of music: reduce or damage any part of it and all would be diminished.

The Trust land agent responsible for the Northumbrian coast is James Cockle, a slightly built, pleasant and humorous man in his thirties. We met in the carpark at Craster: fulmars nested on the cliffs behind and willow warblers sang their cascading song from a patch of scrub. Before setting off down the coast we laid out Ordnance Survey maps and Cockle ran through what the Trust owned. We began at Beadnell, an attractive village a few miles to the south of Seahouses. Most of the tourist developments have taken place in these two villages, and especially at Seahouses, which is liberally sprinkled with fish-and-chip shops and bingo arcades. Both villages are host to large caravan parks, and Cockle was disturbed by the fact that planning consent had recently been granted for another one at Beadnell. Over the last two years Alnwick District Council had given planning permission for holiday developments at Embleton, and for the enlarging of an existing caravan site at High Newton. Whether caravan sites are a good or a bad thing rather depends on how you look at them. On the one hand they provide relatively cheap family holidays, and without them many people simply could not afford to spend time at the coast. But inevitably the larger sites can ruin the appearance of a coastline, especially when prominently placed. At Beadnell the Trust has bought a nine-acre field opposite the Camping and Caravanning Club's site. Cockle said that the proliferation of caravan sites had made the Trust realise the importance of acquiring a field or more of buffer land behind its coastal holdings.

Embleton Bay stretches from Beadnell south to Snook Point and Football Hole. A great sweep of butter-coloured sand is backed by fine dunes which are bisected by Long Nanny Burn. The land to the north of the burn, Tughall Links, is owned by the Duke of Northumberland, who covenanted it to the Trust in 1966, the same year that the Trust bought the links to the south with funds from Enterprise Neptune. Altogether the dunes cover over 100 acres and among the fetching plants which grow in the rich sward are bloody crane's-bill, burnet rose and purple milk-vetch, none of which I saw when I tramped down to the sea. The sand-spit beside Long Nanny Burn supports a large breeding colony of little terns; such colonies are rare on the east English mainland. I didn't see these either, as my passage along the beach led me to a sign which asked walkers to stay clear of the area. The site is wardened throughout the breeding season by two young men who take it in turn to watch over the birds. In 1987 only two fledglings survived from twenty-nine nests; an unruly dog savaged the rest.

There is also a small nature reserve at Newton Pool. The pool supports a good population of breeding birds, a variety of aquatic plants and some insects whose names are probably more peculiar than their appearance, among them the whirligig beetle and the silky wainscot moth. Newton Pool is just a short walk from Low Newton-by-the-Sea, most of which the Trust owns. It is a pretty little place, typical of the small fishing villages which are to be found in Northumbria wherever there are sheltered harbours. The Trust bought twelve cottages, the main square, the local pub and the beach in the early 1980s. 'Our policy,' explained Cockle, 'is to let the cottages to locals whenever we can.' But locals need work, of which there is a shortage, and consequently most of the cottages in Low Newton are second homes.

Forty years ago twenty commercial fishermen worked out of Low Newton; now all have gone. This is a familiar story, not just in the north-east, but throughout Britain. Ports like North Shields and Grimsby supported huge fleets not long ago but now their waterfronts are close to lifeless, and many of the smaller fishing communities have disappeared completely. We should rejoice, I suppose, that any survive at all, and it was good to see fishing boats coming in and out of Craster and Seahouses, and to find fishermen still at work on the beach at Boulmer. One's sorrow at the dwindling of the inshore fishing fleet is tempered by the knowledge that the fishermen themselves are largely to blame for the decline in fish stocks. Yet on the whole it is the larger, high-tech, capital-intensive enterprises which have done the damage; and these are the ones which have survived.

To the south of Newton Haven is Embleton Bay, which can be approached along the beach – from either Low Newton or Craster – or from Embleton village, which straddles a low hill behind the bay. I recommend the latter approach. The road peters out at the club house of Dunstanburgh Castle golf course, a dilapidated wooden-framed shack where you can get a drink, a sandwich or a plate of sausage and beans. From the club house it is a short walk across a fairway and through the dunes to the sea. To the south the bay culminates with a great slab of Whin Sill on which are perched the sprawling ruins of Dunstanburgh Castle. To the north the sands fade into reefs of Whin Sill and limestone. Overlooking the beach from the dunes is a shanty of wooden shacks and bungalows, which endow the area with a thoroughly antipodean feel.

All of this was once owned by the Sutherland family. In 1961 Sir Ivan Sutherland gave Dunstanburgh Castle to the Trust, and it is now administered and looked after by English Heritage. The same year Sir Ivan also gave Embleton Links to the Trust, retaining a forty-year lease over the golf course at an annual rent of one shilling. At present the Trust has no control over what happens on the golf course but it is currently negotiating a new lease which, if agreed, will give the present tenant long-term occupancy in return for substantial conservation measures. Over the past few years the club has widened some of the fairways; this has been good for the golfers, if not for the duneland plants, although in some places the club's mowing regimes have actually encouraged the formation of herb-rich swards. Cockle believes that a golf course can be managed in such a way as to improve the natural habitat.

Before I met Cockle I had spent an hour or so walking round the bay. It was a fine sunny day; a whiff of salt and dry grass eddied around on a stiffish breeze. By Northumbrian standards this was a popular beach, yet there were less than a dozen people here: a woman and child swimming, the others dog-walking or eating sandwiches in the dunes. I was particularly intrigued by the holiday shacks, about forty in all, which were strewn across the dunes. Most

*Bungalows in Embleton Dunes*

had clapperboard walls which were stained or painted white. Some were rather grand, with classical porticoes, shuttered windows and the like. Others were little more than potting sheds. I liked them. I liked their old-fashioned appearance; I liked their architectural eccentricities; and I felt they fitted into the landscape, indeed even contributed to its interest.

The Trust sees things somewhat differently. When the property was accepted, Head Office in London made it clear that the 'bungalow' owners' leases would only run for a further forty years. The bungalows are privately owned, but the freeholders pay a ground rent to the Trust; so when the leases run out in 2002 the owners will be asked to remove their bungalows. If they don't, the Trust will presumably exercise its legal option to undertake the removal itself. The bungalow owners had recently been reminded by the Trust's Regional Committee that this remains the position. When asked what he thought, Cockle said he could see both sides' points of view.

Many families have been using their bungalows – or shacks or whatever you wish to call them – for three generations. Many of them were built by friends of Sir Ivan's father; they came up from Tyneside to play on his golf course, and stayed here for weekends and sometimes longer. Perhaps it would be stretching a point too far to say that the bungalows should be conserved as examples of duneland vernacular architecture, or as a reminder of what used to happen before the introduction of the town and country planning laws, but they are certainly much prettier than Second World War coastal defences, which the Trust preserves on some properties, and in any case what is at stake is not just a view, or a holiday home, but the collective memories of many families. The Trust's biological survey takes a more prosaic view: 'The holiday bungalows, scattered throughout the northern part of Embleton Links, mean that this area is somewhat disturbed and their use should be discontinued at the earliest opportunity.' I disagree, and I hope the Trust will think again.

It was not until James I came to the throne, and the Crowns of England and Scotland became one, that any degree of peace settled on the Border regions. 'In the land of the Border ballads,' wrote G. M. Trevelyan in his *English Social History*,

> all men were warriors and most women were heroines. To Chaucer it was an unknown, distant, barbarous land – much further off than France – 'far in the North, I cannot tellen where'. There the Percys and other Border chiefs were building magnificent castles to resist the siege of the King of Scotland's armies – Alnwick, Warkworth, Dunstanburgh, Chipchase, Belsay, and many more. The lesser gentry had their square 'peel' towers, smaller copies of the castles of the great; there were no manor houses, a product of relative peace. The peasants lived in wooden shanties that the raiders burnt as a matter of course, while the inhabitants and their cattle hid in the woods or sheltered in the peels.

Of all the castles in Northumbria, I think Dunstanburgh is the most alluring, the most dramatic. There have been settlements there of some sort since Roman times. In the thirteenth century the fortifications belonged to Simon de Montfort, after whose death the land was given by Henry III to his son Edmund, Earl of Lancaster. The ruins we see today are relics of the castle

*Dunstanburgh Castle*

which was built by Edmund's son in the early 1300s. On a grey, rainy day
Dunstanburgh Castle can look malevolent and forbidding; it is as though the
damp gloom gives substance to its ghosts. But under a full sun it becomes
another world, full of easy enchantment, its walls sharply etched against the
blue sky and kittiwakes mewing softly on the basalt cliffs below.

At the time of my visit the Trust was negotiating the purchase of the thick
strip of farmland and foreshore which spans the mile between Craster and the
castle, an area of some 280 acres. This would be a magnificent acquisition,
and it would safeguard for ever the approach along the shore. In recent years
the farmer ploughed up some of the grass fields and put them down to corn;
the Trust would return them to grass, which is much more in keeping with the
landscape. The castle itself covers some eleven acres of land. It has a massive
gatehouse, which can be seen from miles away, but little else survives save the
odd tower and the surrounding wall. What the building lacks in substance, it
makes up for in beauty: you should savour every stone.

Craster is an attractive village where everything appears to be cast in
miniature. There is a small harbour, from which half a dozen cobles make
their way out to sea. Lobster pots are piled up at the back of the harbour and

*Boats in Craster Harbour*

*The Whin Sill at Castle Point, Dunstanburgh*

behind them are some tiny gardens, very cottagey with their wallflowers and irises, stocks and fuchsia bushes. Craster always smells good, for across the street from a pub called the Jolly Fisherman is a place which smokes kippers. Craster kippers are smoked over oak chippings and it is hard to tell whether the smell comes from the fish or the wood.

Such is the varied nature of the coast to the south that it must be hard for geologists to keep their hammers to themselves. The Whin Sill continues for a mile south of Craster and culminates in the jointed scarp of Cullernose Point. From here down to Howick Haven the cliffs are made up of limestone, sandstone and shale, sandwiched within which are some thin seams of coal. Then from there down to Alnmouth are large outcrops of millstone grit, some of which, like Marsden Rock, are set a little way off the shore. To the chagrin of the Trust, geologists have employed not only hammers but drills in their quest

*Rocks at Rumbling Kern*                    *Tractors and boats, Boulmer*

to study the rocks near Cullernose Point. Cockle led me down to the shore a little before we reached Howick and pointed out the riddled rocks. This is not Trust land, but Lord Howick and the Duke of Northumberland have given the Trust covenants over most of the coast between Craster and Boulmer.

I had already seen in West Cornwall some of the problems which can arise on covenanted land. Cockle felt that new covenants were better, and less susceptible to abuse or circumvention, than ones made some time ago. 'Obviously,' he said, 'covenants permit the continuation of agricultural practices, and some changes may occur which we cannot prevent. For example, many farmers see sand dunes as sacrificial areas. They drain well and farmers like to put their cattle on the dunes in winter. But they tend to overstock and overgraze them.' The cattle are fed on silage and concentrates, and these, together with the animals' manure, have the effect of raising soil fertility. This leads to coarse grasses crowding out the more subtle members of the duneland flora. 'We've had a chat to Lord Howick about it,' said Cockle, 'and he has said he'll discuss it with the tenants.'

The coast along here, and indeed all the way down to Alnmouth, is rugged and remote. Occasionally the rocky shoreline is interrupted by sandy beaches, but these are often tiny. There is one at Rumbling Kern, which can be seen from a holiday cottage owned by the Howick Estate. Lord Grey of Falloden, the man who piloted through parliament the Great Reform Act of 1832, had this built as his Bathing House in the early nineteenth century. It is small, yet rather grand, with gothic windows, ornate cap-stones at the roof corners, fluted columns by the door, and a flight of steps down to the sea. Unfortunately, it was made of a soft sandstone, which in places has been

*Sands at Boulmer*

almost weathered away, leaving holes in the walls large enough for starlings to nest in.

The road departs from the coast here and loops past Howick Hall and through Longhoughton before rejoining the sea at Boulmer. Boulmer is rather a scruffy place, but that is probably a good sign: fishing villages which are still fishing villages generally are. Wooden boxes were scattered along the shingle beside a row of Second World War anti-tank blocks. The fishermen at Boulmer use tractors to winch their cobles out of the sea: the ones here were old Internationals and Fordson Majors, the sort you'd rarely see on a farm nowadays, except perhaps in the hills. There were several cobles fishing out at sea, and on the shore men in yellow oilskins prepared to join them. Apparently, Boulmer was once a great smuggling centre for gin. This curious fact comes from Edward Grierson's admirable *Companion Guide to Northumbria*, which is just about all the visitor requires apart from an

*St Waleric's Chapel, with saltmarsh behind*

Ordnance Survey map. (Twice I heard people refer to Ordnance Survey maps as 'ordinary survey maps'. They are not ordinary at all: they provide a remarkable amount of information, marking everything from footpaths to forests, tumuli to Roman villas, phone boxes to windmills. They even show whether a church or chapel has a spire, a tower or neither; and they mark most National Trust properties.)

After leaving Boulmer we again drove inland, then dropped down a broad hillside to the River Aln, which snaked its way through a fertile bowl of land devoted to the growing of wheat and rape. The former was a lush green; the latter a brilliant yellow. This is good farming country, as indeed is much of lowland Northumberland: the rich soils have always yielded good crops and last century's landlords celebrated their good fortune (both on the land and as industrial entrepreneurs) by building fine houses, both for themselves and their tenants. Not only fine houses, but good stone barns and dairy parlours

*Church Hill, with Alnmouth behind*

and stock yards; and as often as not there is a chimney beside each cluster of farm buildings, evidence of the steam engines which once powered threshing machines and other agricultural implements.

'Very picturesque,' wrote Grierson of Alnmouth, 'very continental, with its gaily painted houses following the curve of the estuary to the sea.' Cockle led me up on to Church Hill, from whose summit we looked across the river to Alnmouth, a small town which prospered as a Victorian holiday resort after the arrival of the railways. At one time it served as the port for Alnwick, which lies some four miles inland, but during the last century a freak storm diverted the river and Alnmouth's harbour was gradually smothered in silt. The river used to run to the south of Church Hill and through a gap in the dunes, but it was diverted to the north, slicing the hill away from the town. Where the river once flowed there is now a broad expanse of saltmarsh backed by mudflats and fields. On the top of Church Hill there is a large wooden cross, a little way below which are the ruins of St Waleric's Chapel. The Duke of Northumberland leased this land to the Trust in the 1960s and the Trust has recently re-pointed the chapel. Cockle said that there were gravestones dotted around the hill, but such was the density of scrub that he had never managed to find them.

A little way to the south of Church Hill the Trust owns eighteen acres of Buston Links, encompassing about half a mile of shore. To the south of here there are a further two miles of duneland and sandy beach, and then comes the River Coquet and the town of Amble. What Defoe called this 'long coasting county' continues another thirty miles or so to the mouth of the River Tyne. There are considerable stretches – one thinks, for example, of Druridge Bay, where the Trust has a small property – which remain unspoilt, but it is not until one reaches the cliffs at South Shields and, a little further south, the coal beaches of County Durham, that the Trust plays any significant role again in the conservation of the coast.

# 8

# *All on the Grandest Scale*

THE PEOPLE of North Wales make much of their money from sheep and tourists. There are certainly too many of the former – overgrazing has ruined many a heath and wood – and not everyone welcomes the seasonal invasion of the latter. Here, for example, is Jan Morris in *The Matter of Wales*:

> Here, as everywhere, tourism is a corrosion, or a corruption. What farmer can resist the extra income of a caravan site on his stoniest and bumpiest meadow? Why bother to put up your signs in your own language, if all your customers are English? Tourism feeds upon parody, on self-mockery even: ludicrous stereotypes of this grand old country, women dressed up in tall hats and aprons for the selling of fudge, cheap and shoddy love-spoons wrapped in plastic, tea-cloths with ill-printed images of poets and heroes, to raise a cheap laugh in a Leatherhead kitchen. And as it enriches, so it sterilises; there is nothing fertile to it.

Spend a little time in North Wales and you will see what Morris is getting at. Along the north coast, between Chester and Bangor, there is a string of resorts 'with all the statutory accessories of disco, ice-rink, hot-dog stand, indoor surfing centre and trailer camp suburb'. Along the west coast, around Harlech and Aberdovey and Aberystwyth, great swathes of duneland have been flattened to make way for unsightly caravan parks. And in towns and villages everywhere craft shops churn out overpriced and shoddy bric-à-brac.

Elegiac denunciations of tourism may twang our heart-strings, but we should treat them with a degree of scepticism. For one thing, generalisations about tourism (or tourists) simply will not do, any more than will generalisations about farming (or farmers). The difference between a farmhouse bed-and-breakfast and a Butlin's holiday camp is every bit as great as that between a smallholding in the Welsh hills and an arable estate in Eastern

OPPOSITE: *The old brickworks, Porth Wen, Anglesey*

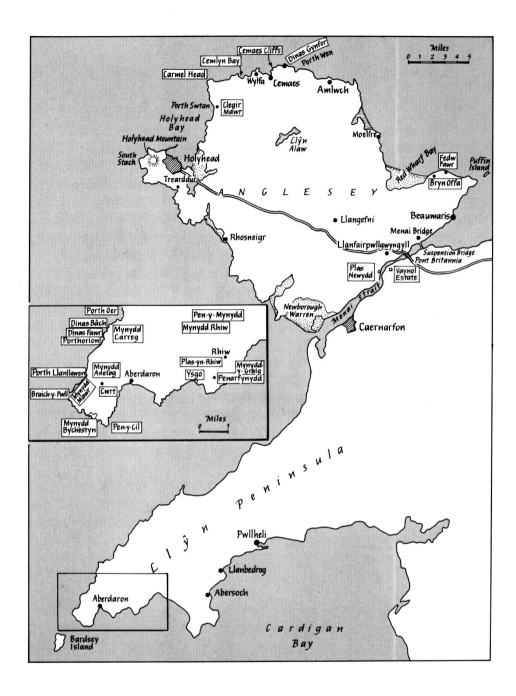

England. Tourism can be destructive, of both landscapes and communities, but there is nothing intrinsically wrong with it (and if there were, then everyone, and especially travel writers, should be encouraged to remain at home).

Tourism corrupts, says Morris, and if one looks at the way in which history has become a commodity, to be flogged, however disingenuously, to the gullible visitor, then perhaps that is true. Wherever the tourist goes in Wales

170

he or she is regaled with stories about saints and bards and druids; in Cornwall, it is pixies, smugglers and the Arthurian legend. We are all suckers for romance and those who promote tourism know it: they dollop it out by the bucketful, with little concern for veracity or realism. With a bit of luck, they can even call upon a local artist, or perhaps a writer or politician, to do a bit of posthumous promotion: Wordsworth for the Lakes, Hardy for Dorset, Constable for Suffolk, Lloyd George for Criccieth. We may find this commercialisation of history – or culture or whatever you wish to call it – galling, but it only matters if it damages people and communities still living, or if it fosters prejudice or causes hardship. I doubt whether it ever does.

Morris says that tourism sterilises, that there is nothing fertile to it. I think this is nonsense. Many of our finest seaside towns are resorts rather than ports: tourism may not have made them, but it certainly endowed them with things which we treasure now, from Regency hotels to piers, beach huts to promenades. Imagine how dull places such as Brighton, Llandudno and Scarborough would be had the Victorians – who virtually invented the seaside holiday – forsaken the coast and chosen instead to go camping in the Pennines or Peaks. Perhaps it is true that many old resorts – once stately retreats for the middle classes – have become noisier, brasher and tackier. But I suspect that a dislike of these places is to a large extent fuelled by snobbery and xenophobia.

I cannot think why Morris says that tourism 'is an unworthy way to make a living, for such a people as the Welsh'. Are the Welsh in some ways superior to other races, and thus unsuited to such tasks as serving food, running caravan sites and selling ice-cream? Without a tourist industry North Wales would be a very different – and much poorer – place. Were it not for the tourists, depopulation, the perennial scourge of rural areas, would increase markedly, and many farming families would not survive were it not for bed-and-breakfast receipts and the caravans parked on their bumpy meadows. It is reasonable to suppose that if a farmer makes some money from tourism, he may feel less inclined to squeeze money out of his land by farming it more intensively. The caravans may be unsightly, but rather their presence than the loss of an old hay-meadow, or the clearing of a hedge.

Tourism has a long history in North Wales. From the Middle Ages onwards vast numbers of pilgrims made their way to the tip of the Llŷn Peninsula, from where they took a boat across to the island of Bardsey, whose monastery was founded in the sixth century, and in whose soil are said to be buried thousands of Welsh saints. As for Anglesey, the town of Beaumaris had become a 'pleasure resort' for the well-to-do by the beginning of the nineteenth century, and from 1822 onwards steamships made regular sailings from Liverpool to

*Aberdaron, looking westward*

the Menai Strait throughout the summer months. When the railways arrived –
reaching as far as Pwllheli on Llŷn, and crossing Anglesey to the port of
Holyhead – many villages which formerly had known little business other
than farming became tourist resorts.

I arrived on Llŷn at the end of June: torrential rain for one day; brilliant
sunshine the next. The Llŷn Peninsula has much in common with Cornwall. It
is roughly the same shape, like an arched foot with rheumatic toes, and like
Cornwall its north and south coasts are dramatically different. The north is
bounded by high cliffs, which are occasionally interrupted by small, sandy
beaches, while the south has few cliffs and many a long stretch of sand. The
climatic variations between north and south are equally great, the north coast
being cool and windy, the south mild and calm. 'Al Llene is as it were a pointe
into the se,' wrote John Leland, who travelled round these parts in the 1530s.
He recorded that there were few woodlands on the peninsula and that the
farmers grew 'good corne, both by shore and almost thorough upland'. In the
far west he came upon 'the smaule townlet of Abredaron, wher is a 30. or mo
housis' and a church to which pilgrims came on their way to Bardsey Island.
Samuel Lewis's *Topographical Dictionary of Wales*, published in 1849,
painted a more detailed picture of Aberdaron: 'The village is small, chiefly
inhabited by fishermen, and, by its isolated situation and the want of good
roads, precluded from much intercourse.' Every week boats left Aberdaron
for Liverpool, loaded with pigs, poultry and eggs. 'The coast scenery,'
commented Lewis, 'is on the grandest scale.'

*Gareth Roberts on Braich-y-Pwll*

The village of Aberdaron is scattered about the confluence of two small streams. There are two pubs, a hotel, a couple of cafés, a post office and a carpark. An old church, anchored on a slope in a sea of gravestones, overlooks a small bay. There is nothing vulgar about the village; like thousands of others round the coast it caters for simple, old-fashioned tastes. In the shop beside one of the cafés you can buy postcards, little plastic windmills, buckets and spades, and shrimping nets. It is good to see that in a rapidly changing world necessities such as these – and for children they are necessities – have scarcely changed in thirty years, the nets still being attached to bamboo canes, the spades much too small to carry out proper excavations of the beach.

Within a few miles of Aberdaron the Trust owns half a dozen properties covering 1,500 acres of magnificent coastal landscape. The Trust's warden is Gareth Roberts, who was raised on a farm midway between Aberdaron and Braich-y-Pwll, the tumultuous tip of the peninsula. His knowledge of the countryside and its people is personal and extensive. Like everyone else here he was brought up speaking Welsh, which remains the first language for most people. Roberts still farms in a small way, rearing beef and sheep, and with his red hair, russet moustache and deerstalker he looks every bit the Welsh farmer. 'Nobody round here is starving,' said Roberts, 'but no one drives about in a Merc either.' We headed past scattered farmhouses, each surrounded by small fields bounded by broad earth banks. 'Visitors bring money in,' he reflected, 'and people think nothing of moving into the garage for the summer to make way for the tourists. I've slept in a hen-house myself.'

The views from Braich-y-Pwll are stupendous. On the northern side of the property – the Trust owns 122 acres here – sheer cliffs fall a great distance to the sea. On the other side, to the south, the land falls gently down to a broad shelf of farmland, across which is cast a network of what look like hedges but are in fact earth walls covered with a mat of vegetation. These *clawdd*s form a crucial part of the landscape – just as the stone hedges do in West Cornwall – and the Trust has recently bought a block of fields (and therefore a great length of *clawdd*s) below Braich-y-Pwll. 'There's one farmer I know down there,' said Roberts, 'who has eighteen fields covering just twenty-four acres.' During the course of one day I jotted down the flowers which I saw growing on the *clawdd*s – red campion, foxglove, pignut, honeysuckle, lady's bedstraw, knapweed, scabious, speedwell, gorse, dog rose, buttercup, white clover, a variety of vetches and trefoils, the odd orchid and much else besides. All of which made driving along the country lanes a great pleasure.

Unfortunately, many of the *clawdd*s have suffered over recent years. 'There are now so many sheep in the area,' said Roberts, 'that in some places they are eating the *clawdd*s bare. Once the vegetation has gone the soil gets worn away and the walls soon crumble.' Under EEC regulations farmers in Less Favoured Areas (in other words, on poorer types of farmland) receive certain incentives which encourage the production of livestock. The EEC allows up to six ewes per hectare in its grant system, which works out at around 2·5 ewes per acre. 'There is no way you'd graze at that level here,' said Roberts, 'more likely you'd have one ewe for every two and a half acres.' But the point is that the system encourages overstocking, and by midsummer much of Llŷn is as bald as a snooker table.

According to Roberts, the local farmers are a conservative bunch with no great capitalistic ambitions. 'They're quite happy carrying on as they always have done,' he suggested. Apparently, they do not feel compelled to modernise their operations as farmers elsewhere often do. 'Every now and again,' said Roberts, 'someone comes in to Llŷn, makes a hell of a mess, flattens the place and then sells up.' One particular farmer went to the extreme of dismantling his half of a *clawdd* which lay between his farm and a neighbour's. And all for the sake of a little more grazing land.

It is this sort of thing which the government's Environmentally Sensitive Areas (ESA) scheme is supposed to prevent. Farmers who join the ESA scheme – which operates in ten areas, one of which is Llŷn – are paid an annual sum, based on the acreage they farm, in return for which they must agree to certain management practices. For example, in West Penwith they must look after the hedges; in the Pennine Dales they must safeguard their hay-meadows; and in Llŷn they must keep their *clawdd*s in good order. Peter Mansfield, the Trust's land agent in West Penwith, considered the ESA scheme a brilliant success. Farmers there were paid £24 per acre if they joined the scheme and some 90 per cent of those who were eligible had done so. From what Roberts said, it was a very different story in Llŷn. 'There are about 900 farmers in the ESA catchment area,' he explained, 'but when I last heard only 200 or so had bothered signing on.' He thought this lack of enthusiasm stemmed from the low level of financial help for the Llŷn ESA: £6 per acre, or £12 if the farmer agreed to certain restrictions. This really does seem ludicrous when one considers that under the Set-aside Scheme – whose purpose is to reduce surplus production – arable farmers in Less Favoured Areas are paid £50–70 per acre not to cultivate their land, and not to produce crops.

From Braich-y-Pwll Roberts pointed out the features of the landscape: across a short stretch of water, away to the south-west, lay the now monkless island of Bardsey; immediately to the south was Bychestyn, a small block of common land and clifftop owned by the Trust; and a little way to the east of Bychestyn was Cwrt Farm, on which we now descended. As Jan Morris says, 'Aesthetically the great merit of the Welsh Sea itself is that land generally shows across it.' From mid-Wales one looks north to the Llŷn Peninsula, and south to Pembrokeshire; from North Anglesey one sees over to Great Ormes Head, and, on a clear day, to the Lancashire coast. From Braich-y-Pwll, when the weather is fine, there are views of the Wicklows and Mournes across the Irish Sea, and of Anglesey across Caernarfon Bay. Today, as it happened, there was a slight haze, and we could see little further than the ridge of land which lay beyond the bay of Porth Neigwl.

Cwrt Farm was one of two properties near the tip of Llŷn which the Trust was trying to buy. It consists of 237 acres of land, including a thin valley of dense scrub which snakes down to a small cove, Porth Meudwy, from where pilgrims used to make their way to Bardsey. A narrow track led us down to the shingle beach: four tractors were parked above the high-water mark beside half a dozen small boats, one of which belonged to Roberts's father. 'They fish in a small way round here,' he explained. 'When they're not too busy on the farms they go after lobster and crab.' Cwrt Farm itself is now mostly down to grass, though the present tenant once grew potatoes and corn.

Porth Oer, the other property which the Trust was hoping to buy, is more commonly known as Whistling Sands. Apparently it gets its English name

OVERLEAF: *The Llŷn landscape:* clawdds *and small fields leading up to Mynydd Rhiw*

*Porth Oer – or Whistling Sands*

from the sound the dry sand makes when trodden on. It is a beautiful place, a small sandy bay backed by scrubby cliffs and defined by rocky promontories. The cliffs hardly deserve the name, for they are very steep banks of no great height. Farmers tend to turn their ewes out on land like this after they have sold their lambs, and there is generally enough fodder here to sustain them through the summer. The plant life on these cliffs is superb and in places orchids are so plentiful that it is hard not to tread on them. Adders are common too and a year never goes by without someone being bitten at Porth Oer.

I went down one evening to the cliffs some way along the coast from here. It was a little before ten o'clock, the sun had long since set and the sky in the west was almost iridescent. Blues, pinks and purples jostled one another in a brief fit of picture-postcard vulgarity, and then darkness slowly seeped across the landscape. After a while a badger poked its nose from the earth and sniffed deeply. It must have got a whiff of me because it retreated smartly. Ten minutes later it appeared again, took another swig of the salty sea air and headed briskly down the hill into a dense stand of bracken. Over the next quarter of an hour three more badgers appeared, one adult and two juveniles; each went quickly into the bracken. Walking back across the fields behind, I picked my way through the chomping sheep; there were hares too, and a tawny owl called from a copse.

In some regions – Cornwall, for example – the Trust seems to have sufficient money with which to buy coastland, but other regions, and North Wales is one, are relatively hard up. When I saw Ian Kennaway, the Regional Director, he was quite candid about it. 'We're comparatively poor here,' he said. There are various reasons for this. For one thing, Wales doesn't attract in any great number the sort of people who give legacies and donations to save particular bits of coast. 'We don't get the Volvo-owning tourists, like Devon and Cornwall,' said Kennaway. Nor does Wales have a large Trust membership. There are approximately 21,000 members in the north, and the same again in the south. Perhaps the Welsh regions should be more aggressive, I suggested to Kennaway. 'Yes, we could be more pushy,' he replied. 'So far we've been more concerned with our Welshness.' But Kennaway was not despondent. 'Despite the financial problems, we haven't missed a lot. Somehow we nearly always manage to find the money to get what we really want. If we work hard we'll get Cwrt, and with luck, if the price is right, we'll raise the money for Porth Oer.'

Mention the National Trust to anyone who has had much to do with it, and certain names crop up time and again. There are the founders, of course: Octavia Hill, Hardwicke Rawnsley and Robert Hunter. Then there are figures from the past who exerted influence both intellectual and administrative: Lord Antrim, for example, and Clough Williams-Ellis. And there are the figures from the present too, some of whom I have written about here. But the history of the Trust is as much the story of those who have given to it as of those who have worked for it.

The manor house of Plas-yn-Rhiw, given to the Trust by the Keating sisters, overlooks the long sweep of Porth Neigwl – or Hell's Mouth Bay – a few miles to the east of Aberdaron. The bay is ill-named, for it is curvaceously feminine and blessed with a mild climate. The house, which sits in sylvan seclusion a hundred feet or so above the coastline, possesses the charm of a mongrel: in origin medieval, it was much added to in Tudor and Georgian times. It is intimate, lived-in and eccentric. The last of the Keating sisters died in 1981 and the house is much as she left it. The hall and sitting-room are spacious and sparse, with stone-flag floors, solid furniture and unplastered walls. The kitchen looks distinctly pre-war, with its remarkable four-ring

*Still life, Plas-yn-Rhiw kitchen*

paraffin cooker, crude Welsh dresser and old-fashioned cooking implements. On the first floor there are some bedrooms and a library, and on the second, more bedrooms and a medicine cupboard full of sensible-looking pills and potions: Universal Embrocation, Vaseline, quinine sulphate, liver pills and aspirin. Surrounding the house is an exquisite garden. It is said to be at its best in spring, when the camellias, magnolias and azaleas are in flower, but it was still a blaze of colour when I saw it in June. Herbaceous beds, full of delphiniums, daisies and mallows – the sorts of flowers one expects in a cottage garden – were restrained by clipped box hedges. There was just the right mix of cultivated formality and untended nature: foxgloves and red campion had taken up residence in some of the hedges; great beards of lichen hung from the trees.

*The garden at Plas-yn-Rhiw*

The three Keating sisters – Eileen, Lorna and Honora – first saw Plas-yn-Rhiw in 1919 when they came on holiday to the Llŷn Peninsula. The house was empty and over the years they watched it fall into a state of dereliction. In 1939 the house and what remained of the estate – it had been whittled down from over 400 acres to about a tenth of that – came on to the market and the Keatings bought it. The Trust still sells Honora Keating's guide to the property. It is charming, not least because it is so curious. The photographs are black and white and of poor quality, and Miss Keating writes about herself in the third person. 'One reason why they bought the property,' wrote Miss Keating, referring to herself and her sisters, 'was for the purpose of saving a unique area of natural beauty to give to the National Trust in memory of their parents.' They moved in with their eighty-year-old mother and set about restoring the house and making it habitable. The Misses Keating gave the house to the Trust along with some 400 acres of land, formerly part of the estate and brought back into it by the Keatings.

John Tetley, onetime Regional Director in North Wales, wrote of the sisters that they 'worked as a very effective team in fighting for the beauty of Llŷn whenever and by whomsoever it was threatened . . . They spoke for the countryside in a way which most men find some diffidence in matching, brushing aside "practical" counter-evidence as of insufficient weight.' It is fitting that after Honora's death the Trust acquired 146 acres of common land on the summit of Mynydd Rhiw, the mountain which rises behind Plas-yn-Rhiw, in memory of the Keating sisters.

Anglesey is slightly larger and more populous than the Isle of Man. Thirty miles across by twenty deep, it supports around 70,000 people. There are a few small towns – the main ones being Holyhead, Llangefni, Amlwch and Beaumaris – and two colossal industrial enterprises: an aluminium works near Holyhead and a nuclear power station at Wylfa Head. The island possesses no rivers worth speaking about and, apart from Llŷn Alaw, not much in the way of open water. To the north and west the country is pleasantly hilly; in the centre it undulates unostentatiously; and in the south it boasts little other than the odd wrinkle, these coming mostly in the form of hedges. To the traveller passing through southern Anglesey on the way to Holyhead, from where the ferries sail to Dublin and Dun Laoghaire, it must all seem pretty dreary. But the island is wholly redeemed by its marine fringe. Along the north and west coasts the scenery is dramatic and in places awe-inspiring; along the south coast it is flat, though not without interest; and along the east there is the leafy landscape of the Menai Strait.

Anglesey has been cultivated for a very long time, and when the Romans took up residence in northern Wales the island served as their granary. Samuel Lewis, writing midway through the last century, praised the native sheep, which were the largest in North Wales, deplored the native horse ('an inferior breed'), commented on the vast numbers of hogs which were raised for the markets in and around Liverpool, and noted that the island was rich in wildlife. For centuries the islanders reared Anglesey black cattle, many of which went for export. Before the building of the bridges over the Menai Strait, the cattle were forced to swim across to the mainland.

There are two bridges linking the mainland with Anglesey. Thomas Telford's suspension bridge, built in 1826, spans the Strait half a mile to the north of Robert Stephenson's tubular rail bridge, which was partially destroyed by fire in the 1960s. Both have received much praise, and the former undoubtedly deserves it. The Strait itself is a most unusual feature. It consists of a thin strip of sea, seldom more than a mile across and about fifteen miles long. Naturally it is tidal, and water is constantly being slopped into the Strait or out of it. The Anglesey coast is best observed from the mainland, and the mainland coast is best observed from Anglesey – and preferably from Plas Newydd.

'One of the most important things about Plas Newydd,' said the 7th Marquess of Anglesey, 'is the view. But you've come on a bad day for that.' Sheets of squally rain obscured the countryside outside the study window, and the mainland was no more than a blur across the Strait. I returned the following day when the sun shone brilliantly from a cloudless sky. 'Most of what you will see,' the Marquess had said, 'belongs to the National Trust.' Over the water from Plas Newydd were the woods and parkland of the Vaynol Estate, behind which were the rugged mountains of the Snowdonia National Park.

The Marquess gave Plas Newydd and 169 acres of woodland beside the Strait to the Trust in 1976. 'What you see now is a late eighteenth-century aggrandisement of a much earlier house,' he explained. James Wyatt and Joseph Potter were responsible for redesigning the house, and Humphry Repton advised on the layout of the parks and gardens. The house was much altered by the Marquess's father, 'who decided to attach a bedroom to every bathroom'; he also removed the battlements from the parapets around the house, took off the gothic pinnacles, did away with the private theatre, and commissioned what is probably Rex Whistler's most famous mural. Even if you have no interest in old houses or fine gardens, you should still visit the Whistler, which was installed in the sixty-foot-long dining-room in 1937. Here is a brief description of it from the guidebook:

The view over the Strait seen from the windows provided Whistler with the basic inspiration for his scheme, which represents a similar stretch of water dotted with islands and with a mountainous landscape rising the other side. In place of the scattered Welsh farmhouses and dark woods of the opposite shore, however, his imagination has created sunlit Renaissance cities with buildings of every period and style jostling each other on the quaysides. Some are recognisable pastiches – the steeple of St Martin-in-the-Fields, Trajan's Column or the Round Tower at Windsor . . . In the centre of the main wall Lord and Lady Angleseys' coats of arms are shown as if carved in stone on the ends of the parapet wall, and here too are Neptune's trident

*Detail from Rex Whistler's mural at Plas Newydd*

and crown carelessly propped up against an urn, with wet footprints leading up the steps from the sea and into the room itself – as if to suggest the sea-god himself had joined the family at dinner.

And there is much else to amuse and divert: a tiny self-portrait of Whistler sweeping a colonnaded passage; the present Marquess's cello leaning against a wall; one of the family dogs with its hindlegs on Lady Anglesey's book; and one of her cigarette butts smouldering nearby.

The Marquess was for many years a vice-chairman of the Trust's Welsh Committee and he remains a staunch supporter. 'It is one of the few great organisations which is almost wholly good,' he said. He has retained the top floor of the house for himself and his family, and he described it as 'rather like living in a howdah on top of a white elephant that is fed by someone else'. He believes that the one and a half miles which he has given to the Trust, taken together with the Vaynol Estate opposite, represent the only parts of the Menai Strait which are safe from undesirable development.

The acquisition of Plas Newydd had nothing to do with Enterprise Neptune, but it was Neptune money which helped the Trust to bring Vaynol (or Glan Faenol as it is now known in Welsh) under its wing. 'It's a good example of what can be done using Neptune funds,' explained Ian Kennaway. 'By 1951 we owned a big chunk of land in the Carneddau mountains, and then in 1976 we were given Plas Newydd, which looks on to Carneddau. We'd been looking at Vaynol, which lay in between, for some time.' In the mid-1980s the executors of the late Sir Michael Duff, the Marquess of Anglesey's brother-in-law, put Vaynol on the market. It was divided into more than twenty lots. 'Although we were interested,' recalled Kennaway, 'we couldn't afford to buy any of the estate at the time.' However, a strip of land at the southern end of the estate went unsold and the Countryside Commission made it known that it would provide some financial help if the Trust decided to buy it. At the same time, the business consortium which had taken over much of the estate announced that it was keen to sell the strip of land to the north. So eventually Neptune funds, with substantial grants from the Countryside Commission and the National Heritage Memorial Fund, helped the Trust to buy both bits of land, thus ensuring the protection of over one and a half miles of coast opposite Plas Newydd. The Trust's warden on Anglesey, Bryn Jones, drove me round the Vaynol Estate one afternoon. Much of it seemed run-down and a bit shabby, but in time it will improve. The Trust is converting arable land back into parkland and replacing conifers with broadleaves. This land is less than a mile from Bangor, and for the first time the public can walk along the shore and see Plas Newydd from across the Strait.

Most of the Trust's holdings on Anglesey are to be found along the north coast. They range from the small to the extensive, from the remote and seldom-visited to the accessible and popular. I spent a couple of days walking the cliffs and bays in the company of a friend, and certain memories remain vivid. There was the sight of a young peregrine awkwardly flapping its wings on a sloping sea-cliff. Every now and then it took off, only to flutter clumsily back to the cliffs a few yards further down, the browns and greys of its plumage in tasteful contrast to the pastel-pink of the thrift and soft greens of the cliff grasses. We saw dozens of other birds too: terns at Cemlyn Bay; choughs off Carmel Head; ringed plover on a shingle beach. There were linnets messing around the ruins of an old brickworks at Porth Wen and fulmars just about everywhere. Off the cliffs at Fedw Fawr a small flock of black guillemots bobbed on the waves, though it was the flowers there that really startled – the orchids and asphodels of the damp heathland.

*Cemlyn Bay; lagoon on the left, sea on the right*

We began at Porth Swtan, a small sandy cove bitten into the island's north-west corner. A steep-spired church overlooked a small village of whitewashed houses. From the village a path led north along the cliff behind the bay. On our left was a thick hedge of honeysuckle and thorn; on our right, small meadows grazed by a herd of suckler beef, mostly Charolais–Hereford crosses. As soon as we reached the far side of the bay we were on Trust land, and for the next seven miles or so – out to Carmel Head, then east along the north of the island – the Trust owns or protects all the cliffs and much of the farmland behind. This stretch of coast is as fine as any you will see in Wales:

magisterial without being bleak, remote without being too inaccessible. One of the great things about the coast here is that you must walk a good distance if you want to see much of it. Once round Porth Swtan the path climbs higher as the cliffs rise, and there are long views to the south: we could see the ferries making their way in and out of Holyhead Harbour; to the east of the town was the huge chimneystack of the aluminium works. For a while we continued beside the rough clifftop hedge, then the path headed through bracken and on to the grassland slopes of Clegir Mawr. Most of the flowers were purple, pink or blue: there were clumps of thrift and thyme on the cliffs;

ABOVE: *Harebells on Anglesey dunes*

RIGHT: *White Lady Rock, Llanbadrig, near Cemaes*

foxglove, crane's-bill and knapweed grew beside the hedges. The sounds were wholly rustic: the beating of waves on the shore below; the piping of oystercatchers; the churring of wrens in the thickets; the grinding of crickets; the mellifluous song of the skylark.

If you follow the cliffs the whole way round you eventually come to Cemlyn Bay, where the Trust owns over 300 acres of farmland, a couple of miles of coast and a nature reserve, all of which was bought in 1968 with the help of the former Anglesey County Council and Enterprise Neptune. There is a large and noisy colony of terns behind a long shingle bank. The views to the east are ruined by Wylfa nuclear power station, and there are plans afoot to build another beside it. The Trust intends to object to the project, on the grounds that there will be much disruption during construction and that the landscape will suffer. After a brief wander along the rocks by the sea we continued east to Cemaes, a pleasant resort-cum-fishing village. Down on the beach families sheltered behind colourful windbreaks. A few people were swimming in the

bay; some men were digging for lugworm; others sat with their Thermos flasks and newspapers; and one or two strode out along the cliffs beyond, which are owned here by the Trust.

Between the Cemaes Bay cliffs and Red Wharf Bay, which lies some fifteen miles to the south-east (or much further if you follow every indentation in the coast), the Trust owns nothing apart from the site of an old Iron Age fort and a few acres of cliff land at Dinas Gynfor. This was given to the Trust in 1913 by the Commons, Footpaths and Open Spaces Preservation Society, an organisation which was set up in 1865, its first Secretary being Robert Hunter, who later helped found the Trust. Though the Trust owns little here, there is a tremendous amount of coast which is worthy of protection, and indeed this part of North Wales is seen as a priority for future Neptune acquisitions. This sounds very matter of fact. However, it's rather like going into an art dealer's and saying, 'I'll take a couple of Van Goghs and a Rembrandt, please.'

One area where the Trust had expressed an interest was Porth Wen. Shortly before my visit part of the bay came on to the market, but later the landowner withdrew it. The bay is as deep as it is wide, its seaward shores rocky and barren, its inner slopes covered with dense stands of bracken and grass. There are a few small lenses of sand at the back of the bay alongside some much larger areas of rock and shingle. All is dominated by the ruins of an old brickworks whose two chimneys rise above the weed-seamed shells of kilns and sheds like a couple of teeth in a wizened mouth. We sat on the cliffs above the works, observing the tongue of seawater lapping against the shore. Cormorants and herring gulls made their way across the bay; oystercatchers piped from the wrack-covered rocks; somewhere behind a curlew called. Beside us were the rusting remains of an old machine on which was stamped 'Baxter's improved 16 × 9 patent knapping motion stone dresser'. It was curious to speculate on how we would rail against the building of a brickworks in a place such as this nowadays, yet these ruins seemed to have coalesced – spiritually, if not materially – with the natural landscape.

The only other Trust properties on Anglesey's north coast lie to the east of Red Wharf Bay on a knob of hilly land which guards the entry to the Menai Strait and from which can be seen, way beyond Puffin Island, the cliffs of

*Fedw Fawr, Gwynedd*                    *Porth Meudwy, south-west of Aberdaron*

Great Ormes Head and the Lancashire coast – weather permitting, that is; which it wasn't when Bryn Jones took me to see Fedw Fawr and Bryn Offa. The latter overlooks the long sands of Red Wharf Bay: our visit was brief and the rain intense. It was raining too when the warden and I reached Fedw Fawr, but we spent longer there and I returned the following afternoon when the weather was fine. On both occasions an English girl who lived in an isolated cottage beside the clifftop common, of which the Trust owns 130 acres, came out to chat. She pointed out the remains of an old limestone quarry below, and she encouraged us to get our noses down into the wet herbage so that we could smell the fragrant orchids. Jones didn't look like the sort of man who would go round smelling flowers – he had spent most of his life working with farmers before joining the Trust – but he obligingly sank to his knees and sniffed. The common was a wonderful sight, and even a philistine would have rejoiced at the flowers: beside the orchids – and there were several species – there were dense patches of yellow bog asphodel and some intriguingly large club mosses.

Unfortunately the common is gradually being invaded by gorse and other shrubs and if nature is left to her own devices these will soon take over and destroy Fedw Fawr's floristic interest. In the old days the heathland was maintained by grazing, but the local farmers are no longer taking up their grazing rights. This leaves the Trust with the task of controlling the scrub, which can be done in two ways: it must either reintroduce grazing, or it must establish a rotational burning regime, whereby the land is divided into plots, each of which will be burnt every six to ten years. The latter course of action sounds more drastic than it is – burning is used as a means of managing grouse moors and lowland heaths – and it is certainly less bothersome than keeping sheep or cattle.

The two wardens I met in North Wales – Gareth Roberts and Bryn Jones – had much in common apart from the fact that they were brothers-in-law. They were raised where they now worked; both had spoken Welsh before English; both had a farming background. Jones had only just joined the Trust, but Roberts had been warden on Llŷn for the past four years. In many ways he was the antithesis of the new breed of Trust wardens. He had received no formal higher education; he had no great expertise on subjects such as botany and zoology; he had a deep aversion to paperwork of any kind. All of which is an excellent thing, for the new breed of warden would be entirely out of place in an area such as this. 'It is of fundamental importance,' said Kennaway, 'that our wardens speak Welsh, and if they come from the area where they work, so much the better.'

On the North Wales coast the relationship between the Trust and its tenants is generally excellent, and much of the credit for this should go to the wardens. Roberts and Jones speak a language the local farmers understand, by which I don't just mean Welsh. 'This job is all about people,' Roberts had said. 'If you do something the farmer wants, then you can be sure that in six months' time he'll help you when you need something done.' Roberts was an intensely practical man and I admired his no-nonsense approach to the job. When I met him he'd recently been on a wardens' course in the Lake District where people were making a great fuss about the problems of repairing eroded footpaths. 'That's not a problem,' he said scornfully, 'it's just something that needs doing!'

To the outsider this part of Wales is very foreign, much more foreign than Scotland, and just as foreign as Northern Ireland. It not only feels distinctively different, it sounds different too: go into any pub on the Llŷn Peninsula and there's a good chance you won't hear a word of English spoken; and if you do you will find that the Welsh, though not a loquacious people, are curiously articulate. I frequently heard people talk about 'Welshness', but Welshness is hard to define, not least because the Welsh have no obvious leitmotifs. I suppose there are the chapels and the grey slate roofs; but the North of England is just as strong on chapels, and the Lake District is long on grey slate roofs. There is no Welsh equivalent of the French baguette or beret; or of the English village green.

One morning I was taken by Jonathan Marsden, the Trust's Historic Buildings Representative for North Wales, to see the landscape artist Kyffin Williams in his cottage overlooking the Menai Strait. Williams was a fine-looking man with grey hair, an imposing moustache and a sharp wit. For a while we talked about the Anglesey coast. He believed that there should be a law to prevent any building between the road and the Strait. 'The edge of the Strait is terribly important,' he said, 'it could easily become a gutter for bad architecture. Just think of that horrible block of flats between Beaumaris and the bridge – it looks as though it was selected from a catalogue. It's got nothing to do with the landscape – it could be in Wigan!' Then Williams went on to talk of other things: of the benevolent feudalism practised by the big estates on Anglesey during the eighteenth century; of the Nonconformist revival during the nineteenth century; of Welsh attitudes towards landscape. He said he didn't think that the Welsh were particularly interested in the landscape; they were too busy fighting against it. 'All the best landscape painters came from areas where the land was fertile, where it was rich,' he suggested. He mentioned Normandy, southern England and Germany. Wales had produced great poets, and music of a certain sort, but little in the way of great painting.

Finally we got round to the business of Welshness. Williams, who had spent time in the late 1960s among the Welsh immigrants of Patagonia, told a story of how he had recently been to the funeral of an old Welsh Patagonian. He arrived at the chapel to find a thoroughly depressing scene, the congregation looking ill-kempt, ill-dressed, dour. And then the service and the singing began, and it became another world. Williams said that had an Englishman stumbled upon the chapel – parachuted from space, so to speak – 'he would have thought he was somewhere terribly strange, somewhere like Bulgaria'. The English would never understand Welsh culture; it was so different from their own. And in any case most English people would probably be unaware of its existence: 'Welsh culture is an underground culture,' said Williams.

Ian Kennaway had explained the Trust's lack of pushiness in North Wales by observing that the Trust was much concerned with its 'Welshness'. This sounds odd – pursue it further and you could easily slide into the quicksands of metaphysics – but I think I know what he means. For one thing he is acknowledging that Wales is a country apart; that it is much more than a geographical appendage to England. He is also affirming that if the Trust is to succeed in protecting the Welsh landscape, it must be sensitive to the needs of those who live there. When the Trust took over Carreg, on the north coast of the Llŷn Peninsula, everyone assumed that it would rent the land out to a large landowner. It didn't. Instead it divided the land into three chunks and rented each to a local farmer, thus bucking the prevailing trend whereby the large farmers squeeze out the small. The Trust did something similar with its farmland at Cemlyn on the north coast of Anglesey; and at Vaynol it has given grazing licences to sheep farmers from the neighbouring hills. All this has endeared the Trust to the people who matter, which is to say those who live and work beside its properties. 'We're very much involved in the Welsh way of life,' said Kennaway, 'we're working for the local people as much as we can.'

# 9

# *Beyond the Valleys*

I HAD HEARD so much about the Gower Peninsula that I felt I half-knew it long before I set foot there. Perhaps its virtues had been too loudly and frequently trumpeted, for my first feelings were of disappointment. Certainly the landscape was pleasant, in places spectacular, but I couldn't fathom why so many people had told me of Gower while failing to mention other stretches of coast which were, as far as I could see, its equal if not its better. However, a couple of days, including one in the company of David Stewart, the National Trust warden, helped to dispel some of my doubts. Much of the Gower coast is memorable; and indeed no other part of Wales possesses a greater variety of scenery. That such unspoilt countryside should be found just a few minutes away from industrial South Wales is in itself astonishing. I suspect that my initial disappointment had little to do with Gower's landscape and much to do with the local architecture, which is generally dull and sometimes hideous. The only really attractive village is Llanrhidian, which overlooks the saltmarshes on the north coast. The rest look like little chunks of suburb, of the nondescript type to be found in the nether regions of Bexhill or Filey.

The Gower Peninsula is roughly rectangular, about thirteen miles from east to west and between three and six miles in depth. It is hard to say exactly where the peninsula begins, for it fits into the body of South Wales like a leg into a torso. Presumably it begins where Swansea ends. No matter which way you approach Gower, you must pass through areas of a densely industrial nature. Coming from the west there is the town of Llanelli, whose lights can be seen twinkling across the Burry Inlet from the north coast of Gower at night-time. And coming from the east you must pass by Port Talbot and the industrial estates of Swansea, which in odour and appearance are as unseemly as any in Britain. Gower's eastern shore backs on to Swansea Bay: here are the small seaside towns of Oystermouth and Mumbles, pleasant enough places

OPPOSITE: *Worms Head, looking back towards the mainland*

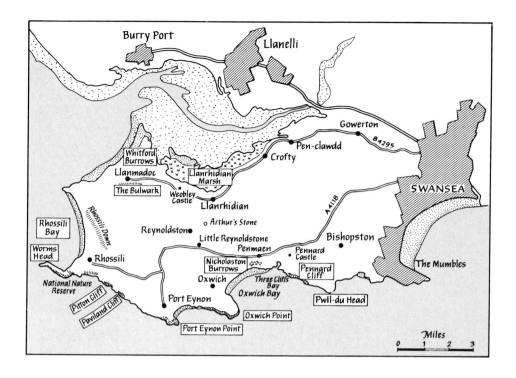

with the statutory endowment of promenades, piers, palm trees and public privies. Gower lies behind all this, its physical nature determined by its geology and patterns of land use.

Reflecting on the legacy which the coal industry had left East Durham, J. B. Priestley commented, 'The Cotswolds were to be congratulated, it seems, on their lack of coal deposits.' Much the same could be said of Gower, for had the South Wales coal measures extended a little way westward, the peninsula would have been turned into something like the valleys round Merthyr Tydfil and Aberfan: densely populated, grimy, slag-dumped, and now, with the recent closure of many pits, depressed and tragic. But the great lens of coal which occupies the hills between Cardiff and Swansea ceases where Gower begins, and in its place are thick deposits of limestone and the occasional outcrop of Old Red Sandstone. Much of central Gower is unenclosed common land, while the fields surrounding the commons are generally small and skirted by high hedges. In places the soils are good and some of Gower's farmers take advantage of the mild, frost-free climate by specialising in early potatoes and the like. Most of the land, however, is used for grazing: this is dog-and-stick country, liberally sprinkled with large numbers of sheep and a good population of semi-wild ponies, which are to be found just about everywhere – on the commons, on the saltmarshes, on the village greens.

Gower holds a special place in the National Trust's affections, for it was here, at Whitford Burrows, that the first acquisition was made with Enterprise Neptune funds. The Trust already owned several blocks of land –

*David Stewart*

ranging from a five-acre plot near the village of Penmaen to 250 acres of cliff land to the east of Pwll-du Head – but the pace with which it bought land on Gower quickened once Neptune was launched. The Trust now owns around three-quarters of the Gower coastline, covering some 5,000 acres.

David Stewart turned up at my lodgings in Llanmadoc – a small village in the north-west corner of Gower – at eight o'clock in the morning. He was remarkably tall, very slim, blond, sharp-featured and bearded. He had about him the air of the compulsive worker. He was busy that day, so he briefly outlined the Trust's work on Gower and suggested what I should see on my own. The following day we would meet again and visit some sites together.

I began at Whitford Burrows. It was now mid-August: the heat and fecundity of summer had waned, but the crispness and mottled colours of autumn were still some weeks away. At this time of the year the countryside often looks scruffy: the harvests are in, the fields have yet to be ploughed and prepared for winter-sown crops, and nature seems exhausted, like a played-out diva. The hedgerows beside the small road which led from Llanmadoc to the Burrows told the story. There were scarcely any flowers left, save for the odd ragwort and the occasional late bloom of bramble. The grass and the leaves on the trees and bushes were a faded green, and the only real colour to be found was in the hedgerows. Berries of various shapes and sizes caught the eye, from the moist red fruits of cuckoo-pint and honeysuckle to the waxy berries of hawthorn and the smoky-blue sloes of the blackthorn. Alongside the hedgerows brittle stalks of hogweed, seeds long since shed from spoked

ABOVE: *Whitford Burrows*

LEFT: *Autumn gentian in dune slacks, Whitford Burrows*

flowerheads, leant against one another or collapsed on tired clumps of nettles and rust-coloured docks. On the telephone wires swallows gathered. After a while the hedgerows and the houses came to an end and a rough track wound its way through a small copse, then skirted past a conifer forest to the dunes, beyond which lay the sands and the sea. The tide was a long way out and I tramped across the milky-green marram and on to the ribbed sands. It would have taken ages to walk all the way out to Whitford Point. Instead I inspected the litter: there wasn't that much, but there was enough to spoil the view.

The Trust owns 670 acres of sand burrows and saltmarsh whose flower and bird life is so rich that this area, along with adjacent chunks of land owned by the Somerset Trust, has been leased to the Nature Conservancy Council (NCC) and is managed as a National Nature Reserve. Altogether the reserve covers some 2,000 acres of dune, marsh, beach and pine plantation. Though only half an hour's walk from the road, it feels tremendously remote. When I was there the beach was empty. 'One of the challenges at Whitford,' explained David Stewart the next day, 'is agreeing a joint management plan with the NCC. Their remit is primarily for nature conservation. We have to think about such things as access and the appearance of the landscape as well.' There are two rare insects which live under driftwood on the beach at Whitford. Though the ground beetle *Eurynebria complanata* and the pill woodlouse *Armadillidium album* are to be found elsewhere in Britain, they are present here in great numbers. Unfortunately, the driftwood is mixed up with other litter, which may not concern the insects, but which the Trust considers offensive. This led to a potential conflict of interests between the two organisations, with the NCC wishing to leave things alone, the Trust wanting to clear things away. In the end a compromise was reached: the litter is now selectively cleared away, with the driftwood being left for the beetles.

During the summer there had been much fuss in the newspapers about the filthy state of Britain's cities, and especially London. Less seemed to be said about the problem of litter in the countryside and along the coast, yet in many ways rural litter is more offensive than urban litter. 'This is the dirtiest place I've been,' announced Stewart, who'd arrived at Gower eighteen months earlier, having spent the previous ten years or so working in Somerset. He showed me a large file of newspaper clippings he had kept on the problems of litter and pollution. Among the summer's headlines and stories were the following in the *South Wales Evening Post*: 'Swansea's biggest toilet – the Mumbles Sewage Outfall' and 'Sunseekers at Gower beaches over the bank holiday needed hospital treatment for gashes caused by broken glass . . . in sand.' One hospital alone treated twenty people.

According to Stewart there are two main sources of litter on Gower's beaches. Most of it comes in from the sea, where it is dumped by local authorities or thrown overboard by ship crews. The beaches suffer most in winter, when storms bring in large quantities of rubbish. 'Different beaches have different tidal systems,' explained Stewart, 'and some are worse affected than others.' Things are especially bad at Rhossili Bay and to the south and east of Worms Head. Then, of course, there is the matter of tourists leaving their own litter behind. In terms of quantity, they leave much less than comes in with the tides, but the casual way in which people discard what they no longer need is unforgivable. I find it extraordinary that people who evidently enjoy the beauties of the countryside wilfully despoil it. One of the places which Stewart suggested I visit on my own was Arthur's Stone, a neolithic burial chamber commanding dramatic views of the Burry Inlet, the estuary of the River Loughor. The stone is about a third of a mile from the road which crosses the common of Cefn Bryn: to find it you do not need an Ordnance Survey map – just follow the crisp packets.

'This year we've had a lot of stick about litter,' said Stewart. This seems unfair, as the Trust can hardly be blamed for the indifference of individuals and the shortcomings of municipal dumping policy. 'One of the reasons why we've had stick,' explained Stewart, 'is that we've raised our public profile – we're in the local press nearly all the time.' The Trust has been fighting an image which in the past had led to its unpopularity among many locals – that of the big estate, run by outsiders. 'What we're saying is, "We're here; we own land; we accept the responsibility,"' explained Stewart, 'and consequently we get the brickbats.' Stewart also felt that the rising tide of support for all things 'green' had led to many people being more aware of the litter problem, and thus complaining about it.

The Trust does what it can to keep its beaches clean. During National Litter Week volunteers had spent over 1,000 hours helping to clear litter from the Trust's beaches, and Stewart and his assistant spend much of their spare time picking up rubbish. Walking along Britain's beaches I feel a certain nostalgia for the litter of my youth. In those days beachcombers could pick their way through the driftwood, the old bits of rope and fishing net, and find interesting lumps of cork, beautiful coloured glass balls, green medicine bottles, desiccated starfish, the egg cases of skate and whelk . . . Now it is all Coke tins, contraceptives and plastic bottles: some of this stuff will last for ever.

Between Whitford Burrows and the small town of Crofty, which lies about five miles to the east, is one of the most forlorn, desolate and inspiring landscapes in Britain. The Trust's biological survey report describes Llan-rhidian Marsh as 'rather monotonous, short, grazed saltmarsh grassland'. It is monotonous in the sense that there is a lot of it – getting on for 3,000 acres is exposed when the tide is out – but it possesses its own very distinctive beauty. Stand beside Weobley Castle, which is perched on a hill a little way to the west of Llanrhidian, and the whole wide landscape, from the long spit of sand at Whitford Burrows to the neck of the Burry Inlet, is laid out before you. Immediately to the west of the castle is some handsome woodland consisting mostly of oak and ash; to the east are commons and pastures, and in the middle distance the small town of Crofty, the centre of Gower's cockle industry. Below the castle the land slopes steeply down to some rush-infested fields, beyond which lies the saltmarsh. On the far side of the estuary are Burry Port and Llanelli; they are a good way off, though the large power station at Burry can be clearly seen with the naked eye. Come here at high tide and water stretches from one side of the estuary to the other; at high spring tides even the coast road linking Llanrhidian and Crofty is under water. Return six hours later and the water is confined to a narrow channel midway across the estuary; the rest is mud and marsh. When the sun shines the crescent-shaped creeks and ditches of the saltmarsh glisten like elvers. At low tide the cocklers of Crofty make their way out to the shellfish beds. Until recently they did their business with horse and cart; today they use Land Rover and tractor.

Weobley Castle, a handsome, grey-stone ruin, has fine views of the marsh, but to get the feel of the place you must explore it on foot. I drove a little way along the Crofty road and walked out almost to where the saltmarsh ended. There was a Ministry of Defence sign beside the road warning of unexploded shells and bombs on Llanrhidian Sands. Further out was another sign carrying a copy of the South Wales Sea Fisheries Committee by-laws, much of which concerned cockle gathering in the Burry Inlet. Scattered across the marsh were a hundred or more ponies: small, tough animals of various colours, ranging from black to chestnut and caramel. There were also some sheep. Half a dozen herons stood peering into ditches, like elderly retainers awaiting orders, while out on the mudflats there was a huge flock of oystercatchers, perhaps a thousand strong, and a much smaller flock of curlews. Starlings picked their way across the marshland, and there were plenty of crows too.

In 1967 the Trust, using Enterprise Neptune funds, bought nearly 1,300 acres of saltmarsh here. Some is leased to the NCC, some to the West Glamorgan Wildfowlers' Association. All of this area – and indeed most of what the Trust owns on Gower – is classified as a Site of Special Scientific

*Llanrhidian Marsh at low tide*

Interest. Llanrhidian Marsh is particularly important for the populations of wildfowl and waders which gather here during the winter months. It seems strange that the Trust should allow shooting on its land, although the biological survey report concludes that 'the present shooting lease/agreement does not appear to be in any conflict with the ornithological interest'.

Next day I returned to the marsh with David Stewart. The Council had told him that there was a dead pony rotting away beside the road, and that it might present a health hazard. It lay twenty yards or so from the roadside, abdomen inflated, legs sticking stiffly into the air, nose and mouth already crawling with maggots. Stewart explained that although none of the ponies belonged to the Trust, the Trust buried the ones which died on its land: 'As the commoners don't bother tagging their animals, responsibility for getting rid of dead animals falls on us.' Stewart's assistant would be down with a spade later in the day.

Some seventy people have grazing rights on the marshes along Gower's north coast, but most of the sheep are owned by two farmers. According to

Stewart there are fifteen active pony breeders. Every now and again the farmers round the ponies up and sell a few – for riding, apparently, though someone in a local pub thought for pet-food too. However, there is little money in the business. 'The farmers who keep ponies are enthusiasts,' said Stewart. 'They and their families have always done it; they like to keep the tradition going.' In fact, farming on Gower remains a very old-fashioned occupation. Most farmers own no more than seventy-five acres: fields – and profits – are small, and many farmers make ends meet by doing a variety of other jobs. Some even go winkling.

The ponies and sheep are – or should be – the principal means by which the commons retain their character. While conservationists in mid- and North Wales worry about overgrazing, on Gower they are concerned with the opposite. 'If all the commoners exercised their rights,' explained Stewart, 'there wouldn't be a blade of grass left. But the problem here is that grazing has steadily declined and we've now got scrub encroaching on to many of the commons.' The farmers are somewhat cavalier in the way they deal with scrub: they set fire to it. 'We get fires all over Gower,' said Stewart. 'It doesn't seem to be carefully managed rotational burning either – it even happens during the nesting season, which, from the birds' point of view, is the worst possible time.'

On my way down to Gower I had stopped off at the Trust's Cirencester offices and spent some time with Jo Burgon, the Adviser for Coast and Countryside, and Katherine Hearn, one of the Trust's nature conservation experts. Burgon spends a lot of his time helping and overseeing the Trust's wardens, while Hearn has done much to raise the awareness within the Trust about the wildlife in its care. Undergrazing, they said, had become a severe worry for the Trust in many places. 'At the moment,' said Burgon, 'we tend to make arrangements with farmers to ensure that grazing continues where it's needed. But in the future we may have to become farmers ourselves.' And indeed the Trust does already own its own stock in some places: for example, it has a flock of sheep in the Chilterns and a herd of Shetland ponies on the Lizard in Cornwall. Burgon concedes that owning stock brings its own problems: 'There are veterinary bills to pay, and you can't just buy animals and dump them on the land that needs to be grazed – they have to be watched over and looked after.'

'There may well be changes in the ways small farmers farm,' said Stewart, 'and if fewer and fewer farmers graze the commons, something will have to be done.' Stewart admits that eventually the Trust may have to run its own sheep – and presumably ponies – on the Gower commons and marshes, but the idea

*Rhossili Bay*

does not appeal to him. 'I'd much rather we encouraged farmers to carry on grazing themselves,' he said. It would be sad if the ponies disappeared from Gower. They are very much a part of its charm.

Few tourists or day-trippers spend time around the marshes; instead they head for the south and west coasts, to the beaches at Oxwich, Port Eynon and Rhossili. Although it was the height of the holiday season, Gower seemed far from overcrowded. Oxwich and Port Eynon were busy, but not overbearingly so, and the beach at Rhossili was so vast that the few hundred people there were no more conspicuous than the fleas on a hedgehog.

Dylan Thomas used to come to Rhossili often in the 1930s. 'The bay,' he wrote, 'is the wildest, bleakest, barrenest I know – four or five miles of yellow coldness going away into the distance of the sea.' The Trust owns most of the beach, the hill of Rhossili Down behind, and Worms Head, the sinuous and lumpy promontory which reaches a couple of miles out to sea, forming Gower's most westerly tip. Worms Head is cut off at high tide. It is just possible, if you walk fast, to make your way to the end, spend half an hour looking around the limestone caves, and return again without being cut off – provided you leave the mainland as soon as the tide is low enough. Dylan Thomas described a trip on to Worms Head in a short story called 'Who Do You Wish Was With Us':

> The sea was out. We crossed over on slipping stones and stood, at last, triumphantly on the windy top. There was monstrous, thick grass there that made us spring-heeled, and we laughed and bounced on it, scaring the sheep who ran up and down the battered sides like goats. Even on this calmest day a wind blew along the Worm. At the end of the humped and serpentine body, more gulls than I had ever seen before cried over their new dead and the droppings of ages.

Some seventy years earlier Kit Morgan, who lived on Gower, wrote the following about Worms Head: 'There are thousands of birds to be found here – gulls, cormorants, lundibirds [guillemots] and puffins. They fly in crowds over your head. If you take a boat and sail round the Head you can shoot away until you are tired.'

Today Worms Head is part of the South Gower Coast National Nature Reserve, managed by the NCC, which encompasses six miles of magnificent, craggy cliff between Worms Head and Port Eynon. Most of the land is owned by the Trust, and two small sections are looked after by the Glamorgan Wildlife Trust. The limestone cliffs on Worms Head are home to large

*The Vile, Rhossili*

colonies of kittiwakes, razorbills, guillemots and fulmars, and the cliffs to the east also support fair numbers of breeding seabirds. Behind the cliffs there is a complex mixture of species-rich grassland and heath, worthy in its own right of inclusion in a nature reserve. 'And on top of all this,' said Stewart, 'this part of Gower is studded with archaeological sites.' There is an Iron Age fort – or the remains of one – on virtually every headland, and there are dozens of old burial mounds and scores of derelict lime kilns. Between Worms Head and the village of Rhossili a rectangular plateau of farmland known as the Vile boasts one of the best-preserved medieval field systems in Britain, and here the farmers still grow their crops in narrow strips, known as landshares, much as their forebears did many centuries ago. The Vile, as it happens, does not belong to the Trust but to a dozen or so local farmers.

The limestone here, and indeed throughout Gower, is pitted with caves which for over a century have attracted archaeologists and palaeontologists. Excavations in the caves have revealed that they were occupied by many creatures as well as by early man. Bones have been found of mammoths and reindeer, which lived here when the climate was sub-Arctic, and hippopotamuses and elephants, which thrived when Gower's climate was tropical. Some idea of what life was like during one of the recent Ice Ages is given in an excellent booklet called *The Caves of Gower*, published by the Gower Society:

We can perhaps picture the scene along what is now the Gower coast in one of the Ice Age periods. The present cliffs would have formed a bold escarpment at the edge of the icy, windswept plateau of Gower, falling towards a wide valley which stretched away to the distant hills of Devon. Many of the cliff caves would have opened on to a scree- and soil-covered shelf at the edge of the valley. In the valley (now the Bristol Channel) would have roamed some of the exotic animals whose remains intrigue us today. It is unlikely that the larger animals actually lived and died in the caves. The presence of their bones there is readily explained as the work of carnivorous animals such as the wolf.

Not only animal remains have been recovered from the caves in Gower. In the later stages of the last Ice Age, and indeed in early historic times, some of the Gower caves were occupied by human families. Paviland Cave, famous as the home and burial place of the 'Red Lady', has also produced a single flint implement left there over 70,000 years ago by a member of the sub-human Neanderthal species. Minchin Hole was apparently used as a refuge by later inhabitants, a mere 1,500 years ago.

*Thurba Head, looking east*

Gower is sometimes called 'the playground of South Wales'. It lies within day-tripping distance of many millions of people: Birmingham is no more than three hours away; Bristol about an hour and a half; Cardiff less than an hour; and Swansea and the valleys are just down the road. Yet there are no theme parks here and no large holiday camps. Hotels and bed-and-breakfasts are surprisingly thin on the ground, though there are sizeable caravan sites along the south coast. In short, Gower has not been spoilt. Swansea City Council has a policy of not widening the roads in Gower or providing any

more parking spaces. This is all to the good. The Welsh Office, however, has suggested that Gower could support more 'executive housing' than it does at present: this is monstrous.

For those of a gregarious nature there are the beaches at Oxwich and Port Eynon. The former was busy and colourful on the day of my visit, but the crowds were confined to the western end of Oxwich Bay. Indeed the sands further east are part of an outstanding nature reserve whose habitats include not only dunes and beach, but saltmarsh, freshwater marsh, fen and

*Three Cliffs Bay from near Penmaen*

woodland. Over 600 species of flowering plant are found here and the reserve is exceptionally rich in birds. Over 400 pairs of reed warblers breed in the reed swamp along with eighty pairs of sedge warblers and forty pairs of reed bunting. Buzzards, bitterns and sparrowhawks are among the visitors.

Further east there are two fine beaches, both owned by the Trust, which are harder to get to and consequently much quieter than the tourist beach at Oxwich. First comes the beach below Great Tor, which had less than twenty people on it when I walked on to the limestone headland above; and then a little further to the east there is Three Cliffs Bay – 'the most photographed bit of countryside in Wales', according to Gary Davies, the Trust's Regional Public Affairs Manager. The combination of steep cliffs, broad sands and winding stream is compelling.

Gower has much to offer besides its beaches. Virtually the whole peninsula is of interest to the naturalist and archaeologist, and many people come here to pursue such sports as hang-gliding, rock-climbing, horse riding and fishing. Every year 300,000 pairs of feet make their way past the Trust's shop and information centre at Rhossili; many come for the walk along the clifftop, and many wander down to the beach to sunbathe or swim, but a good number come to hang-glide, ride or fish. According to Stewart, Rhossili is big enough to cope with these pressures, though naturally both the Trust and the NCC keep an eye on the visitors. Some of the speed-climbers – whose purpose is to shin the cliffs as fast as possible – have ignored voluntary restrictions accepted by other mountaineers and climbed straight through bird colonies, but on the whole the area survives, and survives well.

There has been much talk during the past few years of tourists swamping the countryside. This is nothing new. In the mid-1960s Michael Dower, an influential planner, predicted something he called 'The Fourth Wave'. He foresaw a Britain in which a rapidly rising population (he anticipated a population of 70 million by the year 2000), coupled with increasingly high levels of affluence and mobility, would threaten the whole fabric of the countryside. He warned the planners that they would 'see people like ants, scurrying from coast to coast, on holiday, swarming out of cities in July and August by car, coach, train and aeroplane to a multitude of resorts and hidden places throughout the isles of Britain'. Well, Dower was wrong, although one still hears plenty of grumbling about the hills being worn away by trampling feet in places like the Lake District. No doubt there are some problems, but they tend to be localised and soluble, and anyone who doubts that it is possible for the countryside to support large numbers of visitors without it being ruined should go to Gower.

# 10

# Neptune's Future

THE NATIONAL TRUST took on its 500th mile of coastline during the autumn of 1988 when it bought, for the sum of £1, a mile of Durham coast to the south of Easington Colliery. The previous owner had been British Coal. The beaches here are black with colliery tippings, and the towns and villages look neglected and impoverished. It is the last place in England where you would expect to find the Trust.

At about the same time the Trust acquired a five-mile stretch of coast in North Devon. The previous owner had been Colonel John Pine-Coffin, whose family has farmed the Portledge Estate since Norman times. This is the sort of place an Englishman dreams about when he is stuck in an African desert or a polar wasteland. With its wooded combes, its lonely beaches and high, sweeping cliffs, it possesses all the attributes of a rural idyll. This, one feels, is the England of Keats and Elgar; and it is precisely the sort of England which one expects the Trust to safeguard.

To mention in the same breath two areas as wildly different as these seems almost perverse. I do so because their acquisition by the Trust gives some clue to the ways in which Enterprise Neptune will operate over the next quarter of a century. It goes without saying that the Trust will continue to acquire unspoilt stretches of coast. But how can it justify taking over beaches which have become the dumping grounds of industry?

Some of us, wrote J. B. Priestley in his *English Journey*, are fortunate enough to know West Durham and the magnificent countryside around the upper reaches of the Wear and Tees. 'But who knows East Durham?' he demanded. 'The answer is – nobody but the people who have to live and work there, and a few others who go on business.' I went there twice: the first time alone, the second time with Ian Turvey, the land agent responsible for the Trust's coastal holdings in Durham. On my first visit the coast was shrouded in thick

OPPOSITE: *The coal beaches below Easington Colliery*

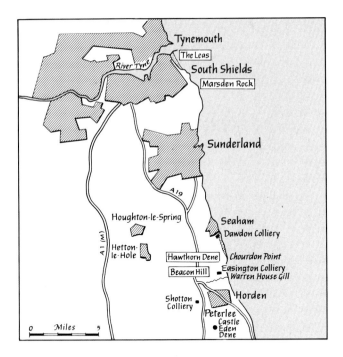

fog. I parked beside a boarded-up row of brick houses at the bottom of Easington Colliery's main street and made my way past some shabby allotments towards the beach. It began to drizzle. On the way down I passed a group of six children. They were struggling up the hill, pushing battered old bikes on whose crossbars were strapped sacks of sea-coal. A little while later I came across two men, both with heavily laden bikes; neither so much as looked up when greeted. Down on the grey-black beach half a dozen men in cloth caps and Wellingtons picked away at the coal tippings which the tide had just brought in. Watching them I felt ill at ease, like a reluctant voyeur: there is something demeaning about this scavenging way of life.

The old colliery towns round these parts are bizarre places. Priestley described Seaham Harbour, which lies a few miles to the north of Easington, as like no other town he had ever seen:

> It is a colliery town on the coast. It looks as weird as a carthorse with scales and fins. Its position on the sea did not relieve it of any of the usual dreariness of colliery towns. In fact, to my eyes it seemed drearier than the ordinary inland mining towns, perhaps because the coast itself there has a dirty and depressing look. The sea was dingy and had somehow lost its usual adventurous escaping quality. You could not believe that by setting sail on that sea you could get anywhere in particular. It was not the kind of sea you wanted to bathe in. Perhaps in summer it looks different, altogether more inviting; but I do not find it easy to imagine that district in sunshine and under a soft June sky.

214

East Durham is no longer as remote and isolated as it was when Priestley visited it in 1933, though even today I doubt if many people ever go to Shotton or Horden or Easington or Seaham unless they have business there. In the 1930s, coal mines were privately owned and living conditions, even for working miners and their families, were wretched: Seaham, according to Priestley, was 'undernourished'. Most of the mines have closed down now, and the only ones still working between Seaham and Peterlee are Easington, Dawdon and Vane Tempest Collieries. I doubt whether there are many who go hungry now, but what Priestley had to say about the appearance of the towns and landscape, about the run-down feel of the streets and the widespread poverty, might just as well have been written yesterday as fifty years ago.

Priestley had seen the coast at its worst, as had I on my first visit. Returning

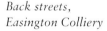

*Back streets,*
*Easington Colliery*

*Horden Point, looking towards Easington Colliery*

with Turvey in midsummer, under clear blue skies and a sweltering sun, it seemed a very different world: tough and poor, certainly, but not without its own peculiar charm. 'When I came to work here as a land agent,' said Turvey as we made our way south from Newcastle, 'I never dreamt I'd be involved with an area like this.' He had expected to spend his time managing large country estates, and indeed he was also responsible for looking after the Cragside Estate in Northumberland. That the Trust has become involved on the Durham coast is largely due to the efforts and ideas of Oliver Maurice, the Regional Director for Northumbria. 'It's a terribly depressed area,' explained Turvey, 'and Oliver Maurice felt that the Trust should be establishing itself in communities like this.' Someone else I met in the region put it more bluntly. 'The Trust is a very middle-class organisation,' he suggested. 'Its members are largely middle-class and so are its tastes and concerns. For once it was felt that it was time things changed; that it was time the Trust went into areas where it had no constituency at all.' At the time of my visit the Trust owned two small stretches of coast: half a mile at Beacon Hill and a mile at Warren House Gill, the former bought from a farmer a couple of years earlier, the latter coming from British Coal. Within the year the Trust expected to acquire a further three miles of coast, thus bringing over half of the Durham coastline into its ownership.

The views from Beacon Hill encompass beauty and dereliction in about equal measures. The hill itself is mostly down to grass, though in places it has been invaded by gorse and scrub. Between it and the sea is the coastal railway line which links Sunderland with Hartlepool: the latter was just visible a long way off to the south. In the same direction, though much closer, we could see Easington Colliery's conveyor belt marching out to sea on sturdy stilts. Below the end of the conveyor was a large pyramid of colliery waste waiting for the incoming tide to wash it out to sea.

We headed north, down the flanks of Beacon Hill, around the edge of a field of honey-coloured wheat and into the thick woodland of Hawthorn Dene. Here is Priestley again: 'The country itself was very queer. Running across it, like great cracks, were the narrow valleys called "denes", where there was usually a rushing stream, and perhaps some trees.' Many of the denes support a rich fauna and flora. Castle Eden Dene, to the south of Horden, is a National Nature Reserve; and a chunk of Hawthorn Dene, part of which is owned by the Trust, is looked after by the Durham Wildlife Trust. The woods were thick and verdurous; there was hawthorn here alongside ash, sycamore and oak. The floor of the wood was carpeted with wild garlic and dog's mercury; in the glades and beside the river were stands of Himalayan balsam, meadow crane's-bill, rose bay willow herb and bell-flower.

Turvey and I followed the stream out to sea, passing under a vast brick bridge which carried the railway line across the dene. The beach looked thoroughly unprepossessing. Scattered across the foreshore were heaps of rusty and fire-blackened rubbish; the ashes of whatever had been combustible clung in a grey slime to the tangles of iron wire and metal junk. Where the waves slopped against the shore all was black; indeed the waves themselves were black.

The magnificently named Blast Beach, set against the backdrop of Dawdon Colliery, a mile or so to the north of Hawthorn Dene, looked even more desolate: it was larger, scruffier and filthier. Yet this beach, like much of the coast, is quite outstanding from a botanical point of view and is part of the Durham Coast Site of Special Scientific Interest. One of the Trust's nature conservation experts wrote: 'If the Trust owned this beach it would probably be the most interesting it owns.' It is very wide, and between the cliffs and the high-water mark there is a range of different habitats. Of special interest are

*Hawthorn Dene, with Chourdon Point beyond*

*Horsetails and willow herb:*
*wasteground invaders*

*Bloody crane's-bill*

the cliffs themselves, which are made of the rare Magnesian Limestone. We were here at a perfect time of year, for the flowers were at their best. Everywhere we went we saw bloody crane's-bill, self-heal, bugle, pyramidal orchid, purple milk-vetch, wild thyme and rock rose. At the foot of the cliffs the limestone rubble supported a similarly rich flora, then further out were lenses of grassed-over rubble beside lifeless spoil. The juxtaposition of fecund nature and drab dereliction was most striking. A curious addition to the landscape were the limestone stacks on the beach. They looked like large chess pieces: it was as though we were watching the conclusion of a game which was down to the last few pawns, the kings and the odd bishop. 'A lot of people just say "ugh!"' said Turvey, 'but there's a lot of fine coast here too.' He explained that the beach, the cliffs and most of the hinterland between Hawthorn Dene and Dawdon Colliery were owned by a company called Necoast. Necoast had bought the land speculatively; it had hoped to get permission to dump coal on its beach, but permission had been refused. The Trust was now in the process of negotiating for the land, which included thirty acres of arable fields and forty acres of woodland as well as two miles of cliff and beach.

After a brief walk on the cliffs behind Blast Beach we headed back to Easington for lunch. These coastal towns are all much of a muchness. Each has a main street studded with chapels and pubs. Prominent too are the working men's clubs – the CIUs – and the low-price supermarkets: in East Durham the Co-op not only supplies people with food, it buries them too. Behind the main streets are rows of back-to-back terraces where the miners, or ex-miners, and their families live. Virtually everything is built of brick, though the public buildings are sometimes embellished with stone. After lunch we headed for Warren House Gill, and then looked at the land to the south which the Trust was hoping to buy. One section was owned by Durham County Council; where once there was Horden Colliery now there was nothing but rye-grass. The other section, just to the north of Castle Eden Dene, belonged to a local farmer.

The Trust, Turvey explained, intended to take on a warden as soon as it had acquired a bit more land. He or she will have to be very tough indeed, for the problems are many and extreme. Signs of vandalism and theft are to be seen everywhere. Sometimes the latter is on the grand scale. In Hawthorn Dene there used to be an iron bridge some thirty feet long and weighing many tons. One day, a couple of years ago, it disappeared. The thieves drove down to the beach, made their way up the dene and used a crane to load the bridge on to a lorry. Turvey showed me a less spectacular example of the sorts of thing which happen here. When the Trust took over the land from British Coal it held a ceremony, which consisted of lunch at the Easington Colliery Institute followed by the unveiling of a plaque at Warren House Gill by the Trust's chairman, Dame Jennifer Jenkins. The concrete plinth was still anchored to the ground above the cliffs, but the plaque had been prised off and dumped in a field.

Fly-tipping is also a major worry. On the track down to the beach there are piles of builders' rubble and household rubbish. Presumably, some people feel they have a *de facto* right to dispose of their rubbish by tipping it here. It would be easy to rail against their behaviour, but I find it unsurprising. For as long as anyone can remember British Coal – and before it, the private owners of the mines – has been dumping waste on the beaches: it may not be poisonous, but it is very unsightly and it smothers the life on the surrounding sea-bed. If our state-owned industries care so little for the environment, is it surprising that others despoil it too?

Turvey and I actually came across a couple of men in the act of fly-tipping. Much to my relief, Turvey decided we should take the registration number of their van rather than confront them. They didn't look like the sort of people who would appreciate being reprimanded. When we reached the beach we came across a couple of young lads riding trail bikes over the limestone slopes. They shouldn't have been there and Turvey had a brief word with one of them. 'We are going to have to tread warily,' he observed later.

Before we left Warren House Gill we went to see the Employment Training team which was laying a footpath through the woods and down to the beach. Half a dozen men were wielding spades, picks and shovels under the eye of Alan Urwin, the supervisor. Urwin was a big, heavily tattooed man with a shock of black hair and an accent which made every other accent I'd heard during the year sound dull and listless. The sort of English spoken round Bedlington, a mining town north of the Tyne where Urwin and his mates came from, is worth going a long way to listen to. Urwin downed tools and accompanied us to the beach. He had a problem, he explained, because he and his men wouldn't be here to take a delivery of topsoil the next day. Why was that a problem? asked Turvey. It was a problem, said Urwin, because if it wasn't immediately spread out, it would be nicked before the next morning. Like some of the fence posts they'd recently put up, the soil would end up in somebody's back garden.

Urwin had been with the Trust for two and a half years. As a young man he'd worked in the pits and then on Icelandic trawlers; he had also driven trucks, and done a spell as a North Sea diver. I asked him how much he thought the coal-pickers on the beach earned. Hard to tell, he said: but in some areas along the north-east coast it was big business. I heard some say that £70 a week was about average; others claimed that some men earned more than that in a day. Urwin remarked that when he worked the trawlers he could make £1,100 on a fourteen-week trip – 'and in those days you could get a house for nine hundred pounds'. A few hundred yards offshore there was a small fishing boat lying becalmed on the murky water. 'What are they fishing for?' I asked, wondering what fish would spend time round these shores. 'Salmon,' replied Urwin. This really is a very queer place.

Below us on the beach there was a pipeline discharging sewage into the sea; certainly the water had a slimy look about it. 'Not swimming, only going through the motions,' said one MP when referring to the problems of sewage pollution round the coast. The Trust rarely owns land below the high-water mark, and though it may deplore the state of the inland seas, it generally leaves the task of agitating for tighter pollution controls to other organisations. Somewhere in the order of a tenth of all our sewage is pumped out into the sea. Around 300 million gallons of sewage, two-thirds of which discharges above the low-water mark, enters the British seas every day. Many beaches stink, and of the 392 beaches registered by the Department of the Environment as bathing beaches, 40 per cent have failed to reach the EEC's minimum standards of cleanliness, largely as a result of sewage pollution. It is said that the presence of sewage in the sea poses a considerable health risk to anyone imprudent enough to swim near an outfall; stomach upsets and ear, nose and throat infections are among the likely consequences. In the old days polio and typhoid could be contracted from swimming in sewage-polluted waters. Together with the run-off of agricultural fertilisers, and especially nitrates and phosphates, sewage contributes to a process known as eutrophication. The influx of nutrients stimulates the growth of seaweed and phytoplankton and can result in algal blooms. When the algae die they form a nasty scum; the oxygen supply is rapidly depleted by bacteria and the animal and fish life suffer as a result.

There are many other sources of pollution apart from sewage. Especially threatening to marine life are heavy metals, some 40,–50,000 tons of which are discharged into the North Sea every year. The worst-affected areas tend to be those round heavily industrialised estuaries such as the Humber, the Meuse and the Rhine. Pesticides, polychlorobiphenyls (PCBs) and radionuclides also end up in our oceans. And then, of course, there is oil, which is a major killer of seabirds.

Seldom did I come across anyone working for the Trust who mentioned marine pollution: litter, yes; sewage, occasionally; but PCBs, heavy metals and so forth, never. Though the Trust owns over 500 miles of coast, it is largely preoccupied with the management of the terrestrial habitats. But the land *is* threatened, if not by the pollutants washing about in the sea, then by the sea itself. For the sea is rising.

A couple of years ago most people probably thought that the 'greenhouse effect' was solely the concern of market gardeners. Now we all know what it is. Scarcely a week goes by without newspapers carrying articles on the subject ('Get your tan on the Costa Manchester,' said the *Sun*, which foresaw Britain becoming a 'sunshine paradise'); and even our leading politicians have expressed grave concern about the rate at which the earth is heating up. Rising levels of carbon dioxide, methane and other gases – coming mainly from power stations, the burning of fossil fuels and car exhausts – are acting as a barrier to the solar radiation which bounces off the earth and back into space. The principle is familiar to cooks: put a lid on the pan and the temperature will increase. As the polar ice caps begin to melt, the sea level rises. Global warming will have dire effects: low-lying islands may disappear altogether, and river deltas – which in many parts of the world are both fertile and populous – may be permanently inundated. Hundreds of millions of people will be rendered homeless, and the consequences for agricultural production will be immense, even in Britain: in fifty years' time Scottish farmers may be growing maize and Welsh sheep-farmers wheat.

Britain's existing coastal defences were built to cope with a rise in sea level of 12 inches every hundred years, which was double the rate which had occurred during the early part of the century. Present estimates now suggest that the sea level is rising at the rate of 4–6 inches every ten years, or 3–5 feet a century. Those areas most at risk of inundation will be East Anglia, and especially the Fens, and low-lying estuarine areas.

As far as I know, no study has been made of the precise impact which the rise in sea level will have on our coasts. But it will be dramatic: saltmarshes and mudflats may vanish altogether in some areas; the erosion of friable cliffs will become progressively more severe. Some beaches will disappear, and new ones will appear. Virtually every area written about in this book will be in some way affected. There is not much that the Trust can do about it. In certain instances it may decide to give nature a helping hand by encouraging the creation of, say, saltmarshes further inland; but if the forces of nature (aided and abetted by man's interference in the scheme of things) are destined to destroy a beach, then that is what will happen.

In some parts of the country the Trust has acquired nearly all the coast which it identified in 1963 as being worthy of Neptune's attentions. By the middle of 1989 the Trust owned 36 per cent of Cornwall's coastline, 43 per cent of Devon's and 27 per cent of Norfolk's. There are still a few miles of coast in these counties which the Trust would like to buy, but there are other parts of Britain – one thinks, for example, of Wales – where vast tracts of unspoilt coastline have yet to be given the sort of permanent protection which the Trust can offer. Some of the land which the Trust earmarked for acquisition under Neptune is no longer worth buying: perhaps it has been marred by industrial development; perhaps it has become home to a golf course, or a boating marina, or a caravan site. Some areas have had the beauty bulldozed out of them; others have been tarted-up beyond redemption. But there are other bits of coast, discounted in the 1960s, which the Trust now considers worth acquiring.

When the Trust conducted its survey of the coast prior to Neptune's launch, its methods of evaluation relied heavily on aesthetic appraisal of the landscape. It was all in the good old tradition of nineteenth-century Romanticism: Wordsworth and Ruskin would have approved. The 900 miles were chosen because they were considered beautiful and unspoilt. Since then perceptions about the countryside have changed: saving wildlife has become as important as preserving landscapes, and nature conservation – which is a form of applied ecology – has taught us to look at landscapes in new ways. Had someone from the Trust visited the East Durham coast twenty-five years ago – and presumably someone did cast an eye over it – they would probably have dismissed it as being ruined and dull. But now the Trust's expert writes in glowing terms of Blast Beach's wildlife, and the Nature Conservancy Council talks of 'the best examples of paramaritime Magnesian Limestone vegetation in Britain'. Durham may lack the aesthetic appeal of Murlough Bay, Worms Head or Golden Cap, but it has other qualities worth conserving. (It goes without saying that perceptions of what is and what is not beautiful vary from person to person. I was raised in the industrial West Riding and I like industrial landscapes: the coast to the south of Seaham is not to many people's tastes, but I found it fascinating, and in places beautiful.)

There is another reason, already mentioned, why the Trust has become involved on the Durham coast: it has decided to move into areas where it has little or no support and where little has been done for conservation. The

*Starfish, Horden*

mining industry is on its last legs in Durham and it is only a matter of time before the collieries at Seaham and Easington close down. When they do, there will be no more dumping of coal on the beaches; after a while the sea – helped by the coal-pickers – will clean the muck away: black beaches will become golden, as they haven't been for many decades. The Trust, by taking over the coast in Durham, is recognising its future potential.

'All this part of Durham,' reflected Priestley, 'had done very well in its time for somebody, but not, somehow, for itself. There has been a nasty catch in this digging-for-coal business. Not for everybody, of course: the ground landlords and royalty owners had not done badly out of it, and I did not notice anyone resembling them hanging around Shotton [a mining village south of Easington]. I fancy they take their sulphur elsewhere and in another form.' There is little enough that can be done to compensate for the hardships which coal mining has brought to this part of the world; but the very least the people here are entitled to is a clean and attractive environment. The Trust, with the help and encouragement of the local councils, is attempting to provide one.

One of the last trips I made was to North Devon, to the five miles of coast which had recently passed from the hands of Colonel Pine-Coffin into those of the Trust. This is a remote coast and difficult to get to: there is a long-distance footpath running above the cliffs but anyone wishing to make a short visit must park on the main road and walk a mile or more down to the sea.

I spent a few hours here in the company of Sally Twiss, the Assistant Regional Public Affairs Manager, and John Gillett, the warden. This was as good a stretch of coast as any I had seen during the year. Some of the cliffs were a reddy-purple; others a sombre grey. On the more gentle slopes there was a dense mat of scrub, and the hills behind were a patchwork of brown and green, cereals and grass. The Trust owns 880 acres of land here stretching from Green Cliff, near Abbotsham, to Bucks Mills. Midway along the coast is the Peppercombe Valley: it is rather like one of the Durham denes, but altogether on a bigger scale.

As we made our way down the wooded valley the warden pointed out the cottages – mostly derelict – which the Trust had taken on with the rest of the property. Just before we reached the sea we came to a couple of small fields which were suffering the first signs of neglect: the grass was rank and scrub was invading from the hedgerows. The oak woods were tremendously rich and mosses and lichens clung to every inch of bark. In among the oak grew ash, sallow, beech and wild cherry. There were plenty of ferns too, and the hedges bore the fruits of black and white bryony, honeysuckle, sloe and

*Cliffs near Peppercombe*

*Peppercombe Valley*

bramble. On the way back up the valley Gillett led us off the path and through a thick tangle of scrub to the ruins of Peppercombe Castle. All that remained were a few walls, some tilting dangerously, and the foundations of what had once been a gentleman's residence. In a small clearing – perhaps once part of a garden – tortoiseshells, peacocks, red admirals and several other species of butterfly fluttered around some flowers. On our return to Horn's Cross Gillett took us to see a shopkeeper who showed us some photographs taken of the valley at the end of the last century. It was unrecognisable: here was Peppercombe Castle dominating the sepia landscape; around the grounds were lawns, a tennis court, a boat house, orchards and fields. All this has gone now, or almost gone, smothered in vegetation.

OVERLEAF: *Tilting rocks, Bideford Bay*

Writing of life in England during the seventeenth century, G. M. Trevelyan observed that the sea was '"the Englishman's common", his way to market, his fishpond, his battleground, his heritage'. It was to be another century or so before fashionable society forsook the inland spas and repaired instead to the resorts of Brighton and Scarborough; and not until Victorian times did people of humbler means travel in any great numbers to the newly constructed boarding houses of Blackpool, Rhyl and Margate. Wandering around the coast today, it is very easy to forget that much of what now seems remote and peaceful was once noisy, busy and dirty. Indeed, there is scarcely a single area written about in this book which didn't support industrial activity well before the days of seaside tourism. Robin Hood's Bay was once dominated by the 'pleasing awful and magnificent' spectacle of the alum works; West Penwith supported a great number of tin mines; the sea-cliffs of Dorset supplied the stone with which Christopher Wren rebuilt London after the Great Fire of 1666. And nearly always there were smaller industries catering for local needs. Since time immemorial men have been making a living from the sea and the land beside it: harvesting fish, cockles, crabs and seaweed; smelting iron and baking lime; carting sand to the cow-byres; digging turfs for fuel and cutting reeds for roofing. Signs of all these activities still abound: the lime kilns smothered with brambles and ivy; the brickworks buried deep in woods; the old houses reduced to rubble; the wharfs and jetties crumbled into the sea.

It is tempting to say that all this is proof of nature's remarkable resilience. And nature does possess a degree of resilience – or at least an ability to absorb, often through modification, the pressures imposed upon it. But nature has no way of dealing with many contemporary threats. Tidal barrages, nuclear power stations, the building of motorways and new towns, the dousing of farmland with pesticides and fertilisers – things such as these are ruinous not just for decades, but for centuries and sometimes for ever. Which is why Britain needed – and still needs – Enterprise Neptune.

# Coastal Properties owned by the National Trust

## ENGLAND

### AVON

MIDDLE HOPE (WOODSPRING) AND SAND POINT, KEWSTOKE 5 miles north of Weston-super-Mare. **Middle Hope** [182:ST335665]. 159 acres stretching over 2 miles of coast, with views across the Bristol Channel to the Welsh mountains and across the Somerset Marshes to the Mendips. **Sand Point, Kewstoke** [182:ST325660]. 32 acres of coastal headland adjoining Middle Hope.

MONK'S STEPS, KEWSTOKE On north edge of Weston-super-Mare [182:ST336632]. The Monk's (or St Kew's) Steps and 2½ acres. Views of the Severn Estuary and towards Bristol.

REDCLIFFE BAY [182:ST440762]. A coastal belt of 2 acres, about 200 yards long, which is crossed by the mariners' footpath from Clevedon to Portishead.

### CORNWALL

BEDRUTHAN (north coast) 6 miles south-west of Padstow, west of the B3276 [200:SW849692]. 60½ acres of clifftop land, including Pendarves Point, overlooking Bedruthan Beach which is reached by a precipitous cliff staircase. Bedruthan Steps are the rock islets and do not belong to the Trust.

THE BLACK HEAD (south coast) 3 miles south of St Austell [204:SX039479]. 11½ acres of prominent headland with signs of Iron Age fortification.

BODIGGA CLIFF (south coast) 1 mile east of Looe [201:SX274543]. 43 acres. 30 acres of rough cliff land overlooking Millendreath Beach, with wide views over Looe Bay to St George's Island, and 13 acres of foreshore.

BODRUGAN'S LEAP (south coast) 1½ miles south of Mevagissey (B3273), just south of Chapel Point [203:SX027431]. 3 acres. From this headland Sir Henry Trenowth of Bodrugan, pursued by Sir Richard Edgcumbe of Cotehele, is said to have jumped into the sea and so escaped to France.

BOOBY'S BAY [200:SW857752]. 2¾ acres of cliff land, including Constantine Island. Tom Parson's Hut, thought to be a fisherman's store or shelter, is let and not open.

BOSCASTLE HARBOUR (north coast) 3½ miles north-east of Tintagel, on the Bude road (B3263) [190:SX0990, 0991,1091,1190,1191]. 116 acres. The harbour, with 61 acres of the adjoining cliffs, including Willapark headland (317ft), 21 acres of Penally Hill on the north side of the harbour and 34 acres of cliff land east of Little Pentargon.

BOSCREGAN FARM AND HENDRA CLIFF (north coast) 2 miles south-west of St Just [203:SW358296]. 69 acres. ½ mile of cliff with farmland behind it on the south side of Polpry Cove, with views over Whitesand Bay to Land's End.

BOSIGRAN AND CARN GALVER (q.v.) 1½ miles north-east of Morvah, 2½ miles south-west of Zennor, on both sides of the B3306 [203:SW425367]. 498 acres of land in the centre of the stretch of coast from St Ives to Land's End. The cliffs run for a mile from Porthmeor Cove westward to Porthmoina Island under the Iron Age cliff castle of Bosigran. **Porthmeor** (q.v.) (north coast) 3 miles north-east of Morvah, 2 miles south-west of St Ives on either side of the B3306 [203:SW431372]. 76 acres. The ancient tenement of Porthmeor, farmed continuously since the Iron Age, comprises 3 'jigsaw' farmsteads, of which 2 are now owned: Higher Porthmeor Farm, with 70 acres of pasture, cliff and moor; and Lower Porthmeor, comprising a farmhouse, cottage and outbuildings with 6 acres of meadow and moor.

CAMEL ESTUARY: FISHING COVE FIELD, TREBETHERICK (north coast) [200:SW927777]. A cliff field of 3 acres between Trebetherick Point and Daymer Bay, with 1¾ acres adjoining and 1½ acres to the south of Trebetherick Point.

CAPE CORNWALL (q.v.) (north coast) 1½ miles west of St Just [203:SW351319]. 78 acres of cliff and foreshore forming the only cape in England.

CHAPEL PORTH (q.v.) (north coast) 1½ miles south-west of St Agnes, 1 mile north of Porthtowan [203:SW697496]. 367 acres of cliff and heath-covered moorland surrounding Chapel Coombe, the wild valley leading down to the small cove of Chapel Porth, including some ruined buildings and engine houses of the now disused tin and copper mines of Wheal Coates, Towanroath, Wheal Charlotte and Charlotte United.

CHYNHALLS CLIFF (south coast) 1 mile south of Coverack, 3½ miles south-west of St Keverne

[204:SW780170]. 52 acres, with ⅔ of a mile of cliff running southward from a point west of Chynhalls Point to Black Head.

CRACKINGTON HAVEN (north coast) 6 miles north-east of Boscastle, 8 miles south-west of Bude [190:SX142968]. 1,003 acres of cliff, farmland and foreshore, including Lower Tresmorn, stretching for 4¼ miles along the wildest part of the north Cornwall coast.

CUBERT (north coast) 4 miles west of Newquay, between Holywell Bay and Crantock, 3 miles west of the A3075 [200:SW7760]. Cliff, farm and common land totalling 569 acres, with sand dunes to the south surrounding the beaches of Porth Joke and Holywell. **The Kelseys** 333 acres, including Kelsey Head, the south side of Porth Joke, Holywell Beach and the island known as The Chick. **West Pentire Farm** 100 acres, including West Pentire Head and the north side of Porth Joke.

CUDDEN POINT 3 miles south-east of Marazion [203:SW548275]. 15 acres of headland closing the view eastward from St Michael's Mount.

THE DIZZARD (north coast) 2 miles north-east of Crackington Haven, to west of coast road from Bude to Boscastle [190:SX160987]. 144 acres. A wild headland overlooking Chipman Strand, running from Dizzard Point south-west to Chipman Point.

THE DODMAN (south coast) 4 miles south of Mevagissey, 10 miles south of St Austell [204:SX0039]. 518 acres stretching from Gorran Haven to Hemmick Beach. Also 276 acres at Dodman Point, including Lower Penare Farm. **Hemmick Beach** [204:SW995407]. 106 acres surrounding the unspoilt cove, and dominating two small valleys behind the beach. **Lambsowden Cove** 1¼ miles west of Dodman Point [204:SX982409]. 70 acres of farmland running out from the coast road (Gorran to Caerhays) to the cliffs. **Lamledra Farm** West of Gorran Haven [204:SX015414]. 66 acres above Vault Beach.

DUCKPOOL TO SANDYMOUTH (north coast) 5 miles north of Bude [190:SS2010, 2011]. 984½ acres, including 2 miles of coast. Steep cliffs rise behind a very large sandy beach. Includes 67 acres of farmland and cliff at Coombe, giving access to Duckpool Beach; Houndapit Cliffs [190:SS2010], 117 acres of open farmland stretching to the cliff edge; and

392 acres of cliff and farmland at Stowe Barton [190:SS210114].

ERTH BARTON AND ERTH ISLAND (south coast) 1½ miles south-east of St Germans, 4 miles west of Saltash [201:SW3856]. 198 acres of saltings and foreshore in surroundings of great beauty at the confluence of the Rivers Tiddy and Lynher.

FAL ESTUARY. **Ardevora** [204:SW875405]. 32 acres of foreshore on the east bank of the River Fal, in the reach known as the Ruan River. **Trelonk** [204:SW885413]. 22 acres of foreshore on the east bank of the Fal.

FOWEY (south coast). 375¼ acres of farm, woodland, creek and cliff at the entrance to the harbour and overlooking the estuary, including 148 acres at Coombe [200:SX112510]; and 105 acres at Pont Pill, Lanteglos [200:SX135115], including Pont Creek Farm and some foreshore.

THE GANNEL, NEWQUAY (north coast) [200:SW7961]. 82 acres, mainly on the south bank of the sandy estuary, Crantock Beach, and forming part of the view from Newquay and Pentire Point East.

GODREVY TO PORTREATH (north coast) On north side of the B3301 [203:SW6043]. 751 acres of cliff and farmland extending for over 6 miles, including (from east to west) Western Hill, overlooking Portreath Harbour, the precipitous Ralph's Cupboard, Porthcadjack Cove, Basset's Cove, Reskajeage Downs, Hudder Downs, Hell's Mouth, Navax Point and most of the Godrevy Peninsula. Several small beaches and numerous coves, the haunt of Atlantic seals and other wildlife.

THE GRIBBIN AND POLRIDMOUTH (south coast) 2 miles west of Fowey [204:SX097496, 105505]. 120 acres of farmland comprising the east side of Polridmouth Cove, including Southground Point and Lankelly Cliff.

GUNWALLOE CHURCH COVE (south coast) 4 miles south of Helston on west side of the Lizard Peninsula [203:SW661204]. 254 acres surrounding the cove beside which stands the fifteenth-century church of St Winwaloe, including the Towans and Mullion Golf Course, and Winnianton Farm.

GUNWALLOE FISHING COVE (south coast) 4 miles south of Helston, on west side of the Lizard

Peninsula [203:SW654224]. 48 acres. 4 acres behind the beach and a further 44 acres of farmland between the coast road and the beach.

GURNARD'S HEAD (north coast) 7 miles west of St Ives on the B3306 [203:SW432386]. 32 acres. The whaleback granite headland is the principal feature between Zennor Head and Pendeen Watch.

HELFORD RIVER (south coast). 592½ acres of estuary, farmland and cliff. **Bosloe** (north bank) [204:SW775275]. 162 acres south-west of the village of Mawnan Smith and joining together the Carwinion and Glendurgan properties. The property includes Bosloe House, the beach below and Bosveal Farm on either side of the road to Durgan. **Carwinion and Chenhalls** (north bank) [204:SW780280, 785285]. 108 acres to the east and south of Mawnan Smith. **Frenchman's Creek** (south bank) [240:SW748258]. 36 acres forming the south bank of this peaceful wooded creek from which Daphne du Maurier's novel took its name. **Gillan Creek** (south bank) [240:SW775251]. 14½ acres of woodland at Tregithy, including ¼ mile of coast, and a 3-acre wood forming the north bank of the creek below the road leading west from St Anthony-in-Meneage Churchtown to Carne. Also 2½ acres on the south side of the head of Gillan Creek at Carne Vean. **Glendurgan** (north bank) ½ mile south-west of Mawnan Smith on the road to Helford Passage, 4 miles south-west of Falmouth [204:SW772277]. 40 acres comprising Glendurgan House (*c.*1820, not open) and the wooded valley garden running down to the estuary and Durgan village, with fine trees and tender shrubs, walled and water gardens, a maze and a Giant's Stride. The property includes the beach. **Mawnan Glebe** (north bank) [204:SW787272]. 43½ acres of farmland and wooded cliff. At the entrance to the estuary adjoining Mawnan Church. **Nansidwell** (north bank) [204:SW790283]. 53 acres forming a valley running down to the sea between Rosemullion Head and Chenhalls. **Penarvon Cove** (south bank) [204:SW757264]. 3 acres to the west of Helford village. **Pengwedhen** (south bank) [204:SW755264]. 34 acres of farm and woodland to the west of Helford village and surrounding Penarvon Cove. **Rosemullion Head** (north bank) [204:SW797278]. 53 acres to the north of the Helford River mouth, with views over Falmouth Bay. **Tremayne Woods** (south bank) [240:SW728257]. 49 acres of mixed woodland stretching for ½ mile along the south bank of the estuary and then up the east bank of Vallum Tremayne Creek, with further

woodland as far south as Mudgeon. **Trewarnevas and Coneysburrow Cove** (south bank) 2 miles east of Manaccan, just east of Gillan Harbour and Cove [240:SW790252]. 5½ acres of cliff, cove and a promontory called the Herra.

HOR POINT AND HELLESVEOR CLIFF (north coast) 1½ miles west of St Ives [203:SW5041]. 24½ acres. A fine stretch of rocky coast with good views.

HORE POINT (south coast) 1¼ miles south-west of Looe, on east side of Talland Bay [201:SX236519]. The headland overlooks Portnadler Bay and St George's Island and dominates this section of the coast. 144 acres of farm and cliff land.

LERRYN CREEK. 111 acres of park around Ethy House and creekside woods above the Fowey Estuary [200:SX1357].

LESCEAVE CLIFF (south coast) 5 miles west of Helston and at the east end of Prah Sands in Mount's Bay [203:SW587275]. 13 acres of cliff.

LIZARD PENINSULA (south coast). 1,165½ acres of cliff, harbour, farmland, shore and woodland; with many headlands, coves and points including Kynance, Poldhu, Poltesco, Carleon and Mullion Coves, the Marconi Memorial and the western corner of Lizard Point.

THE LOE (south coast) 2 miles south of Helston, 1 mile east of Porthleven [203:SW645250]. 1,554 acres, including the Loe Pool, a freshwater lake over a mile long in a landscape of great beauty, separated from the sea by the shingle beach of Loe Bar. Carminowe Creek forms a branch of the lake to the east.

MAER CLIFF, BUDE (north coast) [190:SS200077]. 116 acres of clifftop pasture and foreshore immediately adjoining the town, running northwards for ⅔ mile to Northcott Mouth.

MAYON AND TREVESCAN CLIFFS Between Sennen Cove and Land's End (A30) [203:SW349259]. 57 acres of cliffs, including Maen Castle – a good example of a Cornish cliff castle – and the Irish Lady Rock.

MORWENSTOW (north coast) 6 miles north of Bude on the Devon border [190:SS205153]. **Rectory Farm and Vicarage Cliff**. 234½ acres protecting the surroundings of the church of St Morwenna, made famous by the West Country parson–poet, the Rev.

Stephen Hawker (1835–74), who was the subject of Baring-Gould's book, *The Vicar of Morwenstow*.

NARE HEAD AND VERYAN BAY (south coast) 4½ miles south of Tregony (A3078) [204:SW916370]. 467 acres of farmland and cliffs forming the south-west side of Veryan Bay, including Nare Head and Gull Rock, with views east to the Dodman and west to the Lizard, Blouth Point, Kiberick, Caragloose and Camels Coves. **Portloe.** 7½ acres of grazing land behind the Jacka, south-west of Portloe on the west arm of Veryan Bay.

NORTHCOTT MOUTH (north coast) 1 mile north of Bude and immediately north of Maer Cliff [190:SS202085]. 27½ acres of grassland and foreshore comprising most of this small beach.

PARK HEAD, ST EVAL (north coast) 6 miles south-west of Padstow [200:SW845710]. A wild headland which dominates this part of the coast and forms the backdrop to the view from Bedruthan Steps. 222 acres, including Pentire Farm and Diggory's Island, with eight small coves and a fine rock-arch.

PENBERTH COVE AND TREEN CLIFF (south coast) 4 miles south-east of Land's End, 7 miles south-west of Penzance [203:SW402228]. 198 acres. The jagged granite headland of Treryn Dinas forms the backdrop to the magnificent view from Porthcurno. 36½ acres, including the famous Logan Rock, weighing 66 tons, Pedn-vounder Beach and an Iron Age promontory fort.

PENCARROW HEAD, LANSALLOS, LANTIC BAY AND LANTIVET BAY (south coast) Between Polruan and Polperro [200: & 201:SX1451]. 1,129½ acres of cliffs and farmland, including Pencarrow Head, Blackbottle Rock, Great and Little Lantic Beaches, farmland surrounding Lanteglos and Lansallos Churches and the several coves of Lantivet Bay.

PENDOWER BEACH (south coast) 1 mile south-west of Veryan, 5 miles south-west of Tregony [204:SW902385]. 247 acres, comprising Gwendra Farm, which overlooks the large sandy beach, and the east side of the bracken-covered valley, which opens on to it at Pendower itself; and to the east Carne Beacon, a prominent round barrow and viewpoint.

PEN ENYS POINT (north coast) 3 miles west of St Ives [203:SW491410]. 36 acres of rugged coastline,

comprising Trevelyan Cliff and Trowan Cliff.

PENTIRE HEAD AND PORTQUIN BAY (north coast) 6 miles north-west of Wadebridge [200:SW935803–968805]. Cliff and farmland totalling 723 acres, including Doyden Point, 95 acres of Lundy Bay, Pentire Farm and Pentireglaze Farm.

POLPERRO (south coast). **Chapel Cliff and Raphael Cliff** On west side of the harbour [201:SW205505]. 107½ acres of cliff, coastal scrubland (an SSSI), and farmland, with fine terraced walks on the cliffs.

PORT GAVERNE (north coast) ¼ mile east of Port Isaac, 7 miles north of Wadebridge [200:SX003808]. 16 acres, including the beach, foreshore and fish cellars on the west side of the stream.

PORTHCOTHAN (north coast) 5 miles south-west of Padstow [200:SW857722]. 17 acres forming the north side of the inlet.

PORTHCURNICK (south coast) 9 miles south-west of Tregony, 1 mile north of Portscatho [204:SW880360]. A sandy beach, sheltered by the low headland of Pednvaden. 77 acres with ¾ mile of coast, including all the fields surrounding the beach and southward to the village of Gerrans.

PORTHMINSTER POINT (north coast) On south edge of St Ives; access on foot from Porthminster Beach or from the A3074, past the coastguard station [203:SW525395]. 12 acres of cliffs and small fields between the railway and the sea, with several rocky little coves.

RINSEY CLIFF (south coast) 1 mile south-west of Ashton, halfway between Helston and Marazion [203:SW594269]. 33 acres of heather-covered cliff surrounding the sandy Porthcew Cove, dominated by the dramatic ruin of the engine house and stack of Wheal Prosper tin and copper mine, abandoned in 1860.

ROSEMERGY AND TREVEAN CLIFFS (north coast) 1 mile north-east of Morvah Church, on north side of the B3306 [203:SW415365]. 257 acres of wild cliff, Iron Age fields and moorland overlooking the Brandys Rocks, Porthmoina Cove and Bosigran Head and including four rocky viewpoints.

ST AGNES (north coast) 22 acres of Newdowns Head, 1 mile north of St Agnes Beacon, east of

St Agnes Head, with fine views to the north-east over Perran Bay [203:sw708518]. **St Agnes Beacon** ½ mile west of the B3277 [203:sw710504]. 61 acres of heath-covered land rising to 629 feet.

ST ANTHONY-IN-ROSELAND (south coast) 2¼ miles east of Falmouth (by steamer); 10 miles south-west of Tregony (by road) [204:sw8632]. Coastal farmland and foreshore, forming about half the St Anthony Peninsula. 434½ acres surrounding the hamlet of Bohortha and including, on the Channel coast, Porthmellin Head, Killigerran Head (with views to Nare Head and the Dodman), Elwynick Cove and Towan and Porthbeor Beaches and, on the St Mawes Estuary, a mile of the east bank of the Percuil River and the south shore of Froe Creek. **St Anthony Head** [204:sw846312]. 68½ acres. The headland, which forms the eastern entrance to Falmouth Harbour, was fortified in 1895 and has been garrisoned intermittently ever since. Wheelchair path to viewpoint.

ST JUST-IN-ROSELAND On east side of Falmouth Harbour, 1½ miles north of St Mawes [204:sw848353]. 118 acres of farmland, foreshore, and ½ mile of coastline.

ST LEVAN CLIFFS (south coast) Between Land's End and Porthcurno [203:sw384218]. 9 acres of Pedn-Men-an-Mere headland, including 8 acres of Rospletha Cliff.

ST MICHAEL'S MOUNT ½ mile south of Marazion [203:sw515298]. 102 acres which includes the harbours and foreshore.

TINTAGEL (north coast). 196½ acres of headland, cliff and beach mainly to the south of the village, including Barry Nose, Glebe Cliff and the headland of Willapark.

TREGARDOCK BEACH (north coast) 3 miles south of Tintagel, 3 miles north-east of Port Isaac, 1½ miles east of the B3314 [200:sx040840]. 66 acres of cliffs from Tregonnick Tail southward nearly to Jacket's Point, including Tregardock Beach and Trerubies Cove.

TREGASSICK AND TREWINCE (south coast) On the east bank of the St Mawes Estuary [204:sw865344]. Tregassick Farm, of 143 acres, embraces the hamlet of Porthcuel and includes 1½ miles of the unspoilt shores of this lovely estuary.

TRELISSICK 4 miles south of Truro, on both sides of the B3289 above King Harry Ferry [204:sw837396]. 390 acres of park, farmland and woods overlooking the Carrick Roads (Fal Estuary), including the woods on the west bank of the Fal above and below King Harry Passage, Turnaware Point on the east bank of the Fal, Round Wood at the entrance to Cowlands Creek, and 14 acres at Lamouth Creek, including 3 acres of foreshore.

TRELUGGAN CLIFF (south coast) 2 miles north-east of Gerrans [204:sw890379]. 89 acres. ½ mile of coastal land, part of Treluggan Farm, overlooking Gerrans Bay.

WHITESANDS BAY (south coast) 5 miles west of Torpoint, 3 miles north-west of Rame Head [201:sw390525]. **Sharrow Point and Higher Tregantle Cliffs.** 69 acres of cliffs overlooking Whitesands Bay, including Crowstone and Sharrow Cliffs. **Trethill Cliffs.** 1 mile to the west on the coast road to Porthwrinkle. 69 acres of farm and cliff land between the road and the sea.

ZENNOR (q.v.) (north coast) A stretch of rugged coastline and farmland west of St Ives on the B3306 [203:sw4539]. 846½ acres of cliffs and farmland with fine views; the farms of Treveal, Foage and Bosporthennis, moorland at Pennance, and cliff land at Tregerthen, Zennor Head and Boswednack.

## CUMBRIA

ARNSIDE. **The Knott and Healthwaite** 1 mile south of Arnside [97:SD456774]. 156 acres overlooking the Kent Estuary and Morecambe Bay, with distant views of the Cumbrian fells. An SSSI notable for its flowers and butterflies. **Sandscale Haws** [96:SD1875]. 651 acres of sand dunes and marsh at the mouth of the Duddon Estuary.

## DEVON

BEESANDS CLIFF (south coast) ½ mile south of Torcross, 3 miles north of Start Point [202:sx822415]. 16 acres at the north end of Beesands Beach, as far as the Limpet Rocks.

BIGBURY-ON-SEA: CLEMATON HILL (south coast) 7 acres on south side of the B3392 [202:sx655442]. Views to Bolt Tail and Burgh Island.

BRANSCOMBE AND SALCOMBE REGIS (south coast) [192:SY2188, 1588]. 658½ acres stretching from Branscombe Mouth to Dunscombe Cliff, south of Salcombe Regis and including Southcombe Farm: 111 acres of farmland, adjoining cliffs and foreshore [192:SY143878].

BRIXHAM: SOUTHDOWN CLIFFS ½ mile south of Brixham. 116 acres of cliff and farmland between Sharkham Point and Man Sands, approximately 3 miles south of Berry Head [202:SX927540]. **Sharkham Point** [202:SX933547]. 26 acres of cliffs and farmland between Sharkham Point and the Trust's Southdown Cliffs property. Fine coastal views towards Southdown Cliffs, Man Sands and Scabbacombe Sands.

BURROUGH FARM, NORTHAM (north coast) [180:SS457288]. 44½ acres of farmland running from the edge of the small town of Northam down to the low wooded cliffs along the left bank of the Torridge Estuary, with access to a small cove.

CLOVELLY (north coast)  4 miles east of Hartland on the B3237. **Abbotsham** [190:SS410277]. 16 acres of farmland bought in 1982 with money from Devon funds. Spectacular views of Bideford Bay. **Beckland Cliffs**  2½ miles north-west of Clovelly [190:SS284265]. 140 acres of cliff and farmland of great beauty, including Windbury Point overlooking Beckland Bay, extending the Trust's existing Brownsham property westward by a further mile. **Fatacott Cliff**  4 miles west of Clovelly [190:SS265273]. 165 acres. 153 acres of cliffs and farmland with wide views of Bideford Bay and to Lundy and Morte Point. **Gawlish** [190:SS258274]. 28½ acres of cliff land. **Mount Pleasant** [190:SS317249]. 1 acre just above Clovelly with a view over Bideford Bay.

DART ESTUARY (south coast). **Coleton Fishacre, Coleton Barton Farm and Woodhuish Farm**  2 miles south-east of Kingswear [202:SX918500]. 971 acres. Coleton Fishacre house and garden with 3½ miles of coast. **Compass Plantation**  Adjoining Gallants Bower and Little Dartmouth [202:SX885499]. 2¼ acres of woodland overlooking the Dart Estuary. **Dyers Hill** [202:SX878506]. 11 acres of woodland running up to the skyline opposite Kingswear and including the Old Ropewalk. **Gallants Bower** [202:SX883502]. 29 acres. 28½ acres of wooded hilltop above Dartmouth Castle and dominating the west side of the harbour entrance. **Higher Brownstone**

**Farm** [202:SX901505]. 298 acres of coastal farmland. **Hoodown Wood** [202:SX885420]. 33½ acres of woodland overlooking the Dart Estuary. **Little Dartmouth**  1½ miles south of Dartmouth [202:SX880490]. 165 acres of cliffs and farmland forming the western approach to Dartmouth Harbour. The land runs from Warren Point (off which are the rocks known as the Dancing Beggars) for 1½ miles eastward round Combe Point and Blackstone Point to the harbour entrance. **Long Wood** [202:SX881535]. 101 acres. Oak woodland and 1 mile of foreshore on the east bank of the Dart Estuary. **Nethway Wood, Dragon House Farm, Kingswear** [202:SX906527]. 17 acres of mixed woodland and furze.

EAST TITCHBERRY FARM (north coast)  1 mile east of Hartland Point, north-west of the A39 [190:SS244270]. 120 acres, including 1 mile of cliff, with a very ancient farmhouse and buildings.

GOLDEN COVE, BERRYNARBOR  West of Combe Martin [180:SS565477]. 10½ acres of wooded cliff.

THE GREAT AND LITTLE HANGMAN (north coast)  Between Combe Martin and Heddon's Mouth. 395 acres of coastal heath, with splendid views inland and up and down the coast over the Bristol Channel.

HARTLAND: EXMANSWORTHY CLIFF [190:SS275273]. 40 acres of coastal land.

HEDDON VALLEY: HEDDON'S MOUTH (north coast) [180:SS6549]. 941 acres of woodland and moorland leading down from Trentishoe Common to the sea, with fine views over the Bristol Channel. **Millwood, Martinhoe** [180:SS656475]. 57 acres of mainly deciduous woodland with some rough pasture.

HOLDSTONE DOWN (north coast) [180:SS620475]. 74 acres of coastal heath.

ILFRACOMBE (north coast) [180:SS5047]. 262 acres comprising most of the coastal land from the outskirts of the town west to the village of Lee.

LEE TO CROYDE (north coast). One of the Trust's finest coastal properties, continuous for 5 miles from Lee to Woolacombe, and then with some 'gaps' south-westward to Croyde. Fine cliff walking. **Baggy Point**  At south-west end of Morte Bay [180:SS4241]. 304½ acres of cliffs and agricultural land. Wheelchair pathway. **Bull Point** 2 miles north of Woolacombe [180:ss4647]. A headland of 182 acres. **Combegate Beach** At north-west end of Woolacombe [180:ss455444]. 6 acres. **Damage Cliffs** 3 miles west of Ilfracombe [180:ss470465]. 113 acres of hillocky cliffs, once a golf course, immediately to the west of Lee Bay, with wide views. **Morte Fields** 30 acres at south end of Morte Point [180:ss4545]. **Morte Point** At north end of Morte Bay [180:ss4445]. 168½ acres, with wide views. **Potters Hill** ½ mile south of Woolacombe [180:ss458430]. 30 acres overlooking Morte Bay. **Town Farm** South-east of Morte Point [180:ss457451]. 114 acres. **Vention** Just south of Woolacombe Warren [180:ss451411]. 20 acres of gorse scrub with ruins of a former hotel. **Woolacombe Barton** Just south of Town Farm [180:ss460445]. 545 acres of steeply sloping land. **Woolacombe and Mortehoe** [180:ss454413]. 24 acres. **Woolacombe Warren** 101 acres of sand dunes along the shore at Woolacombe [180:ss4542].

LUNDY 11 miles north of Hartland Point; the nearest ports are Bideford (25 miles), Ilfracombe (25 miles) and Tenby (30 miles) [180:(inset):ss1345]. The island, of 1,047 acres, has a long and romantic history. Its granite cliffs rise sheer from the Bristol Channel.

LYMPSTONE 7 miles south-east of Exeter [192:sx988842]. 6½ acres on the east side of the River Exe, overlooking the estuary.

LYNMOUTH: FORELAND POINT, COUNTISBURY HILL AND WATERSMEET (north coast) [180:ss7449]. 1,487 acres, east of Lynmouth on both sides of the A39. The property includes the cliffs above Sillery Sands which run out under Butter Hill (994 feet) to Foreland Point, which forms the eastern bastion of Lynmouth Bay. 705 acres, with Foreland Point, adjacent cliffs and Town Farm at Countisbury. 52 acres of moorland and cliff on both sides of the A39. 170 acres of coast and woodland at Glenthorne, Lynton, running east from Foreland Point almost to the Somerset border [180:ss7750], a 2-mile stretch of coastline comprising spectacular cliff land.

ORCOMBE AND PRATTSHAYES (south coast) 2¼ miles south-east of Exmouth [192:sy025808]. 126 acres comprising a mile of high Red Sandstone cliff, known as the High Land of Orcombe, and the foreshore east from the end of Exmouth promenade with the fields inland from the cliff.

PORTLEDGE ESTATE, NEAR BIDEFORD (q.v.) [190:ss356237]. 770 acres of agricultural land, cliffs, beaches and foreshore.

SALCOMBE (south coast) About 13 miles of coastline on either side of the harbour. **Bolt Head to Bolt Tail** Between Salcombe Harbour (B3197) and Hope [202:sx7236 or 6639]. 1,055¾ acres of cliff and farmland extending for about 6 miles. The property includes the Cathole Cliffs, Bolt Tail Camp, a promontory fort and Bolberry Down. **Overbecks, Sharpitor** 1½ miles south-west of Salcombe [202:sx728374]. An early twentieth-century house and 6 acres of garden. **Portlemouth Down** On east side of Salcombe Harbour [202:sx740375]. 365 acres extending over 5 miles from Mill Bay, opposite Salcombe, to Venericks Cove beyond Gara Rock. Cliff walks, views and sandy coves, with 50 acres of High House Farm, farmland and rough grazing. **Prawle Point and Gammon Head** [202:sx773350 & 765355]. 132 acres, including 13 acres at Prawle Point, the southernmost part of Devon. 53 acres at Gammon Head, a beautiful rocky promontory to the west. A further 31½ acres of cliff and farmland at Signalhouse Point [202:sx770355]. **Snapes Point** [202:sx735400]. 154 acres of coastal farmland comprising nearly 2 miles of estuary frontage.

SIDMOUTH (south coast). **Peak Hill** [192:sy112872]. 16 acres, including the cliff to the west of Sidmouth.

SOUTH MILTON (south coast) 2 miles west of Kingsbridge [202:sx677415]. 75½ acres. 5½ acres, known as South Milton Sands. 70 acres of Southdown Farm.

WEMBURY BAY AND YEALM ESTUARY (south coast) 5–6 miles east of Plymouth [201:sx530480]. Both banks of the estuary and 5 miles of the sea coast, 915½ acres. **North Bank.** 86 acres, including 26 acres surrounding St Werburgh's Church, with the Mill House and the foreshore. **South Bank.** 470½ acres. 27 acres of hanging woodland immediately west of Noss Mayo. 442 acres of cliff, farmland and woods, including Passage Wood to the west of the ferry landing and then (except for the woodland below Battery Cottage and Cellars Beach) continuously for 2 miles round Mouthstone and Gara Points to Blackstone Point. **Stoke Point, Noss Mayo** [210:sx550460]. 359 acres of cliff and farmland to the south of Noss Mayo, including 2 miles of continuous coastline from Blackstone Point to Stoke Point.

WESTWARD HO!: KIPLING TORS (north coast) [180:SS423289]. 18 acres of gorse-covered hill, at the west end of the town. The setting for much of *Stalky and Co.*

WOODY BAY (north coast)  Between Lynton and Heddon's Mouth [180:SS675487]. 120½ acres. 115 acres of moorland, cliff and woodland on the steep slopes from Wringapeak Point nearly down to the old pier in Woody Bay.

## DORSET

BELLE VUE FARM (q.v.)  On Isle of Purbeck, about 2 miles south-west of Swanage [195:SZ015770]. 51 acres of rough grazing above the cliffs.

BROWNSEA ISLAND  In Poole Harbour, about 1¼ miles south-east of Poole, near Sandbanks [195:SZ0288]. 500 acres. The island is heath and woodland. Magnificent views of the Dorset coast, miles of woodland paths and open glades and one mile of beach for bathing. 200-acre nature reserve, managed by the Dorset Trust for Nature Conservation with access for guided parties at fixed times, containing a heronry, a marsh and two lakes which are sanctuaries for wildfowl.

BURTON CLIFF, BURTON BRADSTOCK [193 & 194:SY483893]. 83½ acres. A high bluff of cliff running west from Burton Bradstock village rising to 100 feet sheer above the sea before dropping down to Freshwater Bay. Inland it slopes to the encircling arm of the River Bride.

GOLDEN CAP ESTATE (q.v.) [193:SY4092]. 1,974 acres of hill, cliff, farmland, undercliff and beach, including about 5 miles of the coast between Charmouth and Eypemouth. **Black Venn** [193:SY356933]. 49 acres, including 29 acres of cliff. **Cain's Folly** [193:SY375928]. 31 acres of undercliff and rough pasture at Charmouth. **Chardown Hill and Upcot Farm** [193:SY395930]. 405 acres with coastal views. **Doghouse Hill** [193:SY432914]. 54 acres. **Downhouse Farm** [193:SY440915]. ¾ mile of undercliff and farmland reaching from Eypemouth to Thorncombe Beacon. **Golden Cap** [193:SY407923]. 26 acres of the summit (618 feet) of the highest cliffs in the south of England. **Hardown Hill** [193:SY405945]. 25 acres of the crest of a flat-topped hill with views south past Golden Cap to the sea. **Ridge Cliff and West Cliff, Seatown** [193:SY422920].

170 acres of cliff, undercliff and farmland on each side of Seatown. **The Saddle** [193:SY408924]. 8 acres forming a col between Golden Cap and Langdon Hill. **St Gabriel's** [193:SY401924]. 192 acres of undercliff and clifftop with steep access to sea reached only on foot from Morcombelake. **Shedbush Farm** [193:SY405935]. A 61-acre grassland farm. **Ship Farm** [193:SY00940]. A 39-acre grassland farm. **The Spittles** [193:SY385935]. 274 acres of farm, undercliff and hill. 59½ acres, including part of the coastal footpath. **Stonebarrow Hill and Westhay Farm** [193:SY385935]. 274 acres of farm, undercliff and hill, and 58½ acres of cliff land, including part of the coastal footpath.

LYME REGIS: WARE CLIFFS [193:SY917133]. 29½ acres, west of Lyme Regis, forming a sheltered valley of unimproved grassland above the Cobb and undercliff.

SOUTHDOWN FARM  7 miles south-east of Dorchester, at Ringstead Bay; access 5 miles from Weymouth along the A353 at the Upton turning past Ringstead RAF camp [194:SY7582]. 273 acres of farmland, with a sea front of 700 yards. Views over Weymouth Bay and Portland Bill. **Burning Cliff and Whitenothe Cliff** [194:SY765815]. 107 acres of cliffs adjoining Southdown Farm, between Burning and Whitenothe Cliffs. The Burning Cliff is said to be so called from shale fires which burned here for six years. Whitenothe Cliff is too dangerous for walkers, although it is the legendary smugglers' escape route chronicled in *Moonfleet* by J. Meade Falkner.

WEST BEXINGTON. **Lime Kiln Hill** [194:SY541871]. 37 acres. 17 acres of former stone workings and rough grazing on the crest of the ridge which overlooks the Chesil Bank to the south and the Bride Valley to the north. **Labour-in-Vain Farm, Puncknowle** [194:SY545865]. 225 acres.

WHITECLIFF FARM AND BALLARD DOWN (q.v.) [195:SZ030810]. On Isle of Purbeck. 108 acres of downland, steep slopes and undercliff with fine views of the Dorset coast and good footpaths. Also 114 acres of undulating farmland.

## CO. DURHAM

BEACON HILL (q.v.)  7 miles south of Sunderland, 1 mile north of Easington Colliery [88:NA440455]. 34 acres of clifftop, pasture and woodland on the

Durham coast, offering spectacular views both north and south; the first coastal property to be acquired in the county.

HORDEN (q.v.) 88 acres of land including Warren House Gill and part of Fox Holes Dene together with clifftop and beach; the 500th mile of coastline bought through Enterprise Neptune.

## ESSEX

COPT HALL FARM, COLCHESTER [168:TL981146]. 400 acres of farmland and saltings, including nearly 2 miles of coastline on the River Blackwater. Important for overwintering birds.

NORTHEY ISLAND, MALDON [168:TL872058]. A 300-acre island in the Blackwater Estuary; a Grade 1 site for saltmarsh flora and overwintering birds. Access by permit only.

RAY ISLAND. A stretch of unspoilt salting in the tidal creek between the mainland beaches and West Mersea, cut off at high tide.

## ISLE OF WIGHT

BACK OF THE WIGHT. **Afton Down** On south-west coast, 3 miles south of Yarmouth, just to north of coast road [196:SZ350858]. 228½ acres. Downland reaching from Freshwater Bay to Compton Farm, with wide coastal views over the island and to the Hampshire coast. **Brook Chine** Astride the Military Road at Brook [196:SZ385835]. 73 acres. A coastal strip of 33 acres and 40 acres of grazing land, including the Chine and 300 yards of shore. **Brook Down** Adjoining Compton Down on the east [196:SZ395851]. 99½ acres of open down rising to over 500 feet at Five Barrows. **Compton Farm** Adjoining Afton Down on the east [196:SZ376850]. 240 acres. The property includes 100 acres of Compton Down, to which there is access from Freshwater by public footpath, giving unrivalled views over West Wight, and 20 acres of pastureland running down to the sea at Compton Chine. **Hanover Point and Shippards Chine** [196:SZ378841]. 26½ acres comprising ¼ mile of coast with low sandstone cliffs.

BEMBRIDGE AND CULVER DOWNS [196:SZ624860]. 104 acres, including the Palmerstonian Bembridge

Fort, which is let and not open. The most prominent feature in the east of the island, the down rises to 343 feet and the cliffs fall sheer to the sea. Wide views.

MOTTISTONE. **Mottistone Estate** [196:SZ405837]. 650 acres comprising farms, woodland and most of Mottistone village, donated by the 2nd Baron Mottistone in 1965. The estate runs from the crest of the downs to the sea. **Sudmoor Point** [196:SZ395828]. 44 acres of farmland and cliff.

NEWTOWN. **Harts Farm** [196:SZ429904]. 36 acres of pastureland, crossed by the coastal footpath. **Newtown River**. The entire estuary of the Newtown River, amounting to some 10 miles in all, and with 4 miles of the foreshore of the Solent, together with Newtown and Shalfleet Quays. The Trust controls all mooring and other harbour rights. **The Quay Fields** [196:SZ420908]. 12 acres of pastureland providing access to the quay and running down to Ducks Cove.

ST CATHERINE'S. **Knowles Farm and St Catherine's Point** [196:SZ595755]. 170 acres of the most southerly tip of the island, from the cliff down to the foreshore. Rugged and undulating land owing to the periodic slips in the blue clay. A wild and beautiful spot. **St Catherine's Down** [196:SZ495785]. 55¼ acres of downland ridge running north from St Catherine's Hill, one of the few places from which the western and eastern extremities of the Isle of Wight can be seen. **St Catherine's Hill** [196:SZ494772]. 24 acres. A very prominent hill with magnificent views over West Wight. Standing on it is St Catherine's Oratory, a fourteenth-century building in the care of English Heritage. It was used as a very early lighthouse.

ST HELEN'S. **Priory Bay, Horestone Point** [196:SZ564907]. 1¼ acres of wooded coastline. **Priory Woods** [196:SZ637899]. 55 acres of coastal woodland at Priory Bay, including Nodes Point and running south to St Helen's Old Church. **St Helen's Common** 1 mile north-west of Bembridge, just east of the B3330 [196:SZ633892]. 9¼ acres and a cottage, with views over Brading Harbour. **St Helen's Duver** [196:SZ637891]. 30 acres. A wide spit of sand and shingle which stretches almost across the mouth of Bembridge Harbour and at its north end adjoins St Helen's Common. Good walking and interesting flora.

VENTNOR. **Littleton and Luccombe Downs** [196:SZ563784]. 92 acres. 12 acres of the crest of the ridge. Accessible by car from Ventnor and providing views both inland and out to sea. 80 acres of the crest of the high downs behind the town of Ventnor [196:SZ573790]. Views south over the Channel, north over the island and the Solent to Hampshire, east over Selsey to the Sussex Downs. **Luccombe Farm** [196:SZ577794]. 244 acres of downland, clifftop and meadow between Ventnor and Shanklin, dovetailing into Luccombe and Bonchurch Downs and leading to ½ mile of beach and cliffs. **St Boniface Down** [196:SZ57782]. Rising to 764 feet, above Ventnor, 221 acres of fine downland, including Bonchurch Down. The highest point on the island.

WEST WIGHT. **Headon Warren and West High Down** [196:SZ310851]. 459 acres of downland, heath and agricultural land in West Wight, extending from Headon Warren on the Solent shore to the chalk cliffs of West High Down in the south. The acquisition links the Needles Headland with Tennyson Down, giving the Trust ownership of most of the peninsula and adding 2¾ miles to its holdings of coastline on the island. **The Needles Headland** ¾ mile south-west of Alum Bay [196:SZ300848]. 39 acres of downland and chalk cliffs forming the westerly tip of the island and overlooking the Needles Rocks. The downs rise to 462 feet and the area is listed as an SSSI. **Tennyson Down** 1 mile south-west of Freshwater [196:SZ330855]. 157½ acres of cliff land, where the Poet Laureate took his daily walk when he lived at Farringford.

## KENT

DOVER. **Great Farthingloe** (q.v.) [179:TR292393]. 67 acres of farm and cliff land extending to just over a mile in length and lying halfway between Dover and Capel-le-Ferne. **Langdon Cliffs and Foxhill Down** (q.v.) [179:TR335423]. 52 acres of cliff land immediately east of Dover. Chalk downland, interspersed with scrub; SSSI.

ST MARGARET'S BAY (q.v.) 4 miles north-east of Dover [179:TR372448]. **Bockell Hill** [179:TR370455]. 11½ acres, adjoining The Leas to the north. Arable farmland, including ⅔ mile of clifftop. **Kingsdown Leas** [179:TR380470]. 11 acres of clifftop between Bockhill Farm and Kingsdown Golf Club. **The Leas**. 10 acres along the top of the chalk cliffs on the west side of St Margaret's Bay. **Lighthouse Down** [197:TR366437]. 10 acres. Just over 9 acres of cliff land on South Foreland, giving ⅓-mile cliff walk.

SANDWICH BAY 2 miles north-east of Sandwich [179:TR347620]. 193 acres of coastal saltings, sand dunes and foreshore lying on the south side of the Great Stour river. **Pegwell Bay** (q.v.) 3 miles north of Sandwich [197:TR343627]. 357 acres of coastline, saltmarsh and mudflats at Pegwell Bay, adjoining NT land at Sandwich Bay. Designated an SSSI, managed by the Kent Trust for Nature Conservation.

## LANCASHIRE

SILVERDALE 4 miles north-west of Carnforth. **Bank House Farm** [97:SD460752]. 57 acres of land, including about ⅓ mile of limestone coastal fringe overlooking the saltmarshes of the Kent Estuary; also George's Lot, some 9 acres of pasture adjoining Bank House Farm. **Castlebarrow**. 21 acres overlooking Morecambe Bay [97:SD462761]. 106 acres of wooded hill, including Waterslack Quarry (1 acre). **Jack Scout** [97:SD459737]. 15 acres of coastal limestone pasture and scrub overlooking Morecambe Bay.

## MERSEYSIDE

FORMBY [108:SD275080]. 494 acres of sand dunes, pine woods, heathland, rough pasture and foreshore west of the town of Formby. Some of the nearest unspoilt coastline to the centre of Liverpool.

THE WIRRAL. **Heswall** [108:SJ246825]. 39½ acres of meadow and arable land fronting the Dee Estuary, with fine views across to North Wales.

## NORFOLK

BLAKENEY POINT 8 miles east of Wells, north of Blakeney and Morston [133:TG0046]. 1,184 acres. A shingle spit of 1,100 acres, with foreshore, saltmarsh and sand dunes. Important for its birds, plants, and a common-seal colony which was hit by the seal virus in 1988. Access by boat from Morston or Blakeney, or on foot from Cley. **Freshes** [133:TG040447]. 195 acres of grazing marshland east of Blakeney. **Friary Hills** 12 acres to the east of Blakeney village. Magnificent views of Blakeney Point and Freshes. Open for informal recreation. No dogs. **Morston Marshes** [132 & 133:TG010445]. 589 acres of saltings interlaced with tidal creeks and backed by scrub-covered grassland forming the whole 2 miles of the south shoreline of Blakeney Harbour between the villages of Blakeney and Stiffkey. **Stiffkey Saltmarshes** On north coast between Wells and Blakeney and north of Stiffkey village [133:TG956439–991444]. 487 acres of saltmarsh, including 2 miles of coastline.

BRANCASTER On north coast between Hunstanton and Wells [132:TF800450]. 2,150 acres, including 4½ miles of tidal foreshore, beach, sand dunes, marsh and saltings opposite Scolt Head Island Nature Reserve.

BRANODONUM ROMAN FORT [132:TF782440]. 23 acres, the site of a former Roman shore fort.

SALTHOUSE BROAD 1½ miles north-east of Cley [133:TG061448]. 29 acres of marsh and shingle, known locally as Arnold's Marsh. A nature reserve important as an adjunct to Blakeney Point. Many migrant waders visit the salt lagoons. **Gramborough Hill** On north coast, ½ mile north-east of Salthouse [133:TG086441]. 70 acres, including the hill and adjacent saltmarsh. **Great Eye** On north coast, ½ mile north of Salthouse [133:TG081443]. About 2 acres of sand and shingle adjoining Gramborough Hill which is gradually being eroded away by the North Sea.

SCOLT HEAD ISLAND 3 miles north of Burnham Market, 1½ miles north of the A149 [132:TF8146]. About 1,620 acres of sand dune, saltmarsh and shingle ridge, with interesting marine flora. Terns (in particular sandwich terns) and oystercatchers nest here.

## NORTHUMBERLAND

ALNMOUTH (q.v.) Access via track from the A1068, 2 miles south of Alnmouth [75:NU241094]. 221 acres of dunes leased from the Duke of Northumberland in 1978.

BEADNELL DUNES (q.v.) ¼ mile north of Beadnell, east of the B1340 [75:NU232987]. 9 acres of sand dunes stretching from the northern edge of Beadnell village to Link House. Also Beadnell lime kilns, a group of eighteenth-century lime kilns by the sea.

BUSTON LINKS (q.v.) [81:NU251085]. 18¼ acres of sand dunes to the south of Alnmouth village, representing approximately ½ mile of coastline.

DRURIDGE BAY (q.v.) 2 miles north of Cresswell village, 1½ miles east of the A1068 [81:NZ2896]. A mile of coastline consisting of 99 acres of sand dunes and grass hinterland.

DUNSTANBURGH CASTLE, EMBLETON LINKS AND LOW NEWTON-BY-THE-SEA (q.v.). On the coast, 9 miles north-east of Alnwick, approached on foot only from Craster to the south or across the golf course from Embleton and Dunstansteads to the north. **Dunstanburgh Castle, Embleton Links and Newton Pool** [75:NU243235/243240]. 617 acres. Dunes and foreshore, including the golf course. Interesting geology and wide range of plants. Newton Pool, near Newton-by-the-Sea, adjoining Embleton Links is a 16½-acre freshwater pool protected as a nature reserve with special ornithological importance. **Low Newton-by-the-Sea** [75:NU241246]. 139 acres. 16 acres, almost the entire fishing village with 12 cottages, including The Square, with the Ship Inn, the beach and other land and buildings adjoining. **Newton Links** [75:NU236417]. 55 acres of sand dunes and rough grazing south of the Long Nanny Burn in Beadnell Bay. **Newton Point** [75:NU242653]. 117 acres of coastal rough grazing and pastureland, including Football Hole; about 1½ miles of coastline between Low Newton-by-the-Sea and Newton Links.

FARNE ISLANDS (q.v.) 2–5 miles off the coast, opposite Bamburgh, reached by boat from Seahouses [75:NU2337]. About 30 islands, some 80 acres in extent. In the seventh century St Aidan and St Cuthbert lived there.

ST AIDAN'S AND SHORESTON DUNES 2 miles south-east of Bamburgh, east of the B1340, stretching from Monk's House to Seahouses [75:NU211327]. 60 acres of sand dunes, with views of the Farne Islands.

## SOMERSET

BREAN DOWN 2 miles south-west of Weston-super-Mare, the southern arm of Weston Bay [182:ST2959]. 159 acres. A bold headland 300 feet high.

EXMOOR. **Greenaleigh Point, Minehead** [181:SS955483]. ½ mile of coast overlooking the Bristol Channel with 46 acres of grass and moorland behind. **Holnicote Estate, Dunkery etc.** Astride the A39, between Minehead and Porlock [181:SS8844]. 12,442 acres, including 4½ miles of rugged coastline.

## SUFFOLK

DUNWICH HEATH (q.v.) Reached by a road turning
south off the Westleton to Dunwich road, $\frac{1}{2}$ mile
before reaching Dunwich [156:TM475683]. 214 acres
of sandy cliffs and heathland with a mile of beach
including a row of coastguard cottages and the
foreshore below high-water mark. Carpark,
information centre, tea-room and shop.

PIN MILL $\frac{1}{2}$ mile north of Chelmondiston village,
5 miles south-east of Ipswich on the south bank of
the River Orwell between Pin Mill and Old Wharf
[169:TM214380]. 156 acres of woodland which was
devastated by the Great Storm of 1987 and replanted
between 1988–9. Marvellous views of the River
Orwell.

## SUSSEX: EAST

CROWLINK, MICHEL DENE AND WENT HILL
5 miles west of Eastbourne, just south of Friston
[199:TV5497]. 632 acres of cliff, down and farmland,
including part of the famous Seven Sisters Cliffs.
**Belle Tout.** East of Birling Gap and forming the cliff
approach to Beachy Head [199:TV557987]. $66\frac{1}{2}$ acres
including $\frac{1}{4}$ mile of chalk cliff. **Birling Gap.** 6 acres,
including the Birling Gap Hotel and carpark, the site
of the White Horses Bungalow, the coastguard
station and 4 coastguard cottages.

EXCEAT SALTINGS South of Exceat Bridge, on west
bank of the Cuckmere River, 2 miles east of Seaford.
$4\frac{1}{2}$ acres overlooking the saltings, and a small piece of
the saltings themselves.

FAIRLIGHT $4\frac{1}{2}$ miles east of Hastings
[199:TQ884127]. 228 acres. 58 acres of cliff land,
including Stumblet Wood.

## SUSSEX: WEST

BOSHAM: QUAY MEADOW 4 miles west of
Chichester, 1 mile south of the A27 [197:SU804038].
1 acre, between the church and the creek.

WEST WITTERING: EAST HEAD [197:SU8724].
110 acres. A spit of land on the east side of
Chichester Harbour entrance, comprising dunes,
saltings and a large stretch of sandy beach; a total
coastline of $1\frac{1}{4}$ miles.

## TYNE & WEAR

THE LEAS AND MARSDEN ROCK, SOUTH SHIELDS
East of the A183 South Shields to Sunderland road
[88:NZ388665]. $2\frac{1}{2}$ miles of spectacular unspoilt
coastline, comprising 282 acres of clifftop grassland
from Trow Point to Lizard Point.

## YORKSHIRE: NORTH

CAYTON BAY AND KNIPE POINT, SCARBOROUGH
[101:TA063850]. 88 acres of cliff and undercliff,
including a popular beach on the northern half of
Cayton Bay.

HAYBURN WYKE 6 miles north of Scarborough
[101:TA010970]. 65 acres of high cliffs overlooking
a small bay and rocky beach.

NEWBIGGIN EAST FARM 1 mile north of Filey Brigg
[101:TA105825]. 500 yards of steep dramatic cliff and
25 acres of clifftop land.

PORT MULGRAVE 10 miles north of Whitby
[94:797177]. 38 acres of cliff and undercliff
surrounding the harbour and the northern headland
of Robin Hood's Bay.

ROBIN HOOD'S BAY (q.v.) 15 miles north of
Scarborough, off the A171. Acquisitions of Yorkshire
coastline under the Enterprise Neptune campaign.
**Bay Ness Farm** [94:NZ958060]. $69\frac{1}{2}$ acres of superb
cliffs and clifftop land forming the northern
headland of Robin Hood's Bay; a further 107 acres
completing the Trust's ownership of the northern
headland of the bay. **Boggle Hole** [94:NZ954040].
8 acres of cliff on either side of a steeply incised inlet
to Robin Hood's Bay. **Ravenscar** [94:NZ980025].
260 acres, including 1 mile of coastline and
spectacular cliff scenery. **Ravenscar: Bent Rigg Farm**
[101:SE995000]. 96 acres of clifftop land, including
part of the Cleveland Way long-distance footpath,
extending $1\frac{1}{4}$ miles above Beast and Common Cliffs.
**Ravenscar Brickyards** [94:NZ973015]. 16 acres.
A disused quarry and site of former brickworks
forming an interesting and important feature in the
scenery of Robin Hood's Bay. **Ravenscar: Church
Farm** [94:NZ973010]. 30 acres of pasture, part of
Church Farm forming skyline to Robin Hood's Bay.
**Ravenscar: Stoupe Brow Farm** [94:NZ966024].
72 acres of farm and coastal land extending the
Trust's holdings at Ravenscar northward into Robin

Hood's Bay. **Rocket Post Field** Adjoining the village of Robin Hood's Bay [94:NZ955058]. 12 acres of coastal land and cliff. **Smails Moor** [94:NZ954070]. A 15-acre cliff field.

SALTWICK NAB 1 mile east of Whitby, off the A171 and the A169 [94:NZ914112]. 7½ acres of cliff land, including a low, rocky nab jutting out into the sea.

STAINTONDALE: RIGG HALL FARM Between Hayburn Wyke and Ravenscar [101:TA005985]. 91½ acres of farmland with superb clifftop views.

**WALES**

DYFED

CEIBWR BAY, MOYLEGROVE [145:SN109458]. 6½ acres of coastal land.

THE COLBY ESTATE [158:SN155080]. 973 acres of farm and tranquil woodland, including ¾ mile of coastland between Amroth and Wiseman's Bridge.

DINAS ISLAND FARM [157:SM0140]. 5 miles east of Fishguard and 18 miles west of Cardigan. 414 acres of farmland, comprising 2½ miles of coastline lying within the Pembrokeshire Coast National Park.

GOOD HOPE. Just to the east of Strumble Head, 3 miles north-west of Fishguard, on the Pembrokeshire coast [157:SM912407]. 97 acres of rugged coastal outcrop and ancient pastures.

KETE [157:SM800045]. 168 acres, with a mile of the coast west of Dale, including a view of the coastline to Skomer and Stockholm Islands.

LAWRENNY [158 & 157:SN17068]. A 71-acre hanging oak wood on the east side of Castle Reach of the River Cleddau.

LITTLE MILFORD [158:SN965118]. 72 acres of mixed woodland on west bank of western Cleddau River, 5 miles south of Haverfordwest.

LLANRHIAN: YNYS BARRI [157:SM805328]. 200 acres of coastal farmland, including 2 miles of coast extending from Porthgain Harbour to Abereiddy.

LOCHTYN, LLANGRANOG Immediately north-east of the village of Llangranog [145:SN315545].

213 acres. A farm with 1½ miles of cliffs, an island, two beaches and a hilltop, Pen-y-Badell, with splendid views of the whole coast of Cardigan Bay.

LONG HOUSE FARM, NEAR ABERCASTLE [157:SM853337]. 151 acres of farmland, comprising 2½ miles of scenic and rugged coastline. Two small islands included with the land: Ynys-y-Castell and Ynys Daullyn.

LYDSTEP HEADLAND 4 miles south-west of Tenby, 1½ miles east of Manorbier, reached from Lydstep [158:SS090976]. 54 acres of headland.

MANORBIER BAY. **Manorbier Cliff** Immediately south of St James's Church [158:SM065971]. 48 acres, including Red Sandstone cliffs, with views westward to St Govan's Head.

MWNT On the coast about 4 miles north of Cardigan [145:SN1952]. 98 acres of coast land. Y Foel is a prominent conical-shaped landmark under which lies the thirteenth-century whitewashed Church of the Holy Cross.

NEWQUAY TO CWMTYDI, CEREDIGION COAST. **Caerllan Farm** [145:SN355577]. A 73-acre farm, with 880 yards of coastline on the east side of the Cwmtydi Inlet. **Coybal** 1 mile south-west of Newquay [145:SN369589]. 37 acres of coastal land adjoining Cwm Soden. **Craig-yr-Adar** ¾ mile to the west of Newquay [145:SN378601]. One mile of cliff land and adjoining Trust ownership at Coybal. **Cwm Soden** [145:SN365584]. 53 acres of partly wooded coastal valley. **Llwynwermod** 1½ miles south-west of Newquay [145:SN372580]. 17 acres of wooded valley and valley-bottom meadow, at the head of the Cwm Soden Valley.

PENBRYN, CEREDIGION COAST. **Llanborth Farm** Immediately north-west of hamlet of Penbryn [145:SN295519]. 95 acres with ½ mile of coastline and including access to Penbryn Beach. **Pencwm** Immediately to the west of Llanborth Farm [145:SN292524]. 29 acres of partly wooded valley, partly pasture, leading to ¼ mile of coast. **Ty Hen** 37 acres of coastal land, ½ mile north-east of Tresaith.

POTTRE, CEREDIGION COAST 2 miles south-west of Newquay [145:SN372579]. 20 acres of partly wooded valley slope, adjoining Trust land at Llwynwermod Wood and running down to the Ferwig River.

ST BRIDE'S BAY. **Carn Nwchwn to Nine Wells** Between St David's and Solva [145:SM775242]. 11 acres. East of Caerfai Bay, rough coastal lands as far east as Nine Wells, including the valley from Pont Clegyr to Caer Bwdy Bay. **Llanunwas, Solva** [157:SM7924]. Just west of Solva, linking Trust-owned Morfa Common and land in Solva on the Pembrokeshire coast. 141 acres of farmland, comprising 2 miles of rugged coastline. **Lower Treginnis Farm** [157:SM725240]. 250 acres. The westernmost mainland farm in Wales. Outstanding coastal landscape with views to Ramsey Island and across St Bride's Bay. **Marloes: West Hook, Trehill and Runwayskiln Farms** 12 miles south-west of Haverfordwest, via the B4327, on the south arm of St Bride's Bay. 524 acres. **Marloes: The Deerpark and Midland and Gateholm Islands** [157:SM758091, 748091, 770073]. 73½ acres of coastal land, comprising over ½ mile of coast at the deerpark, Martin's Haven, together with two islands, completing ownership of the Marloes Peninsula. **St David's** 2 miles north-west of St David's [145:SM740278]. 234 acres, extending from Tywyn Fach to south-east of Carn Llidi (595 feet), with Llaethdy and Trefelly Farms. **St David's Head** [157:SM721278]. 520 acres of common land, including St David's Head. **St Elvis, Solva** Immediately to the east of Solva Harbour [145:SM810240]. 276 acres. The southern boundary is 1½ miles of spectacular coastline. **Upper Solva to Cwm Bach, Newgale** [145:SM802238]. 203 acres, which includes the immediate coastal strip. **Upper Treginnis Farm** 2 miles west of St David's on the St David's Head Peninsula. 116 acres of farmland with a range of nineteenth-century farm buildings. Adjoins Lower Treginnis. **Whitesands Bay to Porth-clais** [145:SM7323]. 81 acres of cliffs.

ST DOGMAELS: CIPPYN FACH AND GERNOS [145:SN122488]. 106 acres of land comprising 1 mile of coastline. Just to the west of Cemaes Head, near St Dogmaels. A coastal footpath traverses the property and affords views north to the Llŷn Peninsula and south to Strumble Head.

STACKPOLE 4 miles by road south of Pembroke [158:SR977963]. 1,992½ acres, including the site of Stackpole Court, the freshwater lakes, woods, 8 miles of cliffs, two beaches, farmland and dunes. Carparks at Stackpole Quay and Broadhaven.

TREGONING HILL On east headland of Towy Estuary, 1 mile south of Ferryside [159:SN362087].

20 acres of cliff land and fields, good views of the whole of Carmarthen Bay.

WHARLEY POINT, LLANSTEPHAN [159:SN340093]. 386 acres of farm and cliff land at the confluence of the Taf and Towy Estuaries, including Lacques Fawr and Lords Park Farms.

WILLIAMSTON PARK The promontory between the Creswell and Carew Rivers south-east of Lawrenny [158:SN030057]. 52 acres. One of the two deerparks of Carew Castle in the Middle Ages, extensively quarried in the eighteenth and nineteenth centuries and now managed as a nature reserve by the Dyfed Wildlife Trust.

## GWYNEDD

BRAICH-Y-PWLL, NEAR ABERDARON (q.v.) [123:SH140254]. 122 acres including Mynydd Gwyddel and part of Mynydd Mawr. Celtic pilgrims embarked from here for Bardsey Island. There is a holy well.

CAE GLAN-MOR On the Menai Strait in Anglesey, between Telford's road bridge and Stephenson's railway bridge, on south side of the A4080 [115:SH546718]. 11 acres given to preserve the view over the strait and the Snowdon range. **Ynys Welltog, Menai Bridge** [115:SH549717]. A ½-acre rocky island in the Menai Strait.

CARREG FARM, DINAS FAWR AND DINAS BACH, ABERDARON (q.v.) [115:SH162292]. 184 acres of land designated an Area of Outstanding Natural Beauty and part of the Heritage Coast and Special Protection Area.

CEMAES (q.v.) On east side of Cemaes Bay, Anglesey [114:SH3794]. 51 acres of cliff and agricultural land, including parts of two small bays and the carpark below the village. **Tyn Llan, Llanbadrig** [144:SH376945]. 2 acres. Two small coastal fields.

CEMLYN (q.v.) 2 miles west of Cemaes Bay on north coast of Anglesey [144:SH325933]. 321 acres of agricultural land and about 2 miles of coast. **Felin Gafnan and Trwyn Pencarreg, Anglesey** [114:SH340937]. 36 acres. A coastal smallholding and a rocky headland.

CLEGIR MAWR, ANGLESEY [114:SH315913].
151½ acres, including the farms of Clegir Mawr and
Pen-y-Foel, ½ mile of coastline and the viewpoint of
Mynydd-y-Garn, inland.

DINAS GYNFOR  2 miles north-east of Cemaes,
Anglesey, 5 miles west of Amlwch [114:SH392951].
4½ acres of cliff land, the northernmost point of Wales.

DINAS OLEU (q.v.)  Above Barmouth, at its south
end [124:SH615158]. 5 acres of cliff land overlooking
Cardigan Bay. **Cae Fadog.**  12 acres of cliff land above
Barmouth and adjoining Dinas Oleu, overlooking
Cardigan Bay and the Mawddach Estuary.

GLAN FAENOL (q.v.)  3 miles south-west of Bangor,
7 miles north of Caernarfon [114:SH530695].
314 acres of farmland and woodland adjacent to the
Menai Strait and opposite Plas Newydd, stretching
from Vaynol Wood in the north to the outskirts of
Port Dinorwic in the south.

LLANDANWG: Y MAES  Immediately south of the
village of Llandanwg and adjoining the Artro
Estuary [124:SH570270]. 24 acres surrounding the
medieval church of St Tanwg.

LLANDDONA: BRYN OFFA & FYNNON OER,
ANGLESEY [114:SH579817 & 578815]. 11½ acres of
common land and an adjoining clifftop field, overlooking Red Wharf Bay, also known as Traeth Coch.

MORFA BYCHAN  1¼ miles south-west of Porthmadoc
[124:SH550368]. 85 acres. Golf course and sand
dunes with about ½ mile of seashore.

MYNACHDY, LLANFAIRYNGHORNY, ANGLESEY
[114:SH295920]. 412 acres of coastal farmland
including 3¼ miles of coastline.

MYNYDD ANELOG, ABERDARON [123:SH158240].
116 acres, part of Mynydd Anelog Common.

MYNYDD BYCHESTYN, NEAR ABERDARON
[123:SH217265]. 46 acres of common land between
Mynydd Gwyddel and Pen-y-Cil.

PENARFYNYDD, RHIW [123:SH158240]. 245 acres of
agricultural land and rough clifftop grazing.

PEN-Y-CIL, ABERDARON [123:SH158240]. 8 acres.

PLAS NEWYDD, ANGLESEY (q.v.)  1 mile south-west

of Llanfairpwll; 2½ miles from Menai Bridge; 5 miles
from Bangor [114 & 115:SH521996]. 169 acres. The
house stands on the edge of an unspoilt stretch of the
Menai Strait with magnificent views to Snowdonia.
The grounds include a spring garden with massed
shrubs, rhododendron garden, woods, fine trees and
lawns sloping down to the strait.

PLAS-YN-RHIW ESTATE (q.v.)  In Llŷn, 416 acres
(of which 410 are coastal land) in the parishes of
Rhiw with Llanfaelrhys, Aberdaron, Llanengan and
Llanbedrog. **Plas-yn-Rhiw** [123:SH236283].
Charming eighteenth-century small country house
and garden. **Mynydd Cilan** [123:SH290249]. 70 acres.
Cliffs rising from the eastern arm of Porth Neigwl
with extensive views across Cardigan Bay and the
Irish Sea. **Mynydd-y-Graig** [123:SH2327]. 201 acres
on the west side of Porth Neigwl rising from the sea
to the rocks, Creigiau Gwineu, 800 feet above the
sea. **Penrallt Neigwl** [123:SH248287]. Seventeenth-
century farmhouse with 9 acres of cliff land
adjoining Porth Neigwl Rhiw. **Porth Orion**
[123:SH156285]. 10 acres, 9 acres of cliff land
adjoining Mynydd Anelog. **Porth Ysgo**
[123:SH206266]. 22 acres. Sandy beaches surrounded
by cliffs, with waterfall and stream, on the south
coast of Llŷn between Rhiw and Aberdaron,
approached through Ysgo Farm.

PORTH GWYLAN  1 mile east of Tudweiliog on the
Llŷn Peninsula [123:SH215365]. 54 acres, including
the former harbour of Porth Gwylan.

PORTH LLANLLAWEN  2 miles west of Aberdaron
[123:SH145265]. 41 acres, including ¾ mile of the Llŷn
coast between Mynydd Mawr and Anelog.

TYWYN-Y-FACH, ABERSOCH  North-east of
Abersoch, 6 miles south-west of Pwllheli, between
the Llanbedrog road and the sea [123:SH317292].
19 acres of sandhills covered with thorn scrub and
bracken.

YNYSGAIN  1 mile west of Criccieth [123:SH480375].
198 acres, comprising about 1 mile of coastland and
foreshore including the mouth of the Afon Dwyfor,
with farmland between the sea and the main
Criccieth to Pwllheli road.

YNYS TOWYN  On south-east side of Porthmadoc,
near the harbour entrance [124:SH572385]. 2 acres.
A small rocky knoll with magnificent views of the
Glaslyn Estuary and the Snowdon hills.

## WEST GLAMORGAN

GOWER PENINSULA (q.v.). **Bishopston Valley**
6 miles south-west of Swansea [159:SS575894].
153 acres. A narrow valley running from Kittle to
Pwll-du Bay, with hanging woods. **Llanrhidian
Marsh** 6 miles west of Swansea [159:SS400932].
1,271 acres of extensive saltmarshes on the north
coast of Gower extending westward from the village
of Crofty. **Nicholaston Burrows** [159:SS530877].
278 acres of fine cliffs, including Great Tor to the
west of Three Cliffs Bay and an area of sand burrows
and beach. **Paviland Cliff** 15 miles south-west of
Swansea [159:SS442856]. 80 acres of cliff with fine
views. **Pennard Cliff** 7 miles south-west of Swansea
[159:SS534875]. 248 acres extending from the east
side of Pwll-du Head to Southgate on the west.
**Pilton Green and Pitton Cross** [159:SS434789 &
447874]. 23 acres. Two small commons on the
B4247. **Pitton Cliff** 1 mile north-west of Paviland
Cliff [159:SS427865]. 38 acres. **Port Eynon Point**
1 mile south of the village of Port Eynon
[159:SS468845]. A limestone headland of 43 acres.
**Whitford Burrows** [159:SS445951]. A peninsula of
670 acres with sand burrows and saltmarsh of
particular interest for its birds and plants. National
Nature Reserve. **Rhossili Beach, Down and Raised
Terrace, Worms Head and Mewslade Bay**
[159:SS383878]. 1,479 acres. The bracken-covered
down is the highest point on Gower and is the
dominant feature of West Gower. The Worms Head,
the prominent island and headland of the south-west
corner of Gower, the cliffs from Rhossili village to
Mewslade Bay and the lake foreshore including most
of Rhossili Beach from Diles Lake southward round
the Worms Head to Mewslade.

## NORTHERN IRELAND

## CO. ANTRIM

CARRICK-A-REDE (q.v.) 5 miles west of Ballycastle,
55 miles from Belfast [D0622450]. 30 acres of grazing
and cliff, including a salmon fishery and the famous
rope bridge, access to which is from Larrybane only.
The bridge is taken down from mid-September until
early May and is closed during bad weather.
**Larrybane.** 58 acres of coastline, including the
disused chalk quarry and limeworks adjacent to
Carrick-a-Rede rope bridge and fishery.

CUSHENDUN (q.v.) 23 miles north of Ballymena,
on east coast of Antrim, at the foot of Glendun
[D248327]. 62 acres of the picturesque village and
bay, and 2 acres adjoining the beach with about
½ acre of the foreshore and bed of the River Glendun.

DUNSEVERICK CASTLE (q.v.) 3 miles east of Giant's
Causeway [C987445]. 5 acres. The rocky peninsula of
1 acre, upon which the few remaining stones of the
ancient castle stand, and Dunseverick Harbour, a
further 4 acres.

FAIR HEAD AND MURLOUGH BAY (q.v.) 3 miles east
of Ballycastle [D185430 & D199419]. 764 acres. One
of the most beautiful coastal areas in Northern
Ireland. The property includes part of the wilderness
area of Fair Head and Murlough Bay with its
woodlands. It holds outstanding interest for the
ornithologist and botanist. **Benvan** [D203415].
181¼ acres. Farmhouse and ¼ acre adjoining existing
property at Murlough Bay. 181 acres of coastline and
woodland to the east of Murlough Bay. **Murlough
Cottage, bothy and land.** 17 acres of coastline in
Murlough Bay close to Fair Head.

GIANT'S CAUSEWAY (q.v.) 9 miles from Portrush
[C952452]. 96 acres. A unique basalt rock formation
resulting from prehistoric volcanic action, with cliff
land.

LAYDE 2 miles north of Cushendall [D245289]. A
path leads from a carpark to a small beach, passing
the ruins of Layde Church, probably twelfth century.

NORTH ANTRIM CLIFF PATH. A 10-mile footpath
along spectacular cliffs from Runkerry to White Park
Bay. 104 acres.

PORTSTEWART STRAND (q.v.) [C720360]. 185 acres
of duneland, including a 3-mile strand to the west of
Portstewart.

WHITE PARK BAY (q.v.) 1½ miles west of Ballintoy,
7 miles north-west of Ballycastle [D023440].
179 acres of sandy shore, flanked by white chalk
cliffs, on the North Antrim coast.

## CO. DOWN

BLOCKHOUSE ISLAND AND GREEN ISLAND. Two
islands lying off Cranfield and Greencastle at the
mouth of Carlingford Lough [J254097]. 2 acres.

Important nesting site for common, Arctic and roseate terns. Leased to RSPB.

CASTLE WARD (q.v.) 7 miles north-east of Downpatrick, 1½ miles west of Strangford village on the A25; entrance by Ballyculter Lodge [J752494]. 794 acres. Picturesquely situated on the south shore of Strangford Lough. Built by the 1st Lord Bangor in 1765.

KEARNEY AND KNOCKINELDER 3 miles east of Portaferry [J650517]. **Kearney.** 31 acres of foreshore. **Knockinelder.** 8 acres of beach and adjoining land.

LIGHTHOUSE ISLAND, COPELAND ISLANDS 3 miles off the mouth of Belfast Lough [J596858]. 43 acres. The island is managed by the Copeland Island Bird Observatory.

MOURNE COASTAL PATH [J389269]. 64½ acres. One section of the path runs south along the sea from Bloody Bridge at the foot of Slieve Donard, passing the site of St Mary's, Ballaghanery, an early Celtic church associated with St Donard. Another section leads up the valley of the Bloody River, giving access to the mountains.

MURLOUGH NATURE RESERVE (q.v.) 2 miles north-west of Newcastle, 28 miles south of Belfast [J410350]. 938 acres. Sand dunes and heathland containing many interesting botanical, zoological and archaeological specimens. Ireland's first nature reserve. **Dundrum Coastal Path** [J410350]. Part of the Ulster Way along the old railway line and along the shores of Dundrum inner bay between Dundrum and the Blackstone River.

ORLOCK POINT 2 miles west of Groomsport on the A2 Bangor to Donaghadee road [J539838]. 52 acres of unspoilt coastal land with interesting flora and fauna.

STRANGFORD LOUGH WILDLIFE SCHEME (q.v.) [J560615]. 5,400 acres. Initiated in 1966, this conservation scheme embraces most of the foreshore of the lough. **Anne's Point** [J558686]. 35 acres of agricultural land, water marsh and conifer woodland on the shores of Strangford Lough; includes shooting rights and ¼ mile of shoreline adjoining the existing National Nature Reserve and refuge area at the northern end of the lough. **Ballyhenry Island.** A 5-acre rocky island of considerable scientific interest, situated near the narrows of Strangford Lough and overlooked by Castle Ward. **Barr Hall and Green Island** [J625455]. 17 acres in a narrow strip above high-water mark but including some foreshore and saltmarsh. The coastline lies on each side of the Ards Peninsula. **Darragh Island.** A 21-acre island north of Ringhaddy Sound. **Gibb's Island.** 13 acres of island and mainland, linked by a causeway. **Greyabbey Bay.** 3,608 acres of land, foreshore and sea-bed. **Salt Island and Green Island.** 68 acres. Salt Island (52 acres) for its great ornithological interest, and Green Island (16 acres) for amenity use. **Taggart Island** [J585518]. 26 acres of meadow and woods north of Portaferry overlooking the Narrows of Strangford Lough. Many other islands are either leased or managed by the National Trust, either because of their wildlife or scenic value. A number of these can be visited.

## CO. LONDONDERRY

BAR MOUTH (q.v.) 3 miles east of Castlerock, 7 miles north-west of Coleraine, at the mouth of the River Bann [C782365]. 45 acres. A wildlife sanctuary with observation hide, and about 26 acres of agricultural land bordering the River Bann and the wildlife refuge.

DOWNHILL (q.v.) 1 mile west of Castlerock, 5 miles west of Coleraine on the Coleraine to Downhill coast road [C758363]. 110 acres. Part of the demesne laid out by Frederick Hervey, Earl of Bristol, Bishop of Derry. The property includes the ruins of Downhill Castle, built in 1770, the Mussenden Temple, Bishop's Gate, an ice house, walled garden and woodland and coastal walks, with views along the Donegal and Antrim coasts.

# Index

# Index